RING MASTER

THE INCREDIBLE STORY OF WELSH RUGBY'S CLOWN PRINCE

MARK RING
WITH
DELME PARFITT

MAINSTREAM
PUBLISHING
EDINBURGH AND LONDON

First published in Great Britain in 2006 by
MAINSTREAM PUBLISHING COMPANY
(EDINBURGH) LTD
7 Albany Street
Edinburgh EH1 3UG

ISBN 978 184596 231 9 (from January 2007)
ISBN 1 84596 231 1

A catalogue record for this book is available
from the British Library

Typeset in Rotis Serif and Sans Serif

Printed in Great Britain by
Clays Ltd, St Ives plc

To my dad, Brian, who encouraged me to play; to my mum, Christine, who taught me to sidestep in the living room; to my brother, Paul, and sister, Carmel; and finally to Lisa, Madison and Luca, all of whom I hold so close to my heart.

Mark Ring

Thanks to Tony Woolway of the *Western Mail and Echo* library; Alan Evans, media manager for Cardiff RFC; Ray Ruddick, Pontypool RFC stats man; and Howard Evans.

Delme Parfitt

CONTENTS

FOREWORD

Players and characters like Mark Ring don't come along very often and when they do, they should be savoured. I think we can safely say that anyone who saw Ringo play will remember him as a maverick, a guy who was never afraid to try something different, whether it came off or not – and most of the time it did. There have actually been times when I have been in awe of some of the little tricks he has executed. That's the type of player he has always been.

I first met Ringo when I played against him for the West Wales Under-11 team at the old Cardiff Arms Park ground and I tracked his name from then on. He was a little like me in his younger days – he always seemed to miss out on the Wales age-group teams, too – but I suppose we were together where it mattered most: at senior level.

I have nothing but fond memories of playing for Wales at outside-half with Ringo on my shoulder at centre. He was extremely talented and oozed confidence. You always knew that he would not only back himself to succeed, but also every single one of his teammates. His personality, not to mention his skills, rubbed off on everybody. If ever I wanted to try something, I knew Ringo would be right there behind me to support me.

Though his record commands the utmost respect, I have often wondered just what he would have achieved had he not suffered such serious knee injuries during his career. He performed miracles when he came back from virtually destroying his left knee in a match for Cardiff back in 1985, but that, and future problems, held him back. I think with more luck he might have won far more than his 32 caps for Wales. Who knows, he could have been a British Lion as well. I'm sure that, had he not been recuperating from another knee operation in 1989, he would have gone to Australia to play his part in that marvellous series win against the Wallabies.

And, of course, having gone to rugby league myself, I have often wondered what Ringo could have done in the 13-man code. He had his chance to go north, though perhaps the time he was virtually out-sprinted in a training session by the Wigan prop/second row Andy Goodway put him off! That said I'm sure there are countless rugby union fans glad he stayed in Wales because the game here would definitely have been poorer for his absence.

While I admired his playing ability down the years, I have also valued his friendship. Ringo is one of those guys who are fun to be around. He is generous and well meaning and people seem to want to be in his company all the time. We have always been on the same wavelength off the pitch – as much as we were on it. All I hope now is that he goes on to be a success as a coach and finds a way to harness the huge potential he has in that role while working in Ireland. There is no doubt he continues to have much to offer the game of rugby.

Ringo deserves some luck because he is simply a great bloke. A maverick, a magician or just a friend, call him what you will, but there is only one Ringo – a lot of people may say thank God for that!

Jonathan Davies

PREFACE

MY JOURNEY

....

The Devil climbs onto everyone's shoulder from time to time and he found mine during the 1990 Five Nations Championship. The offer was simple: accept a sum of money that would have a huge impact on your life. In return, betray your teammates and your country.

'Make sure Wales lose to Ireland and we'll give you £35,000.' That was the message from the shadowy London underworld just days before I was to go into battle in the red jersey against Ireland. I could never have done it – and I never entertained it. Though those who, in later years, believed I had stolen money from Pontypool Rugby Club may, even now, choose not to believe that. They can believe what they like.

You can never put a price on the honour and responsibility of representing your country, in sporting terms or otherwise. I've been fortunate enough to taste the ultimate at senior level on thirty-six occasions – thirty-two in rugby and four in baseball. I count the friends I have made along the way as perhaps the most precious thing of all and had I succumbed to temptation in 1990, I know I could now never look any of them in the eye.

If you could experience changing into a Wales strip alongside the great David Bishop, the dual code rugby and baseball international, you would know that playing for your country draws emotions from deep inside you that money will never be able to buy. Such emotions do not rise to the surface in all of us, least of all myself in my playing days, but they are there. And if they are not, then there is something dramatically wrong with your character. The three feathers of Wales used to turn Bish into a wide-eyed monster who wouldn't have sold out his country no matter how many millions of pounds anyone had placed in front of him.

History tells us, though, that not everyone has the same set of values. And while there remain people who are vulnerable, the offers will continue to be made by those who see making money as the be all and end all. Earning money playing sport is one thing, betraying teammates and the very code of integrity all sport must operate under is quite another.

As it turned out, we lost the match I was asked to throw against Ireland at Lansdowne Road anyway. I felt the usual emotions in defeat that day: deep disappointment, frustration, anger even. But deep down inside there was a tiny speck of relief.

Relief in knowing that I had given my all, had stood shoulder to shoulder with my teammates and stayed true to the values that had been instilled in me by my mum and dad when I was a kid growing up on the tough streets of Cardiff's Splott district. Those who had sought to influence me did not know the real Mark Ring.

The same applied to those at Pontypool Park who branded me a thief a few years later. They clearly didn't know me at all. I was supposed to have stolen money from an account set up to raise funds for an end-of-season tour. I never did anything of the kind, nor would I ever have contemplated it. Yet circumstances conspired to leave me with a stain on my character which I'm not sure has been completely scrubbed away to this day.

I have faults, like any human being, but I am not a cheat and I am not a thief. Before anything else, I'm a rugby player: a rugby player who, in his 43 or so years on this planet, has known some thrilling highs and desperate lows. If you could bottle the elation of beating England at Twickenham, as the Wales team I was a part of in 1988 managed to do, it would be a commodity worth breaking the bank for. The old enemy, not just downed in their own backyard but downed by a Welsh team who pretty much knew they were going to do it from the word go. A Welsh team who knew that they could prevail by staying true to the rugby mantra that has underpinned our little country for decades, playing with style, skill, cunning and a willingness to try the unexpected.

The 2006 Wales team said publicly they believed they could beat England at Headquarters by running them all over the park. They failed, emphatically. Our class of 1988 said the same thing amongst ourselves – and we delivered. It will have been at least 20 years before our achievement is matched, with Wales not due back in south-west London for a competitive match until the winter of 2008.

Yet the nature of a sportsman's lot has despair stalking him relentlessly. And I've had my fair share of it jumping on my shoulders and pulling me down. A hospital bed, a destroyed left knee and a man in a white coat telling me I would never play rugby again – it doesn't get much worse than that for anyone who lives for running around a field with a ball in their hands. Yet for all the injuries, all the games I have lost, all the times I have been left out of sides and felt like the most hard-done-by man in the world, they can, of course, never compare to losing a child. That's an experience I wish I could say I know nothing about. But I cannot.

1

CARDIFF BORN, CARDIFF BRED

I was born and bred in the tough Cardiff district of Splott, a sprawling suburb of terraced housing on the south side of the city, just east of the docks area. I played my first game of rugby for my school, St Alban's Primary, at about the age of seven. I was fortunate that rugby had always been, and continued to be, the dominant sport at the school; in fact, all the Catholic schools seemed to play baseball in the summer and rugby in the winter.

We lived at number three Vale Road, a street containing only three terraced houses opposite the Moorlands pub and a biscuit factory that was later to become a Leo's supermarket. There was also a dangerous railway line nearby that carried materials to the steelworks. A few of the kids I used to play with actually died on that line through not taking enough care as they played either close by the tracks or on them.

I was given a solid Catholic upbringing, the product of a strong Irish background in my family – my mother's name is Christine Mary O'Reilly. My dad, Brian, was from the Canton area of Cardiff, but when he met my mother he moved to Splott, where her family lived.

My talent for rugby obviously comes from my father. When I was a kid, he had stints with the local St Albans and Old Illtydians clubs, but he made his name playing centre for Leicester between 1959 and 1961 before I was born. I still have boxes and boxes of his old press write-ups.

How did he find his way to Leicester? Well, he went there because he was offered work in the area. He started to play for one of the local clubs up in the East Midlands before being spotted and asked to go along to the Tigers. Dad played alongside some great players, including the scrum-half 'Chalky' White and Tony O'Reilly – now Sir Anthony O'Reilly of Heinz fame – many of whom took the field for England, like the fly-half Phil Horrocks-Taylor.

I watched Dad play a couple of times later on in his career and he was a fantastic evasive runner. People still tell me today, 'You were good, but you were never as good as your old man.' To be honest, I love hearing that. Dad played into his 40s for not only the local teams but also clubs like Maesteg, Penarth and Glamorgan Wanderers. Like me, by the time he finished his knees were shot to pieces.

The tragedy now is that Dad has Alzheimer's disease. It's toughest on my mother, who looks after him 24 hours a day, clothes him and bathes him – basically, she does almost everything for him. She gets respite every now and again when Dad goes into a home for a week or so, but even then she visits him every day. That's real unconditional love for you. That's the type of person Mum is.

The most frightening thing about it all is how quickly the disease came on with Dad. Only a couple of years ago, he was right as rain. He had a mild stroke followed by some heavy falls that resulted in a couple of nasty bangs to his head, but nobody envisaged what lay around the corner. Dad is 71 now, but every morning of his life, he would get up in the morning and put on his shirt and tie. He would always look smart in an old-school type of way.

He was a member of Cardiff RFC for years and years and would always pack as many of us as possible in the car to go and watch matches as kids. Then later, when I was playing, I would always have this ritual before games that the last thing I would do would be to ask Dad for some advice. He was only ever critical when I played really well – when I played badly, he went out of his way to be supportive. Whether that was just how he was or whether he was deliberately trying to use a bit of positive psychology on me, I don't know, but it worked for me.

He used that sort of thing to his advantage when I was young by asking me to go for his newspaper every morning, saying he would time me to see how long I would take. None the wiser, I would burst out of the front door, trying to break the four-minute mile – Dad usually got his paper more quickly than the previous time.

He would quite often take me over to the park and belt the ball up high in the air so I could catch it when it came down. I have since used that method when coaching youngsters myself: it's a good one for improving hand–eye coordination and also puts a bit of pressure on the kids. What's more, it's a fun drill to do. They always get very excited about it.

Dad's idol was Wales's greatest-ever fly-half Barry John, so later on Barry also became my idol. I remember writing a letter to the great man, saying how much I admired him and wanted to be like him when I was older. Barry saw my note and I've been told by some that 'the King' remembers it to this day. I was first captivated by Barry during the victorious British Lions tour to Australia and New Zealand in 1971. In my mind, every time I went over to the park with a rugby ball I was a British Lion myself. I was basically living my life through him, he had such an effect on me. It was the evasive running that did it for me and my dad always encouraged me to watch players of his ilk. Dad also loved Irishman Mike Gibson and players like Welshmen Gerald Davies and John Bevan.

The sidestepping was the big thing for me: I always wanted to master that art and so every morning when I was running for Dad's newspaper, you could bet I would be sidestepping every lamp post, and even crisp packets or pieces of trodden-down chewing gum that lay on the pavement.

I'm sure I was also helped by the cramped schoolyard at St Alban's. Not only would we be playing what seemed like about 64-a-side games of football with tennis balls, but we would also have to dodge around girls playing hopscotch in the middle of our pitch. It meant that you had to keep your wits about you and watch where you were going, with sidestepping being a key element of it all. The funny thing though is that, to this day, Mum insists she taught me to sidestep in the living room when I was a young lad. I'll take her word for it!

Dad's illness began with him suffering memory loss and, since they diagnosed him, he has become progressively worse. When it was first starting to hit him, he used to go missing for large chunks of the day and he would always end up in the Canton area of Cardiff, where he grew up. I would get telephone calls from friends of his saying he was wandering around down there.

It is difficult for me to handle Dad's condition at times, especially as I have a young family of my own, which demands so much of my love, care and attention. My mother is the rock behind the whole set-up and my brother, Paul, will take him out for a pint every now and then. I feel guilty at times when I think I should spend more time with him. He was always a regular drinker – every day of his life he was in the pub – so on a couple of occasions I took him out for a pint, but we've stopped going now because once or twice I gave him too many down at my local and he got sick when we went back up to the house. The whole situation gets me down terribly from time to time.

Dad lived for his old club, Leicester Tigers, which has always been brilliant at keeping in touch with ex-players, inviting them to reunion functions every now and then. What makes the Alzheimer's hard to deal with for everyone who knows him is that when he was healthy he was such a character, he would light up a room with his presence and he was somebody in whose company people just loved to be. He was a great storyteller and never more fun than when he was with his pals reminiscing about old times. He loved going to stand on the North Terrace at the Arms Park with his big group of mates, who used to love the banter at the games.

There was one guy known as 'the Heckler', who used to have people in stitches during games with some of his witty remarks; even the players at times were creasing themselves. At one game, referee Clive Norling was showing off his new perm hairstyle and the Heckler shouted out, 'You can't fool us, Norling, we know it's you!'

Unfortunately, this heckler drifted away and was replaced by another who was a nastier piece of work. I remember during one game a Cardiff teammate of mine, a full-back called Chris Webber, was given a terrible ride by this fellow.

At another against Bedford, this fellow got on Chris's case so badly that he was close to jumping over the fence and smacking him. At the end of the game, the wag bellowed out, 'Don't forget, Cardiff, when you pack up the kit, pack Webber with it!'

I felt terrible because a lot of our shortcomings had been down to me, but, as I was flavour of the month at that particular time, I just didn't seem to attract criticism. Poor Chris took enough for both of us. When we got back into the dressing-room, he broke down in tears.

I couldn't look him in the eye, knowing I was largely to blame, and although I tried to offer some consoling words, he was devastated and there was no talking to him. The horrible heckler got his comeuppance one day, though, when one of my dad's mates threw a fag butt that obviously hadn't been totally extinguished into the hood of his coat. Before long, I glanced into the crowd and there was this mouthy bugger standing there completely oblivious to the fact that smoke was billowing from his hood.

I remember when we were kids, Dad would always get us into games somehow, even though money was tight. In those days, everyone used to be on the take on the turnstiles, so as long as you knew somebody, there was always a chance you could wangle your way in. We saw so many great Wales games that way.

I was at the famous Barbarians match in January 1973 when Gareth Edwards scored a try against the All Blacks, still held up by so many people as the best-ever scored. I actually couldn't see a thing, standing as we were on the old West Enclosure. If you ever look at the footage, you will see a big inflatable sheep bobbing up and down on the terrace as Edwards jogs back. Well, that's where

I was standing. I was picked up a few times by blokes who were kind enough to put me on their shoulders for a better view.

Standing in a crowd like that was certainly an experience. These were the days when it used to be absolutely chock-a-block in the standing areas; guys used to come out of the pubs with their bellies full of beer and such was the squeeze that there was no point trying to make it to the toilets, so they just used to urinate where they stood. The story always used to go that if you were unlucky, you might get someone filling up your pocket!

Dad was a bit of a character. He used to go the rugby league Challenge Cup final at Wembley every year and I recall one particular time, when it was broadcast on the television, my mother calling me in to see something. The Queen was meeting the teams and a guy dressed up as a clown, carrying a huge leek, was running around on the pitch accompanied by a gorilla. Dad was the clown and his mate, a guy known as Slogger Slocombe, from Splott, was the gorilla! They must have blagged their way in once again and ended up within a few yards of Her Majesty. I couldn't get over it.

Another time when he got into a Wales game, obviously by dodgy means, he was caught on television being frogmarched out by a policeman.

Dad became a rep for a local rubber company and went on to become a director before setting up his own business. As for Mum, she did a range of menial jobs when times were hard. She worked in Leo's and the biscuit factory and also served in the university restaurant in Cyncoed, a more upmarket area of the city, where we moved when I was aged about 11.

We were never flush with money, as I remember, but my younger brother Paul, who later played number 8 for Cardiff and Newport, made sure little sister Carmel and I never went without. I was certainly never short of a pair of rugby boots.

Mum and Dad used to go nuts because they would never last long, as I used to kick them to pieces, wearing them, as I did, every day. Paul and I were always playing various sports together as kids and we were very competitive. The problem between us, more often than not, was my total hatred of losing and, as the older brother, I used to bully him a bit.

We would play cricket in the summer up against a wall in Splott Park, on which we had sprayed some wickets. If the tennis ball hit me on the back leg and it was a plum lbw, I would never take it, despite Paul's passionate appeals. Even when I was approaching my treble century, having been in for two days smashing the ball all over the place, I wasn't inclined to walk. As the park layout went, the easiest place to hit a six was on the offside, the aim being to smack the ball square on top of the toilet roofs. It was naturally a favourite shot of mine.

Almost everything we did as kids involved the outdoors and almost always a sport of some sort. We used to play football into the twilight over at the park with plenty of other kids, which is so different to today, when there are so many other things to distract kids' attention.

There is too much emphasis these days on children sitting in front of a computer screen playing games, or doing something else that keeps them idle, for my liking. All I can say is that even if computers had been around when I was younger, I doubt I would have gone for them over a kick around in the local park.

Even though I very much wore the trousers as the eldest sibling, in terms of my relationship with Paul, there was one occasion when I found myself at his mercy. Paul had bought a table-tennis bat – not an ordinary one, like we were used to using, with a thin layer of dimpled rubber on top of the hardwood, but one with thicker padding around it and a smooth rubber surface. He had saved up £5 from his pocket money and was naturally as pleased as punch with it. He couldn't wait to try it out on the table-tennis table we had set up in our garage.

Of course, as soon as I saw it, I wanted it. I didn't hesitate to take it from him and make him use the old dimpled bat we'd had to make do with for so many years. To my dismay, the change of bats didn't make any difference because Paul beat me even though

I was using his prized new acquisition. I was furious and, in a fit of pique, threw his new bat across the room in his direction, snapping the handle off it in the process.

Well, that was it for Paul. He totally flipped. I saw the rage in his eyes immediately. I had always pushed him about, but that particular day he came towards me looking like he was going to murder me on the spot and I realised that, despite my elder years, I could be about to take a pasting. I quickly began to talk myself out of the situation, as I have done more often than not on such occasions my entire life.

Thankfully, whatever I said did the trick because I escaped physical punishment. But I make no mistake: Paul was going to batter me that day and, from then on, I never bullied him again!

Since I was good at sport at school, I was often challenged for fights by other kids. You would get the message that someone or other wanted your blood and there was no way you couldn't turn up to meet the challenge in the appointed place after school. But I always managed to use the gift of the gab to talk my way out of any fisticuffs. It would be along the lines of, 'You're very lucky today, you know. I would take you, if it came down to it, but today I'm feeling tired, so I'm going to let you off.'

I've never been a fighter – as a kid, competitive sport was all the buzz I ever needed, and playing with and beating Paul was the icing on the cake.

These days, we are not particularly close in a social kind of way. For example, we don't drink together and we mix in different social circles. But I feel we do have a strong and loving bond, as all brothers should.

I also have an equally strong bond with my sister, Carmel. Married to Liam and with a son, Joseph, and daughter, Kate, she also has the Ring sporting genes, having played tennis to a high standard when she was younger. She plays baseball these days for Cardiff side Master Gunner.

Paul and I played together for Cardiff, him at number 8 and

me in the centre, in our early days, although Paul never quite managed to stay at the very top end of the game. He could have done, mind you, if he'd had a bit more luck and been in the right place at the right time on a few more occasions because he had genuine ability. Paul was man of the match in the St Peter's side that famously beat Cardiff in the Welsh Cup back in 1993, but only a few weeks later fell ill and had to give up playing regularly. He was in and out of hospital for about four years and had twelve operations, which must have been tough for a young, fit, healthy man to deal with.

I am immensely proud of him and he is a fantastic husband to Angela and father to his son, Christy, a promising player who made the Cardiff Under-11s squad last season, and daughter, Cara. Not only that, Paul puts in hours coaching the youngsters at St Peter's, combining it with running a successful windows business. He is truly remarkable.

I'm just glad I was able to play a part in what must surely be one of the most memorable triumphs in his rugby career: that cup win at Cardiff. I was in my second spell at Pontypool at the time and was only too pleased to pass on some information and advice about the players the Blue and Blacks picked that day, although I am in no way claiming any of the credit! I felt Cardiff disrespected St Peter's by fielding an unduly weak team and the fact that they put three digits on the scoreboard next to their name really fired up Paul and the boys when they ran onto the pitch. I can remember playing for Pontypool up at Colwyn Bay that same day and when I rang to find out the score, I simply couldn't believe St Peter's had won. I just felt chuffed that my brother and I had been able to share a triumph like that together, even if the part he played in it was far bigger than mine.

Whatever was on the television when Paul and I were kids, we would be out playing it: if it was Wimbledon, you couldn't move on the local tennis courts; if it was a Test match, then there would be any number of cricket matches going on. I remember one day during the Olympics, we decided we were all going to run a marathon and marked out a route over two miles or so. That kind of life allowed me to become skilful at so many sports, but, funnily enough, like many rugby players, I preferred football at first. Like I have said, it was only because I went to a primary school, then a secondary – Lady Mary High School in Cardiff – where the dominant sport was rugby that I found myself pushed in that direction.

Leeds United were my passion for years – it just so happened that as soon as I became old enough to appreciate football clubs, Leeds were in their heyday in the early '70s. Players like Gary Sprake, David Harvey, Norman Hunter, Jack Charlton, Terry Cooper, Terry Yorath, Johnny Giles and Billy Bremner were my heroes. I remember crying my eyes out when Sunderland beat them in the 1973 FA Cup final. I vowed at the time never again to watch the winning goal, which was scored by Ian Porterfield.

I also followed Celtic, but only because one day my mother informed me that Celtic were a Catholic team. The Celtic shirt was, however, the first I ever had, even before I had a Wales rugby jersey.

Catholicism is something that I grew up with and still hold dear to this day. We always went to St Alban's church in Splott, every week without fail. I went out of respect to my family, but my faith has always been important to me. Believe it or not, my proudest moment is not a sporting one but linked to the church – the day my mother received Holy Communion from the Pope.

During the early '80s, the Pope came over and held a Mass at Pontcanna Fields in the city. My uncle Malcolm, who was high up in the police force at the time, was in charge of the whole security operation for the Pope's visit to Pontcanna and he managed to arrange a ticket for my mother. Among many others, she received Holy Communion while we just stood in awe watching.

In many ways as I was growing up, the Catholic school I went to was as big an influence on me as my parents. There was one teacher by the name of Austin Camp at St Alban's who used to frighten me to death. He was one of the older guys, who used to wear shiny, polished black shoes with steel toecaps and drainpipe black trousers, a black waistcoat with a pocket watch and a black blazer. He stood about 6 ft 4 in. tall and had jet-black hair. He was a real serious olde-worlde schoolteacher. You would never think of crossing him, but he turned out to be a really good influence on me and I did well at primary school because of him.

He was a disciplinarian but a brilliant teacher. He could read you a book and, where I wouldn't normally bother with them, he would have me avidly listening to the words as if I was watching a good film. There would be days when he would take the whole class down to the school hall and have us listen to an LP by Elgar, Beethoven or Bach – bear in mind we were just ten years old. He would then give us a brief résumé of what the piece was about and then hand us each a piece of paper and tell us to write down our thoughts about it. I used to love doing that because I found that I did indeed have lots of thoughts on the music that I could easily write down. I wouldn't go out and buy classical music, but even now I can remember all the names of the composers and I could put on paper my thoughts on what they have produced. In fact, it's one talent, other than sport, that I have: I can write creatively. Even today, I sometimes pen a poem or a song.

I played age-group rugby for Cardiff schools all the way up through my school years and for most of that time I was tiny. I was only ever picked for my ability, never for my size. I did end up suffering for my lack of stature in later years, when I believe it cost me Wales Schools caps. I became frustrated that I used to play a part in winning everything with Cardiff and then see lads from other areas get picked for the national squad ahead of me.

I remember playing for East Wales Under-11s against West Wales as a curtain-raiser to a Wales game against Tonga at the Arms Park in 1974. At the time, I had never experienced what it was like for an opponent to get the better of me, but there was a little outside-half from Trimsaran called Jonathan Davies in the West Wales team and this kid took all the tap penalties and jinked his way though all of us the entire game. It really opened my eyes and I saw I had to acknowledge that there were good players out there other than me. Jonathan would later have the same problem with his size because he never seemed to be picked for the national sides either.

On another occasion when I went for a Wales Schools Under-15 cap, which was my dream, I lost out to a fellow called Jonathan Morgan from Neath, even though we had played the side earlier that season and had beaten them by forty-odd points, during which I had scored two tries.

My schoolwork went down the pan after I moved up to secondary school because my life became totally about sport. I was attending Lady Mary, the Catholic school, rather than nearby St Illtyds, where most of the St Alban's primary kids naturally went, so I missed the friends I had made there, especially my pals in the rugby team. The fact that two of the other primary schools whose pupils also went to St Illtyds had good rugby teams made it worse because I knew that St Illtyds was bound to have a really great side that I wasn't going to be able to play in. It was all down to our move to Cyncoed, a suburb that fell into Lady Mary's catchment area, and there was nothing I could do about it.

At Lady Mary, I started in the top stream, but gradually I fell down the ladder. I ended up doing nine O levels and only getting three passes, in religion, maths and English, the only ones I didn't have to revise for. I ended up re-sitting some of them, but my lack of commitment meant I got nowhere.

My mother used to go nuts with me for not revising, but she was fighting a lost cause because sport had taken over. The extent of my love for sport is probably no more evident in the fact that even when I was playing rugby for Wales I was still having the odd game of Sunday League football at the local parks the day after.

My failure at school dictated that my immediate future, before I was ready to make my big break in sport, would be a tough introduction to the real world.

2

FROM THE POST ROOM
TO THE ARMS PARK

I got my first job in August 1980 working as a civil servant at Companies House in the centre of Cardiff. I applied for it simply because the advert in the local paper said it required only two O levels, one in English and one in maths.

At the interview, I was asked a load of silly questions – one being whether or not Sikhs should be made to wear crash helmets when riding motorbikes in the UK. I was sure afterwards that my answers had done me little good, but, to my amazement, I got the job and was put to work in the post room, where I was basically opening letters all day and was bored senseless. We would sit two facing one way and two the other, operating in little cubby holes. To be honest, it totally did my head in.

One positive was that I met all sorts of characters there – it really opened my eyes to the big wide world – but it wasn't long before I came close to the sack. In my boredom, I had been saving up elastic bands and had made them into one big ball. One day, I threw it out of our first-floor window onto a concrete patch just to see if it would bounce up for me to catch, which it did. It was all harmless fun, but I got reported. I think it was a security guard who claimed it had just missed his head, although I swear there was nobody about when I let it drop. To this day, I reckon he saw it from a distance and just wanted to stir up some trouble.

Initially, it was believed that the ball had come from the second floor, but after something of a witch-hunt the finger was pointed at me and I admitted it. I had to travel to London with the union rep

27

for a disciplinary hearing, with the prospect of the sack hanging over me like a dark cloud. In the event, I just managed to keep my job, for which I was grateful.

The one good thing to come out of it was that my bosses realised I was a young man making my way in the sporting world and needed to be doing something that I was going to find more of a challenge. Their answer was to place me in the mortgage department – unfortunately, I found that only slightly more interesting. There was salvation on the horizon, mind you.

I began to fiddle my hours. I was on flexible time, which meant I could key in for work anytime between 7.30 a.m. and 9.30 a.m. and likewise key out for lunch between noon and 2 p.m. So, if workers wanted to, they could key in at 7.30 a.m., key out at noon and back in at 12.30 p.m. after a half-hour for lunch. This meant that they could leave at 3.30 p.m., having done a seven-and-a-half-hour day.

Employees had to work seven hours and twenty-four minutes a day and we could be behind on our hours or ahead every month, though we couldn't be behind by more than fourteen hours and forty minutes – the fact that I can still remember these figures proves how ingrained they were in my mind so that I could have the system totally sussed.

My mother used to wake me up with a wet flannel in the week just to get me up and out of the house to work and I would then catch two buses to Companies House. I would key in at 9.30 a.m., the latest possible time you could get away with, and then work until noon. Then I would go downstairs for a bite of lunch and then key back in at 12.30 p.m. But instead of going back in, I would take my kit bag and head over to Maindy Stadium in the city where, every day except a Friday, I would do sprints and all manner of running exercises. The important thing in my mind was that I had keyed back in at 12.30 p.m. and so my working hours were still ticking over as I was training. I would then slip back into work at 2 p.m. and stay until 6 p.m. after all the bosses had gone home, when I could skive around. The schedule meant

I actually ended up appearing to work overtime, which left me with a surplus of hours, and eventually days, that I could take off to do even more training. It was getting to the stage that even though I had a full-time job, I also felt like I was training full-time as well.

In those days, I was very fit. I was doing 16 on the bleep test, 110 kilos as a one-off maximum on the bench press and I quickly moved up from 12 st. 4 lb to a fit 13 st. 7 lb. I was in great nick, even though I was drinking hard in town quite a few nights a week and having an all-day session on a Sunday. Throughout the week, I could be pissed several times up until a Thursday, although I would never drink on a Friday night before a game. I was young enough and fit enough to be able to carry it off.

Yet my prolonged absences from the office around the middle of the day were bound to get noticed sooner or later – and when they were, it was lucky I had a friend who worked there who used to tip me off every time my line manager started asking suspicious questions. The crux of the bosses' enquiries surrounded their confusion about how I seemed to accrue time owed to me despite the fact that I was hardly ever there!

I would always buck up my ideas when I was tipped off from this friend and break my routine until the pressure lifted, then I could go back on the fiddle. Believe it or not, this continued for the eight years I worked there and that was why I was up there among the fittest lads in the Welsh squad – certainly the fittest in the Cardiff squad bar none.

In the end, one of the reasons I left school to work in the civil service was that I had been tipped off by one of the Welsh Youth selectors that if I did I would definitely get a cap for the youth team. I did, too, against England at Oxford University, and scored a try in a 13–10 defeat that saw us battered up front.

I was still playing for Cardiff Youth when I first got called up to the senior Blue and Blacks squad at the age of 18. We won the Esso Youth Cup final against Newport at Caerphilly's Virginia Park on the Wednesday night and I was asked to go on a trip the next day to the Basque country in southern France to play a game for Cardiff against a combined Basque team. It was John Ryan, who would later become Wales coach, who gave me the opportunity, basically so I could have the experience.

I came on at half-time as fly-half, but had a stinker of a 40 minutes. We weren't the strongest Cardiff team, while our opponents played the incomparable French full-back Serge Blanco on one wing. He scored three tries in what was ultimately an easy victory for the hosts. I can recall on my first touch feeling really confident, but I kicked the ball straight into the arms of Blanco, who proceeded to make about 40 yards with an attacking run.

Things progressed from there. I began training on the track with a proper athletics coach, Walter Thomas. I used to see Colin Jackson and Nigel Walker there, too. There was one occasion when I got chatting to a fellow at the track and I remember him saying, 'You see that guy over there in the long jump sandpit pissing around with all the girls?' I looked over and saw it was Jackson he was referring to. 'He could be the greatest decathlete this country has ever had if only he would stop pissing about,' he continued. He said Jackson could do every event well and as it turned out, he was right. Jackson went on to hold the world record for the 110 metre hurdles, so he must have done a hell of a lot right in his early days.

As for Nigel, well, he failed to get past the semi-final of the hurdles at the 1984 Los Angeles Olympic Games. I knew he wasn't going to make it big in track and field after that because his times were not up to it. We remained good friends, though, and I was the one who was influential in helping him make his break into rugby in later years.

I had played with Nigel at youth level and when he realised he wasn't going to make it big in athletics, I asked him if he would like to make a comeback in rugby. He practically bit my hand off. I introduced him to Alec Evans, who was the coach of Cardiff at that time, in the early to mid-'90s, whose first question was how fast could he currently run the 100 metres. Nigel told him 10.7 seconds.

Moments later, after Nigel had gone, Alec turned to me and without hesitation said, 'We'll take him.'

At the age of 17, I was courting my first serious girlfriend. It was just me and her going to parties and it was all laid-back and very nice. Then Cardiff took me on tour to South Africa. It proved to be a trip that would be the death knell for us for six very good reasons.

I was really chuffed that at such a young age I had been asked to make the trip for what was a kind of world club tournament out there. The competition was due to take place at Loftus Versveld in Northern Transvaal, but we stopped off in Durban first of all for a warm-up game. Now, I was incredibly naive at the time, so two senior guys, the England number 8 John Scott and the coach Roger Beard, took me under their wing.

One evening in the hotel bar, a guy introduced us to some women whom he claimed were 'semi-professional dancers'. Before long, I was showing off. I was performing magic tricks and I was messing around doing sleight-of-hand stuff with glasses and spoons, all the while being egged on by Scotty and Roger. Those two, who were far more worldy-wise than me, were never going to get involved, but they could see I was making a bit of an impression with the girls and they didn't exactly drag me away.

Anyway, the end result of these tricks and more flirtatious behaviour later on during the tour was that I went off with about six different girls on that three-week trip. When I came back, I had a diamond ring for the girl, which I had bought at a special diamond sale. I told her we were over because of the experiences I had been through. I had to be honest with her and didn't regret it – even though she chucked the ring away while we were strolling around Roath Park in Cardiff and I ended up frantically searching for it in the bushes!

For a while after that, I was a bit of a playboy with a mullet hairdo, doing the rounds of the nightclubs in Cardiff. On a Sunday, we would end up looking for something different to do and quite often headed up to the valleys to rugby clubs in places like Tredegar, Abercynon or Tonyrefail. More often that not, it was me; Glenn Webbe, the Wales and Bridgend wing; Martin Daly, a close pal of mine who played for Cardiff; and a big second row who also wore the blue-and-black jersey called Tony McLean, who we nicknamed 'Clubber' because of his resemblance to Clubber Lang in the film *Rocky III*.

At some of these clubs, you would have to queue from 6.30 p.m. if you wanted to stand a chance of getting in and quite a few times we couldn't make it by then. On one occasion at Tonyrefail, we were refused permission, so Webby did his 'Do you know who I am?' bit on the door. He claimed he was to be the guest speaker at the place in a week's time and put on an act of being furious at not being allowed in. After he stopped for breath, the doorman asked him which club he was due to speak at. Webby answered, only to be told that club was half a mile down the road!

My drinking in those days, while probably not great for my health, has provided me with some happy memories, but there was one incident which left me wishing I could turn back the clock, ending as it did with a criminal conviction against my name. It happened over a weekend, when I would not normally have drunk so much. I played darts for a team at the City Arms pub, a famous drinking hole just over the road from the Arms Park that is always packed to bursting on match days, and there was a match scheduled for that particular Friday night, normally my non-drinking night.

I had become a pretty decent darter since my mother bought me a proper Nodor bristle board, which I had set up in the garage. I used to spend nights on end in there until I got to the standard where I was regularly hitting 180 and had become adept at thinking my way to finishes and knowing where to go around the board as my score got lower and lower. I loved spending my evenings in the garage, the only hiccup being the rollicking I got from my mother when she discovered I had been putting on the tumble drier every night for months to keep warm, leaving her with an enormous bill to settle!

I needed a few beers inside me to help me to relax and throw my best, something I know a lot of match darts players will understand, so that night I downed a few, even though I was playing the next day for the Cardiff Athletic team, popularly known as the Rags, which was more or less Cardiff seconds.

I used to love playing for the Rags because there was a mixture of youth players and experienced old heads who had been in the first team most of their careers and were now on their way down. It meant that whenever we went up the valleys to play a club that wanted our blood just because we were Cardiff, we always had a few tough nuts on our side who we could rely on to look after us if things got nasty. That gave us the confidence to go out and play. The idea was to take that confidence with you into the first team if and when you got the chance.

After the Rags game that Saturday afternoon, I had a good few drinks along with a few of the lads in the clubhouse – I was topping up from the night before. By the time we left the ground, we were the worse for wear, having all sunk a good few pints. We then headed out onto the streets of Cardiff in our club jumpers and ties looking for more action. Most Saturdays, the general rule was that we would stay out in town – there was no going home, at least not unless you were prepared to take terrible stick for doing so.

As we were walking past the Park Hotel on Queen Street, right in the middle of the main shopping centre, we could hear one hell of a party going on inside with singing and music playing, the works. It was a group of Maori supporters with guitars and they seemed to be halfway through what was clearly going to be an almighty knees-up.

Well, us lads were like kids in a sweet shop. We were straight over to the Park and in there like a shot, joining in the festivities with gusto. There were many more beers and plenty of sing-songs and by the time we rolled out of there in the early hours of Sunday morning, I could hardly stand. By this time, I was so tired from having first played darts and had a drink on the Friday night, then taken part in the rugby match the following day and then gone on the mother of all piss-ups that all I wanted to do was go to sleep there and then. I looked down the road and saw what looked like a caravan.

'Come on, boys, let's break into that caravan and get our heads down for the night,' I slurred. Yes, I was actually considering spending the night in what I thought was a caravan in the middle of the busiest part of central Cardiff. I staggered over to it and started pulling at the hardboard panels, trying to get in. Of course, it wasn't a caravan at all but a fruit and vegetable stall that had been left overnight. I realised as much when I got inside and fell over next to a pile of cabbages.

Next thing, I heard voices from a group of people in the distance who were shouting and telling me to get away from the stall, so I picked up a load of onions and started pelting the group with them. That persuaded them to slope off, but my problems were not over by any means.

I decided to take something home for my mum, so I stuffed a melon and a cauliflower into my kit bag. Unfortunately, we soon ran into a police car – the officers had probably been tipped off by the guys we had pelted with onions – and we were hauled off to the central police station. It was clear one of us was going to have to take the rap for the whole business. Before I knew it, I was providing fingerprints and having my mugshot taken: all the things that make you feel like a real criminal.

When I went to court, my appearance was given prominence in the *South Wales Echo*, the main evening paper for Cardiff and South Wales, which took me by surprise given that I was still only a young player just making my way out of the Rags. There was obviously going to be no hiding place. My mother was crying her eyes out.

To make matters worse, one of the Cardiff rugby backroom staff, a chap by the name of Tom Holley, worked at the court. Before

I realised it was going to be all over the papers anyway, I had tried to hide from him to lessen the chances of the club finding out about the affair, but he eventually spotted me and told me the club must not find out. Then before I knew it, he was organising legal aid for me. He then led me into a room where the Cardiff secretary, Alan Priday, was sitting! In the event, I had to pay £25 costs and a £20 fine to a Mr M.J. Holmes.

I was terrified that Cardiff would react badly to my misdemeanour and possibly even throw me out of the club, as I had ended up with a conviction for theft, but thankfully after a meeting the directors decided to take no action and let the matter go, despite the fact that the headline in the local paper had screamed: 'Player Steals Melons!'

Thinking back to it now, it is comical, but at the time I felt it left a stain on my character. I'm not sure whether it played a part in how I was viewed by certain people at the club in the future, but I have always felt that there is someone behind the scenes at Cardiff who has worked against me down the years. I've felt resented by some of the more old-school types there who I felt believed that I was not the sort of person that should be at a club like Cardiff.

However, if my court appearance has sullied my name in the eyes of some people, it did nothing to halt my immediate progress up the Cardiff ranks. In February 1983, at the age of just 20, I received a shock call-up to the Wales team to play in the Five Nations opener against England at Cardiff Arms Park. I had played only 12 games for the first team at Cardiff when the call-up came, coach John Bevan, who tragically died of cancer a couple of years later, having faith in me. I wasn't picked originally but got the nod when Robert Ackerman got injured in training, damaging his thumb.

I had been out drinking on the Sunday that my selection was announced and when I went back to the house, my father said Clive Rowlands, the Wales team manager at the time, had been on the phone bidding him congratulations that his son had been selected to play against England. It was an incredible feeling, a total shock to the system, even though I had played in the final trial for the Possibles team that had beaten the Probables. However, it ended up being a bit of an anticlimax. My naivety was very much to the fore as soon as I linked up with the squad.

Before the match, I was put in a room at the Angel Hotel, which is just across the road from the Arms Park, with Terry Holmes. Terry did all he could to help me settle down and take things in my stride, telling me that the main things I would notice would be the pace of the actual game and how quickly it would pass me by. He was certainly right on the second score because it was half-time seemingly in a flash and then game over. I played at right-centre and I think I touched the ball four times.

It ended up a 13–13 draw. The England try, scored by their right-wing John Carleton, was my fault because I got caught out of position, though I didn't dwell on it during the game. They were ahead for long spells, but we gradually crept back into it through our forwards, with Jeff Squire, the Pontypool stalwart who played at blindside flanker that day, leading the charge with our only try that afternoon.

Eddie Butler, Squire's Pontypool teammate, was captain, but Eddie didn't inspire me; in fact, he set the tone with his team talk, saying how he wasn't the type to launch into Churchillian speeches or start beating his chest. Fair enough, but it was hardly the best start in my eyes.

There was one moment when I took a quick throw in to second-row Bob Norster, who scored, only for it to be disallowed for reasons I am still not aware of to this day. But perhaps the most frustrating thing was that my midfield partner, Dai Richards, kept telling fly-half Malcolm Dacey, who also won his first cap that day, to kick for position deep into English territory: it was a safety-first game plan that I didn't have a lot of time for. Dai was a great player with silky running skills, but he was clearly low on confidence at the time and when he found himself in good attacking positions, he was tending more to duck out and go for safety instead of backing himself.

It could all have been so different for me that day. I could have been the hero rather than the youngster who had just come in and made a rather nondescript sort of debut. Along with the disallowed score that I created for Norster, there was another incident late on that sticks in my mind. The score was level and we were pressing them. Everyone had been sucked into this one play but I didn't commit myself to the breakdown, instead putting myself in position, even though we were fairly wide out, to drop a goal that would win us the game. It was all down to Terry Holmes as his head came up and he looked me straight in the eye, seeing I was in the pocket just waiting for the chance. But he chose not to pass it, instead feeding it short to Squire for him to carry on bashing into the English at close quarters.

I suppose Terry played the percentages like the experienced pro he was. If I had sliced a drop-goal effort, there was every chance England could have gathered the ball and gone down the other end through their backs given that so many of ours had been sucked in. Yet me being me, I was deeply frustrated because I was convinced I could have sent it sailing through the sticks. Perhaps Terry didn't have enough confidence in someone who was winning his first cap.

I was dropped for the next game as Robert Ackerman regained fitness and I didn't play again for my country until November the following year when I was part of a Wales team that was trounced 28–9 by an Australian team who went on to clinch a Home Unions Grand Slam inspired, as they were, by David Campese at his very best. But there were no hard feelings on my part. I had only been brought in originally because of an injury, so I didn't really feel that I was out of favour when Ackerman was fit again. And thinking back, I wasn't ready physically for the Test arena: I was so under-developed in terms of my upper-body strength.

I didn't really feel part of the scene, even though I had enjoyed the England game. I hadn't been overly nervous beforehand despite the magnitude of a 20 year old playing for Wales at Cardiff Arms Park, though that's not to say I wasn't keyed up like never before – I can remember that the adrenalin was pumping so hard I could feel my pulse pounding in my ears as I ran around during the game.

When the anthems were being sung, I can remember thinking about my family and friends, the people who had done so much to put me there, and I imagined all those who would give their right arm to be where I was. I thought about my days watching these matches from the terraces and it was hard to believe that here I was, boots on, jersey sitting proudly on my back, three feathers on my chest, actually playing for Wales.

Then I thought about how proud my mother would be – that's when the tears kicked in. I'm an emotional kind of guy as it is – I'm a real baby – so I guess there wasn't much hope for me in a situation like that!

Ultimately, it was the same as any other big game I had ever played in – I was nervous until I got out onto the pitch, then concentration just took over. Terry had told me that everything I did would be instinctive and he was right. Young players, however, need time for that instinct to develop at Test level: it's a bit like getting your bearings in a foreign country and assimilating into the culture. The more familiar you become with the way things are done, the more confident you are. The biggest thing that does for you in rugby terms is buy you time on the field. So much of the game, particularly when you are an outside-half or a centre, is about speed of thought, which is the number-one hallmark of all the greatest players. The more used to the pace of the Test arena you are, the quicker your thought processes become. If you are talented, that process will happen faster.

There was a nice touch for me after the final whistle when my opposite number Paul Dodge, a Leicester player, came over to me, looking as if he wanted to swap shirts. Now, I was very reluctant to let my jersey go, as it was my first cap, but Paul stunned me with what he said next.

'Don't worry, you can keep my shirt, I don't expect you to give me yours. Just pass on my regards to your dad. He's still a legend up in Leicester.'

It was a lovely moment and somehow appropriate that, as I savoured such a landmark event in my career, Dad's influence should be brought into the picture like that.

After the game, all I wanted to do was get over to the Cardiff clubhouse and have a couple of beers with all my mates, but first there was a post-match function to go to – and a Wales cap to collect.

3

BREAKTHROUGH, THEN BREAKDOWN

Much has been made at times of how Cardiff Rugby Football Club once styled itself as the greatest club in the world. Some scoff at the idea, but to me there is no doubt that there was a time when such a claim rang true. Cardiff in its old form was undoubtedly a great club. As for the greatest, well, you could have that debate a million times over with fans from around the globe, though being Cardiff born and bred I would always make the case for my club.

So many great players have worn the blue-and-black jersey – the '70s legends Gareth Edwards, Barry John and Gerald Davies may be the first that spring to mind, but when I was making my breakthrough in the early '80s, names like Adrian Hadley, Gareth Davies, Jeff Whitefoot, John Scott, Alan Phillips, Ian Eidman, Alun Donovan, Owen Golding and Bob Lakin ruled the roost. In my view, Cardiff were the dominant force of the '80s, an era before official league tables when clubs drew up their own fixture lists and the Welsh Cup, for so many years called the Schweppes Cup, was the one pot everyone wanted to win.

I played for Cardiff sides throughout my junior and youth days, from under-11s upwards. I'd play every Saturday morning, then go to watch the senior side play at the Arms Park in the afternoon and sell programmes on the gate. The beauty of doing this, of course, was that as well as earning a couple of quid pocket money, I was allowed into the match for free.

I was fanatical about Cardiff and had been ever since my dad first took me to games when I was young enough to sit on his shoulders. All I wanted was to one day play for Cardiff; at times, it was all I ever thought about. I remember coming back from a family holiday in West Wales and seeing signposts that told us how many miles there were to go to Cardiff and Newport: Cardiff 30, Newport 43. I always used to see it as the result of a rugby match and be disappointed that we had lost to our great rivals. Of course, it was different if ever we were coming over the Severn Bridge from England!

So many times in my younger days I was concerned about whether my lack of size and stature would prevent me from making the grade. When I was trying to make the step up from Cardiff Youth to the Rags, everyone seemed stronger, bigger and faster than me – I only managed to bridge the gap because of the training I did on the track at Maindy Stadium when I should have been working. It must have done the trick because I recall going back for pre-season training just before the trials for the Rags and suddenly feeling as though I could compete as an equal: I felt as though I'd bridged the gap.

The Rags was the perfect place to start a rugby career because, as I've explained, you had older seasoned stalwarts who were on their way down from the top of the game mixed with youngsters trying to make their way up. Older heads like Ian Robinson, who is now a great friend and was then renowned as one of the hardest players ever to lace up a pair of boots, and captain Terry Charles were the kind of people who had a huge influence on me, not just as a player but also as a person. The mixture of youth and experience meant that we had a good rounded side and could look after ourselves.

I can't stress enough how often we would go away to places up the valleys and the crowd would be baying for our heads: Cardiff were the team everyone wanted to beat. With guys like Robinson alongside you in the trenches, though, you always knew if there was any rough stuff, you could give as good as you got. It's something Cardiff's Welsh Premiership side, which has naturally taken the place of the Rags, has lacked in recent times. The team has been made up of youngsters and while they may have talent, they seem to lack good old-fashioned dog.

Yet as well as being able to mix it, the Rags philosophy was to always try to play a bit of rugby when we could and the older guys were selfless in the way they nurtured the youngsters like me. For example, Julian O'Brien played fly-half, but he was always prepared to move across to the centre position and let me wear the number 10 jersey when I took the field.

I was very respectful of the older players, but at the same time very confident in my own ability. I made a conscious effort not to be the cocky, mouthy new kid on the block when I first began to play for the Rags – I was always very polite and watched my Ps and Qs – though my natural character came to the fore as I began to establish myself.

At that time, there were trials to get into the Rags squad. You would have the boys coming up from the youth section and outside applicants – in other words those who had simply answered the club's annual advertisement in the press urging lads who thought they were good enough to come along and try out for the club. The trials were staged at Sophia Gardens, where Glamorgan play cricket. This was in the days when there were rugby pitches at the side of the square and you would turn up and be given a shirt number and a team to join. Only if you made it to the final trial would the Rags side come along and play those selected.

I played in this final trial in my first year out of the youth team in 1980 and there was a fellow playing on the wing called Gerald Cordle, who would later go on to become a superb wing for Cardiff. He had dreadlocks at the time and was a rough-and-ready lad from the tough Butetown area of Cardiff near the docks. Gerald had had a tough upbringing but was a really great bloke at heart and I could see he had serious pace. He scored three tries in the trial game after I had told him that his marker, a bloke called Steve Pill, whose father, Don, had been a committee man but had passed away when Steve was younger, would not fancy it if Gerald ran hard at him. Gerald was grateful for the tip-off and from that day on, me, Gerald and Kevin Trevett, another great friend of mine who I will mention again later, formed a close friendship.

As for me, I breezed in because I played really well on the back of feeling fitter, stronger and more confident than ever following my summer of training. By then, I knew I was going to make it as a top player with Cardiff and had so much drive and will to succeed. I just couldn't fathom why others weren't the same as me. Take the centre Pat Daniels, who had been capped by Wales. He seemed to have the rugby world at his feet for a time and then, for a couple of years, just stopped playing. When he came back to pre-season training, having put on a load of weight, I just thought it was a massive waste of talent.

'What are you doing?' I asked him. 'Why are you just throwing away your career?'

'Well, one year on, one year off!' was all he could say.

There were other guys who had looked like world-beaters in their earlier days who just faded away. One was a centre called Mike Murphy. Mike once forged a superb centre partnership with Pat Daniels and it was he who provided the perfect foil for Pat's power surges – as later Alun Donovan would for me. Mike suffered from constant hamstring problems and put on a lot of weight, but he was the best timer of a pass I had ever seen. He was squeezed out of Cardiff a couple of years later and went off to Pontypridd. I played against Mike with Cardiff and made numerous outside breaks past him, but the game was tinged with sadness for me because I felt Mike wasn't half the player I always thought he could have been. Mike taught me so much.

There were so many characters at Cardiff in the early days. Paul 'Pablo' Rees was one, a full-back who was always the life and soul of the party. He was established in the first team when I was still in the Rags and you could always guarantee that if the Rags had arranged a tour somewhere and were staying at a nice hotel with a beer kitty sorted out, Pablo would go down in training a couple of weeks before with a knock so he could coincide his comeback with the Rags match away on tour.

On one trip to Leicester, we arrived back at the hotel in the middle of a presentation for a cycling event. The announcer said, 'And in third place, with a cheque for £35 and a special Raleigh jacket, is [so-and-so – I can't remember the name].' Pablo, who had nothing whatsoever to do with it, just walked straight up onto the platform in his Cardiff blazer, shook the fellow's hand and walked off with the cheque and jacket!

After being nudged in the back by his wife, the fellow who should have collected the prizes came up to Pablo to ask what he thought he was doing, but he didn't get what he was hoping for. 'You can have the cheque, but I'm keeping the jacket,' Pablo said, before stomping off.

By spring 1985, my rugby career was a tale of happiness and success. I had made my Wales debut and had established myself as a first-choice centre for my beloved Cardiff. I'd had some great moments in the blue-and-black shirt as well – beating the Australian team that had won a Home Nations Grand Slam in October 1984 was definitely one highlight. We took the honours 16–12 at the National Stadium, emulating the Cardiff teams of 1908, 1947, 1957, 1966 and 1975 in having not lost to the Wallabies. We gave an immense display and showed enormous guts to hang on at the end when Australia hammered at our line. I was particularly pleased with the way I played. I was only 22 at the time, but, after my anticlimactic Wales debut, I now felt as though I had proved I could cut it in the highest company.

Adrian Hadley got the all-important try in the club match. The forwards were immense and Gareth Davies' display at fly-half made a mockery of the fact that he was at the time out of favour with the Wales selectors.

There was also our Schweppes Cup-final win against Neath earlier that year. We didn't play particularly well in beating the Welsh All Blacks 24–19 – they got amongst us well and our pack achieved nowhere near the dominance it expected – but Gareth Davies' extraordinary kicking that day helped see us home and ensure a fine note on which John Scott could step down as Cardiff captain.

I was a huge fan of Gareth's. Some people thought he was a fly-half who kicked it too often, but, having played on his shoulder for club and country, I can tell you that he had sublime skills and a fantastic rugby brain. There was nobody more delighted than me when he came back into the Wales team for the 1985 Five Nations. He'd been frozen out during the period John Bevan coached the side, with Bevan preferring the Swansea stand-off Malcolm Dacey. In my view, there was no comparison between the two players.

I was full of confidence as Gareth got changed next to me ahead of the championship opener that year against Scotland at Murrayfield and I had a great game in our fabulous 25–21 win, with David Pickering scoring two tries. It was one of my best-ever games for my country and it was no coincidence, as far as I was concerned, that it came playing next to Gareth Davies.

At club level, since the break-up of Mike Murphy and Pat Daniels, Cardiff had struggled to find the combination of a secondary play-maker to the fly-half and strike runner. They tried various characters in midfield – Neil Hutchings, Dave Barry and Chris Webber, to name a few – but without any real success. The press criticised Gareth's supposed inability to break and the harder he tried the more he highlighted his failings.

Subsequently, I was given a chance in the centre for Cardiff and with what must have been the confidence of youth, I demanded the ball all of the time and always offered a kicking option when nothing else was on. This, I feel, gave Gareth an outlet and also the confidence to go back to doing what he did best: controlling the game whether passing or kicking. His form flourished and he was soon back at fly-half for his country.

I remember the farcical situation in the dressing-room at Murrayfield before the Scotland game when Gareth lifted his jersey off the peg. There, in all its glory, was the number '1' with no '0' next to it: the Welsh Rugby Union had failed to sew a zero onto his shirt. Not that Gareth was unduly worried. When he picked up his shirt, he tipped me the wink, saying, 'Ringo, the boy's back – I'm still number one!' That made me chuckle. I sensed that Gareth was relaxed about coming back into the team, which I admired because had it been me in his shoes, I would have been feeling like it was my first cap again and busting a gut to prove a point.

To solve the shirt-number problem, someone had to hastily tack on a zero borrowed from the Scottish camp, although their numbers were a different shape and material to ours, which meant Gareth took to the field with a zero bigger than the number one on his back. I've often wondered how much that particular jersey would fetch at auction these days: a real collector's item if ever there was one. Yet despite the nonsense, after five minutes he dropped a goal and we were on our way to a great victory.

One of Gareth's real strengths was his ability to land drop goals. On one occasion against Ireland that same season, in a match we lost 21–9, he lined one up and I was convinced he was going to have the effort charged down by on-rushing defenders. I even altered my position outside him in anticipation that I would have to get back and cover. Gareth just stretched his arms out to his right and swung his leg in a kind of hooking motion around the on-rushing opponent, sending the ball spiralling towards the posts. It wasn't a perfect connection, but it went over and, as he ran back in his calm and stylish manner, I went over to ask him how he had done it. He was entirely nonchalant. Although it is not all that evident from the television pictures, I was next to it and know what a piece of genius it was. He was one of the finest exponents of the art of dropping goals.

On one occasion, I was practising drop goals before a big cup game for Cardiff and was sending most of them to the right of the posts. Gareth was watching and offered me some advice. He said that I was bringing my kicking leg through too slowly, so there was too much time between the strike and the bounce of the ball. 'The second that ball hits the floor, you must strike it,' he stressed.

I promptly struck six out of six straight through the middle of the posts from thirty-five metres.

A couple of years later in 1987, I was able to pass on the exact same piece of advice to Mike Rayer ahead of our cup final against Swansea. Mike dropped a crucial goal that day which put us two scores ahead late on at 16–9 (this was in the days when it was four points for a try). It turned out to be the kick that won us the game because Swansea grabbed a last-gasp try to get within a point of us. At the end of extra-time, the score was 16–15.

It's funny how little moments like the one I had with Gareth that day always return to pay dividends. I have to say I am a firm believer in the mantra offered by golfer Gary Player, who once said, 'The more I practise, the luckier I get.' I always trained for countless hours on my own on a Sunday with the ball and if something started feeling good, then I could always turn to it in games.

The cup finals were always the biggest occasions of the year for the club and I remember being gutted at having to sit out Cardiff versus Llanelli in 1985 when I was injured and see their fly-half Gary Pearce drop a late goal to win it 15–14 for the Scarlets. We always approached every cup game with respect, no matter who we were playing, because of the importance of getting to the final and I remember facing some incredibly fired-up smaller teams from the valleys in the earlier rounds of the competition.

Then came 13 April 1985, the fateful day when I destroyed my left knee playing for Cardiff against Swansea at the Arms Park. I was feeling tired, even though it was a full two weeks since I'd been one of Wales's better players in a 14–3 defeat to France in Paris. I really didn't fancy playing, which was so unlike me because throughout my career I have always wanted to play all the time.

I remember the day so well. David Bishop's brother, Terry, was having his wedding party at a place on Womanby Street just over the road from the Arms Park before the match, so I popped in to say hello, although, of course, I didn't drink.

I felt flat, for some reason, when the game kicked off. Perhaps subconsciously I was preoccupied with the following week's game, when England were due in Cardiff for the final tussle of the Five Nations. Whatever, the circumstances of the horrific knee injury I suffered that day were, typically, not helpful to my state of mind in the aftermath. My knee buckled in a double tackle put in on me by scrum-half Robert Jones and flanker Mark Davies, who is now the head physiotherapist with the Wales team. The ligaments just went on me.

The worst thing was that it happened while the referee was still playing advantage on a Cardiff penalty even though we had retreated about 40 yards back towards our own line. I thought about that for a while after the incident, replaying it over and over in my mind and wondering what might have been had he just blown his whistle a bit earlier. But more than that there seemed to have been something in my mind beforehand that day which had never been there before, telling me not to play. Why that was, I can't explain, because up to that point I had enjoyed my best-ever season.

I was later named Cardiff's player of the year, an award voted for by the supporters, as well as the *Western Mail*'s Welsh player of the year. The paper's rugby correspondent at the time, John Billot, reported that the decision was no surprise considering the 'fresh adventure' I had brought to the game in that campaign before the injury. Without wishing to sound big-headed, I thought it was a pretty accurate observation because even though I missed the last Five Nations game of the season against England, I had played very well in the others, particularly the games against France and Scotland in which I made numerous clean breaks. We only lost 14–3 to the French in Paris and I cut them on several occasions with evasive running. The only trouble was that every time I found space, the only person on my shoulder onto whom I could offload was the prop Jeff Whitefoot!

As for my knee injury, I was lucky on the one hand because John Fairclough, the surgeon who carried out the operation, who has since gone on to become a consultant, was hugely positive all the way through. He was at the match when it happened and knew exactly what was required.

I was under the knife within three hours of the match, needing total knee reconstruction. My anterior cruciate ligament had snapped, the medial ligament had gone and the cartilage had also torn. It was a mess. Where it had dislocated, my lower leg bone had actually dropped down a number of inches. The exact moment it occurred was captured by the photographer Huw Evans, now the most well-known snapper in the Welsh game. It looks horrific and I can clearly be seen screaming in pain. And I had good reason, I can tell you. Between sustaining the injury and John Fairclough performing the operation, I was in total and utter agony.

I knew it was bad as soon as it happened; even when the operation was done, the pain didn't go away. Furthermore I had problems with the blood clotting while I was in plaster, so the cast stayed on my leg for around eight weeks. It was straight into rehabilitation after that with a brace around the knee joint.

It wasn't so much the sheer challenge of recovering physically that was hard for me but the mental battle. After the operation, I was told by a consultant at the hospital that I would never play again. To hear those words devastated me. Later, without a shred of exaggeration, I began to think about people who kill themselves because of severe depression. I'm not sure if that's what was going on with me, but I was having suicidal thoughts. One minute I would be saying to myself, 'I don't want to be here any more'; the next I would be telling myself not to be so silly and to snap out of it. It was as if I had a devil on one shoulder and an angel on the other. I just could not come to terms with never being able to play rugby again.

All the while, the pain was excruciating. It felt for all the world as if the plaster had been put on too tightly, and the throbbing was unbearable.

Then John Fairclough came round and my outlook changed. Having been the man who actually did the operation, he assured me that there was no way I wouldn't play again. He told me he had heard of patients who had recovered from the same injury and were fit within as little as six months.

That was it: I decided to work towards regaining my fitness by that November. Being able to set a target changed my mindset completely: suddenly, there was light at the end of the tunnel.

That said, I didn't hit that six-month target because of problems resulting from an infection I contracted when I came out of plaster, which set me back time-wise. But I got on with the rehab as best I could. My leg was incredibly skinny and needed to be built back up. I went to a centre in Talygarn where Terry Holmes had recuperated and although I wanted to go to some top-notch place in Surrey where I'd heard all the professional footballers went, I ended up telling myself that if it was good enough for Terry then it was good enough for me and I knuckled down.

To start with, the physiotherapists taught me how to walk again. There were times when I used to get terribly down because my progress just wasn't quick enough for my liking. Then on odd days I would make a breakthrough, like managing to do something I couldn't do before, and my spirits would be lifted. I was doing all kinds of stretching and weightlifting exercises.

I owe a huge debt of gratitude to Tudor Jones, the Cardiff and Wales physiotherapist at the time, who had also worked at Cardiff City Football Club. He must have knocked on my door every morning to ensure I was up, out and training. Tudor put me through hell, but he knew what was good for me. There were times I was so down I was desperate not to do anything, but Tudor was always there, insisting I just got on with it. He got me running for the first time, as I made even more progress, and I was in the pool twice a day doing remedial exercises to bend the leg.

As well as Tudor, I had my own personal motivation to get back and play for Wales, but there were good days and bad days on that front, too. I was often frustrated at the repetitive exercises, and the boredom I felt doing gentle moves compared to the type of training I was used to got to me on occasions.

In the end, I was out of the game for eleven months, though I would have recovered in nine had it not been for the trouble I had with the infection. In hindsight, I think six was a bit on the optimistic side. Even with the advances in the medical world these days, they say you need a minimum of seven months with that type of injury for fear of coming back too soon.

I desperately wanted to play before the end of the 1985–86 season to get my confidence up for the next campaign, and I did come back in March 1986 for the Rags against Ebbw Vale, which was the perfect reintroduction. And there was an unexpected bonus for me before that season was out: a 28–21 Welsh Cup-final win against our old rivals Newport in which my pal Adrian Hadley scored three tries. It felt great to get back for that game.

It was also good to read comments from the captain, Alan Phillips, after the match about how much he felt Cardiff had missed my creativity in the midfield. One of our tries that day was as clinical as you will ever see, coming direct from a lineout. Terry Holmes and Gareth Davies worked it from half-back, with Davies missing me out and feeding my centre partner Alun Donovan. I looped around Alun and popped a pass for full-back Mike Rayer to split the Newport defence and put Hadley in. You simply don't see tries scored from such first-phase situations these days.

When I watched a video of that game, however, I looked at myself and it was as if I was playing on one leg: I still didn't have the full range of movement and I looked as though I was limping, even though I felt I was putting my full weight on the leg. In a sense, I was never able to leave that injury behind because I convinced myself that I had lost a yard of pace because of it. There are those who would say I had.

One result of the match was that I decided from then on to concentrate on being a second five-eighth, or an inside-centre, because I didn't think I had the pace to play in the number 13 jersey. I was fearful of being exposed in defence by the very quickest outside-centres. I subsequently developed my kicking game and ability to pass off both sides, making the inside-centre my specialist position.

They say lightning doesn't strike twice in terms of injuries the like of which I suffered on 13 April 1985. Well, that was true for me to a degree, although a few years later I was to endure another injury that meant knee problems would haunt me later in my career.

It was Boxing Day 1988 and the traditional fixture of Cardiff versus Pontypridd at the Arms Park was being played. I took a heavy tackle from the Ponty scrum-half Keith Lee and again I knew I was in trouble. Don't get me wrong, this time it was nowhere near as bad as the first time: the damage to the medial ligaments was nowhere near approaching the scale of April 1985. The initial diagnosis was that I would be out of the game for three months, and bang went another Five Nations campaign and the chance to add to the 16 caps I had amassed by then. Bang, too, went any chance I had of touring Australia with the British Lions the summer of the following year.

I was never going to be faced with the Everest I had to climb in 1985 and I did get back in approximately three months, but the irony is that although it was the lesser of the two knee injuries, it is the one that gives me the most trouble to this day because I wasn't as diligent in my rehabilitation as I had been with my left knee. I didn't build up the muscles around the joint sufficiently before returning.

Even now it's my right knee I have to keep moving and keep supple, otherwise I start to experience severe pain. I have to take tablets every day in order to try and keep the joint as flexible as possible. I still have screws in my left knee and I can still run and sidestep off it even now, but when it comes to doing the same on the right one, something tells me not to risk it. I just can't put it down too firmly on the floor. There is no cartilage in my right knee, which means when the bones interlock it just goes into a spasm. It kills me to go down on both knees and it takes me ages to get back up. I could be sitting at an awkward angle and the two bones will lock up on me. Maybe it was because coming back from the injury the second time was so much easier that I couldn't motivate myself to put in the required work, I really couldn't say; but the long, lonely road to recovery was what I just couldn't deal with and again I sank into bouts of being really low psychologically.

I remember once agreeing to do an interview with Eddie Butler for the BBC. I told him to meet me at the gym of a hotel called the Inn on the Avenue on the eastern outskirts of Cardiff. He arrived with a camera crew all ready to go, but I just couldn't face doing it. I apologised to Eddie, but I just could not bring myself to go through with the interview; my head was just so scrambled I don't think I'd have been able to string two worthwhile sentences together. I couldn't concentrate. I couldn't do anything.

Of course, I know I am by no means the only sportsperson to have experienced nasty knee injuries. One of the most recent victims was England footballer Michael Owen at the 2006 World Cup. I knew how devastated he must have felt when he sustained his injury, especially as it happened in such innocuous circumstances. He wasn't even being challenged at the time: it came about as a result of his body twisting awkwardly.

One thing a sportsperson like Michael Owen would have over a younger Mark Ring is that Owen is a professional who is used to the environment of rehabilitation from injury. It comes with the territory. People in his position don't just have access to the very best medical advice, they are completely surrounded by it. Whatever can be done to aid recovery, you can be sure the specialists are doing it, even if it means going to the other side of the world to see the top surgeon in a given field.

For me, playing in an amateur sport back in the '80s, there was just not the support network in place. I was working in the civil service when I was first injured and had to go on half pay after a certain number of months, which meant money became tight and gave me a whole new headache to contend with.

I am not really one for crying over spilt milk and I am big

enough to accept that the knee injuries I suffered were part and parcel of me playing a physical, collision sport, so on that score I have no regrets. People still say to me if it hadn't been for my knee, I would have got loads more caps for Wales, but I won 32 in all. I had four when the first knee went and I got another twenty-eight after that, including sixteen after the second injury, so ultimately I don't believe my knees were that costly. Furthermore, I played for Wales from 1983 to 1991 and to miss just two seasons through injury wasn't that bad a return.

For anyone who suffers a similar serious injury, I would just advise them to be prepared to go through hell in order to recover. There is simply no other way. You have to dedicate yourself 100 per cent to getting the range of movement going and sticking strictly to whatever programme the specialists give you. Anything less and, like me, there will be a price to pay, not just in your immediate future but in later life as well. You have to be professional about it. You cannot afford to get too down if you want to play on the biggest stage for your capabilities, something I managed to do in two World Cups, the first of which was a real step into the unknown.

4

WORLD CUP 1987

I suppose you could have called us guinea pigs going into the 1987 World Cup. Nobody quite knew how the first-ever tournament between teams from across the globe would be received and certainly as players, we were unsure of what to expect.

These days the World Cup is the absolute pinnacle and competing nations are forever banging on about development programmes that are in place supposedly to ensure the team peaks at the right time every four years. Look at someone like Graham Henry, the New Zealand coach, who is pulling players out of the Super 14 as and when he sees fit and virtually developing multiple Test teams that are providing the All Blacks with extraordinary strength and depth. In this sense, perhaps there is too much importance attached to it.

Meanwhile for us in 1987, it was more of an adventure. Our attitude was, 'Let's go down there, give it a whirl and see what happens.' We were genuinely optimistic about going a fair way in the World Cup and we always knew there was a strong chance we might play England in the quarter-finals.

Of course, the game was still amateur. We all had full-time jobs and, to me, it never felt as though we were doing something that was the ultimate in our career. There wasn't even any guarantee the World Cup would happen again if that one didn't prove to be a success.

Our third-placed finish had to be judged as a huge achievement at the time, though we were by no means the third-best team in the world, especially given that the Springboks weren't competing.

It's been said enough times down the years that coming third merely papered over the cracks in Welsh rugby that became chasms only a few years down the line, and in my opinion it's a view that is spot on. The 49–6 annihilation – that is exactly what it was – at the hands of New Zealand in the semi-final was all the evidence anyone needed to prove the point. Whatever else we achieved in those four weeks or so, it was put into sobering perspective by that defeat and the manner of the beating, which I will return to later.

However, we pitched up at Wellington's Athletic Park for the first game of the tournament against Ireland, knowing that beating them held the key to all our hopes – we were very confident of getting past our other two pool rivals, Tonga and Canada.

I got our try in the 13–6 victory that settled us down nicely, then we came through a horrible match against Tonga at the Showgrounds in Palmerston North. We were criticised for our display in the 29–16 win, but the critics appeared to ignore the fact that the game was played in a dreadful swirling wind that was always going to prevent us from turning on the style.

Another thing that went over their heads was the fact that this was our second Test match in four days. Back then, that was something completely alien to us. All we had ever known was the Five Nations in which we would always have a fortnight between games, sometimes a month, which gave us lots of time to organise ourselves and get mentally attuned to the task ahead. We found it tough to adjust and it meant we were not sharp in that clash with Tonga.

You wouldn't have thought it, mind you, looking at the way my best mate on that trip, Glenn Webbe, performed that day, as he ran in a hat-trick of tries. But it was his third score that I will never forget.

Webby had been poleaxed shortly before by a head-high tackle from their full-back Tali Ete'aki, which was just the latest in a long line of questionable challenges from the Tongan boys that had gone on all game. Webby was smashed in the jaw in the challenge and when I looked at him as he pulled himself to his feet, I knew straight away there was something not right with him. Yet I was the only one who seemed to realise it.

I told our captain, Richard Moriarty, that Webby had a problem.

'There's not long to go,' he replied. 'Look after him and just get him to the end of the game.'

Now, ever since we had arrived, Webby had been going on about the 'try of the tournament' prize that had been put up by one of the sponsors and was rumoured to be a Mazda car. Typically, Webby reckoned he had a chance of winning and vowed to conjure up something sensational, even though in a pool match New Zealand's John Kirwan had already caught the ball under his own posts and jinked his way through the entire Italy team to run the length of the field and score. Nothing deterred Webby, though, and in training he was always trying to drum up flamboyant moves that would culminate in him taking the scoring pass.

However, although we didn't know it at the time, the blow from Ete'aki had left Webby severely concussed. Looking at him, I didn't think he would make the end of the game, let alone score a try that would be a contender for the Mazda. I was trying to keep the ball away from him, but then in the last few minutes Tonga put a kick behind our defence and I was the one left chasing back. As I gathered the ball, the only man in support and in space as their attackers bore down on me was Webby, so, somewhat reluctantly, I threw out a long pass to him. I tore over to him so he would be able to offload it back to me and get out of harm's way, but I needn't have bothered. Webby went on the most incredible run I have ever seen, going through the entire Tonga team to score under the posts. Though I don't think he won the Mazda!

I was the first to congratulate him, but as he looked at me, he burst into tears, genuine heartfelt tears from a guy who I had never seen cry in my entire life.

'Ringy, I know you, but I don't know anyone else here, I don't know where I am,' he said. He was petrified and clearly in a different world.

Webby was fine an hour after the game, but he was told to pack his bags and go home because he would be out of action for a minimum of three weeks. It was a loss to us, not just from a playing point of view but also because he was the life and soul of the party and always did so much to keep up people's spirits.

The pair of us teamed up in the first week of the trip to arrange something that boosted morale no end. Quite often in New Zealand we found ourselves in these small hotels where there was next to nothing for us to do to pass the time when we weren't training. Consequently boredom set in amongst the boys and never more so than during our first week in Wellington. You can imagine my excitement, then, when I spotted a pool table in one of the downstairs rooms: I immediately suggested to Webby that we organise a pool tournament. He was all for it and so were the management, who I think realised that us players needed a release mechanism.

Webby and I could both play a bit, but some of the others were not quite so keen, with the likes of the Neath hooker, Kevin Phillips, refusing to play because he said he was no good. We quickly passed a rule that everyone had to play, whether they liked it or not, and before long we had done a draw for a knockout competition – which we fiddled to ensure I met Kevin Phillips in the first round.

Naturally, we had to run a book on the whole business and so I installed myself as the bookmaker and Webby became my runner. The only other rule was that every player had to put NZ$25 on themselves, which immediately gave us a nice kitty with which to run the book. A lot of people had bet on me, so I slashed my odds to 6–4 favourite. The prop Stuart Evans was also highly fancied.

There was an early shock, though – or what was believed to be an early shock – when I lost to Kevin. I was more concerned with running the book, so had deliberately let myself be beaten: in the end, I gave up leaving him easy opportunities because he was so bad he kept missing them and instead I made it appear as though I had potted the black by mistake. There was uproar amongst the boys at what they were convinced was a genuine giant-killing. Stuart Evans then had a genuine off-day and was beaten early on.

Come the final, there were two people left who would never have been fancied – full-back Paul Thorburn and second-row Phil Davies, now coaching Llanelli Scarlets. It was best of five frames – with beer mats covering the pockets to save money. The names went up on the board as Paul 'Cliff' Thorburn and Phil 'Steve' Davies. To make an occasion of it, we made them play in their tour dicky bows and shirts. The Wales touring party turned up en masse to watch the game as if it was the final of the World Championship at the Crucible Theatre.

Glenn as referee was even wearing his WRU blazer and a pair of white gloves – he looked like one of the black and white minstrels. To top it all off, I had carved out a semi-circle in a wooden doorstop so Glenn could use it as a marker to clean the ball. When he brought that out, the rest of the boys couldn't believe the professionalism of it all!

Earlier at the quarter-final stage, I had noticed that there were still no bets on Phil Davies even though he was 8-1, so Glenn and I had piled a load of money on Phil and slashed his odds back, so were desperate to see him win in the final. He went 2-0, Paul pulled it back to 2-2 and then the decider went to the black with Phil winning it. As Webby and I danced around the room in elation, I think some of the boys began to suss out that they had been tucked up. The tournament was a roaring success, though: it did so much to break the ice among everyone in the squad, including management, and it certainly broke the monotony.

Other times we lightened the mood with more basic, off-the-cuff pastimes. Webby made up a game while we were on the bus back from training one day which involved one of us calling assistant coach Derek Quinnell a name, then the next person having to say it that little bit louder and so on. Conveniently, Webby said that he would start off. And guess who was last to have his turn? Yes, yours truly. I practically had to bellow the immortal line 'DQ's a t**t!' at the top of my voice, which inevitably landed me in trouble with the management.

We had imposed a drinking curfew on ourselves during the World Cup and the management encouraged us to stay in our hotels, but on one occasion while we were in Invercargill in the South Island of New Zealand before the match with Canada, we were so bored that Webby said he was going out and I agreed to go, too. We didn't intend to get up to any mischief, we just wanted a stroll and possibly a couple of quiet beers if we came across a bar.

Everything around us was dead, the weather was awful and, to add to our frustration, we were watching matches being played over in Australia in warm sunshine. Then we spotted a light that hinted at a bit of life. It was a little wine-bar-type place and as we got closer, we saw practically the entire Scotland and Ireland squads inside. While our boys were holed up, they were all out having a great time.

We went in and had a good old chinwag with them all and before long our idea of one or two pints became three or four and we decided to play the 'Itchy-coo' game. I won't try to give a detailed description of the affair, suffice to say it is one of those classic drinking games that involves a chairman – Webby – and the participants having to memorise a series of actions and sayings based around the phrase 'Itchy-coo, coo, coo, coo'.

It was going along fine until Webby introduced rubbing his fingers across the cheeks of the guy sitting next to him, who happened to be Scottish flanker John Jeffrey, otherwise known as 'The Great White Shark'. The trouble was, unbeknown to Jeffrey, Webby had dipped his fingers in an ashtray, so it wasn't long before the Scot's face was covered with black stripes. Jeffrey was totally oblivious and couldn't understand why everyone else was giggling so much: he thought it was something to do with the game. Even after a few comments likening him to Glenn Webbe, he didn't twig, and we were amazed to hear a few days later from the Scottish boys that he had turned up for breakfast at the team hotel the morning after still sporting the black marks – he'd obviously just gone straight to bed the night before and had got up in an early-morning daze.

When Wales played Scotland in the Five Nations in Cardiff the following season, Webby was on the bench and as we were strolling around the pitch in our blazers, we spotted Jeffrey doing the same with the Scots boys down the other end of the pitch.

'Oi, JJ!' Webby yelled, at which Jeffrey looked up. 'Itchy-coo, coo, coo, coo!' Webby shouted with a big toothy grin. Jeffrey, obviously keyed up for the game, could only offer a two-word expletive.

Webby's the salt of the earth. He was a great player in his time, but it's his personality that's worth so much. He'll stand his ground in the face of anything – nothing fazes him – yet he is the kindest, most genuine guy you could wish to meet. And his sense of fun is legendary. He's done me a couple of times, none more so than when he took it upon himself to use a tab I had earned for myself at Dorothy's Fish Bar in Caroline Street in the centre of Cardiff.

Any Welsh rugby follower will know Caroline Street as Chip Alley, the place where you go for a tray of chips and curry sauce to soak up a bellyful of beer on international match days, not to mention Friday and Saturday nights out. Well, I had become such a regular customer of the place in my later playing days that if I had ever spent everything in the casino and was hungry, I would go to Dorothy's and be given credit – they knew I was good for the money. One evening, I put enough behind the counter after a decent win to give myself four curries in credit, but I made the mistake of telling Glenn about it. A couple of weeks later after I hadn't been so lucky on the tables, I headed for Dorothy's confident that even though I was penniless there would be a good bit of grub there for me free of charge.

'Sorry, there's no credit left,' I was told to my amazement, having already selected my plastic fork.

'How come?' I asked.

'Your mate, Glenn Webbe, was here last night with his three pals,' came the reply. Webby had done me up like a kipper!

As players under head coach Tony Gray during the World Cup, we had a big input into how we played and this was particularly the case ahead of our final pool win when we trounced Canada 40–9. Tony was a nice fellow, very laid-back and was one of the few coaches of those times who didn't insist on trying to rule with an iron fist. For instance, when a group of us expressed our concerns before playing the Canucks that we were trying to play a wide game, even though Paul Thorburn was a full-back whose style was not suited to that tactic, we were subsequently given licence to have Ieuan Evans and Adrian Hadley hitting the line like the full-back according to which side of the field we were on. For all the talk of player power that hit the Welsh game during the saga over Mike Ruddock's departure in 2005, it has always existed to a degree.

Fair play to Tony for understanding where our strengths lay – in pace and running angles. I think that meeting may later have played in his thoughts when he rather controversially dropped Thorburn in favour of Anthony Clement at the start of the 1988 Five Nations.

Our tactic obviously worked because we ran in eight second-half tries for our most emphatic victory of the tournament – even though I was left out!

Tony was always one of these fellows who tries to get into the mindset of the players and quite often he would approach us informally for ideas and feedback rather than us having to go to him. Throwing it around was what that team was all about.

In the build-up to the tournament, JJ Williams had come in to work with us on our speed, which was the first time specialist attention had been paid to improving speed among the team – although in the run-up to the '87 World Cup, I do remember one day of fitness testing at the old National Stadium after they had put in a three-lane tartan track around the pitch. It was to be a day when David Pickering, who made his Wales debut in the same game as me against England in 1983 and is currently the WRU chairman, made a bit of a spectacle of himself in front of the lads. Pickering struck me as a bit of a flashy type, so it was no surprise to me that when our fitness instructor, who had been brought in from the Cardiff sports college, now known as UWIC, asked who had done proper weights, Pickering was the first with his hand up.

I had never done weights in my life before then, which I know will amaze some people, given the emphasis there is on that side of things in the game these days, but I just never felt it necessary. I was happy with my physique and the way I played the game. I did start doing more as these sessions continued and I worked hard with Bob Newman, an old teammate of mine from the Cardiff Rags, to play catch-up: I was bench-pressing 105 kilos before very long as I bulked up. My defence was criticised at times, though in all the tight matches in which I played I always made my tackles. There were instances when I was trying to protect a sore shoulder and hung back a little, but I never ever did so when the result of the match was still in the balance.

Anyway, Ray Giles, a scrum-half from Aberavon who was in the squad at the time, had done weights to quite a serious level, so when he gave the first demonstration on the bench press it was textbook stuff. Pickering volunteered to demonstrate a press-behind-neck lift. Those who know anything about weightlifting will be aware that to get the bar to this position it should be cleaned (lifted from the floor to the chest), then pushed over the head to rest on the back of the shoulders. But he tried to snatch it (lift it off the floor and over the head in one movement) and, with the bar being too heavy for this movement, he soon began to stumble. All the boys cried with laughter.

We then went out on the track. Pickering was the only one who wore running spikes, silky shorts and a vest and timed himself as he crossed the finishing line, as if to make a point to people that he was the type of guy who did his own work. He shot off like Sebastian Coe when we had to do a long-distance run around the track, but I think we had more or less lapped him by the time we finished.

Even when we got out on the training field, instead of just going off to get on with his work with the forwards, on many occasions he would be trying to drop goals and do skills.

In terms of running, I was never the quickest off the mark – though stamina-wise I was among the best, as my stats proved. While someone like Jonathan Davies was like lightning over 60 yards, I could offer other skills: vision and evasive running were my strengths.

At times, John Devereux managed to combine pace with brute force to devastating effect. Devereux had almost everything a rugby player could want: he could kick the ball miles and was a colossus in defence. I would put him in the mould of Wales captain Gareth Thomas today. I saw John as an ideal full-back and could never understand why he didn't play there. John was always pushed as a centre. He had some great games, no question, but the one thing I didn't rate about him was his passing ability. You could never expect a real money pass off John that would open up a defence, or a little deft offload when it was required. John was a different sort of player to me in that his game was based around power and crashing into defenders. I never liked that way of playing: I've always felt that three-quarters should seek to avoid contact in attack whenever possible. It should be the flankers and the full-back who set up rucks and suck opposition defenders in, leaving three-quarters to then stretch what cover there is left.

In 1987, I didn't regain my place for the England quarter-final in Brisbane, having to be content with being one of the replacements. I was disappointed but lost out because I hadn't been part of the 40–9 win against Canada. We registered a 16–3 win against the old enemy with Robert Jones, flanker Gareth Roberts and Devereux all scoring tries, but quite frankly the victory surprised nobody in our camp because we didn't rate England back then. But the bubble soon burst, or should I say exploded.

The crushing nature of the semi-final defeat to New Zealand

left us demoralised. The All Blacks 49–6 win was an embarrassing result for us by any standards in what was meant to be a last-four encounter. We were simply out-powered and out-manoeuvered in every phase; they were light years ahead of us in their organisation and their structures.

I've always hated sitting on the bench, but that's where I was that day. I have to admit a part of me wondered whether I was better off staying there. We were so far behind them that day it was jolting, and it was the physical difference as much as anything. Our second row that day, Neath player Huw Richards, was sent off for throwing punches at their lock forward, Gary Whetton. Afterwards to cheer him up, I gave him the shorts the great All Black winger John Kirwan had worn during the game, which Kirwan had given to me as a momento. Huw was chuffed and tried them on straight away – but they were too big for him! Their wing's shorts were too big for our second row: enough said.

I got on well with Kirwan; in fact, all the New Zealand boys were fantastic socially, along with being the best team on the planet. They were old school and made a big effort with us, something you don't see nowadays: players might have a quick drink with their opponents after a match and then scarper.

Yet when it was anything to do with the rugby ball, the Kiwis set all the standards. I remember that as soon as the whistle went at the end of that semi-final game, their subs, led by the legendary Zinzan Brooke, shouted across to our subs to play touch rugby as a means of exercising the lungs. They had five, we had six and it was the most serious game of touch rugby I have ever played in my life. And guess what, we beat them – though we did have the extra man!

After the match, the International Rugby Board representative who had been following us around the tournament, an English bloke by the name of John Kendall-Carpenter, got up to make an address. Sensing our lads needed some cheering up, I decided to set myself a challenge. I turned to Richard Moriarty and bet him

NZ$25 that while Kendall-Carpenter was making his speech, I could pinch the handkerchief, which was always there come hell or high water, from his blazer pocket. I went to the salad bar, picked up a pair of tongs and sneaked behind our man, with the rest of the boys looking on in amazement. I was determined to pull off the feat, as Moriarty had given me 6–1 odds.

As Kendall-Carpenter turned one way and then the other, my silver salad tongs were ducking and diving as I tried desperately to swipe the handkerchief. Eventually, I got hold of it and went to yank it out only to discover it was sewn in. I ended up almost pulling the poor bloke's blazer off. Everyone collapsed in hysterics and the stunt was taken in good spirits by one and all. The atmosphere was so convivial and laid-back.

Moriarty was a brilliant person. I first met him on a Wales B tour of Spain back in 1983. He very quickly became a good mate, touring Western Province with me on the first World XV tour I went on in the same year. Richard was one of those guys who could drink one night and then get up and train the next day without seeming to feel it at all.

As we left Brisbane en route to Rotorua in New Zealand's North Island for the third-place play-off against the Wallabies and what would be the last match of the tournament, we found ourselves in a pretty remote part of Australia. We were on a bus heading for Sydney airport when, all of a sudden, Clive Rowlands spotted a shop at the side of the road and ordered a stop for ice lollies in what was pretty savage heat. It had just been announced that the Swansea flanker Richard Webster, who had been sent out to the tournament after Richie Collins had been ruled out of playing due to an injured back, would win his first cap against the Aussies and the boys were all really chuffed for him, but when an opportunity arrived for a wind-up we couldn't resist it.

Outside the shop was one of those old red telephone boxes, so Bleddyn Bowen decided to get to work. Bleddyn took down the number of the phone box and went to call it from the shop, making sure Webster didn't see anything.

Moments later, it conveniently rang. Webster and I were standing right outside the booth, so I walked in and picked up the receiver. Bleddyn explained his joke, so I stuck my head out of the door and said, 'Webby, you're not going to believe this, but it's Peter Jackson from the *Daily Mail*. He's tracked us down and wants a word with you about winning your first Wales cap!'

Webster spent about ten minutes on the phone, talking about what a proud moment it would be for him and how his mum and dad and the rest of his family would be chuffed to bits, thinking he was actually giving an interview to the *Daily Mail*. Neither Bleddyn nor I had the heart to tell him straight after: I don't think he found out until we got home.

We were understandably underdogs in the play-off, but there were a number of things in our favour. One was the fact that the game was back in New Zealand, which meant we would have all the support of the home crowd, who hated the Aussies. The other was the differing mental state of either side. Australia had just lost what was an epic semi-final to France, when they believed they had one foot in the final. They were now so deflated they were even coming out with comments in the press that they could barely be bothered with the game against us.

We had to pick ourselves up after what happened to us against New Zealand and because of that the management decided to tinker with the team, giving me the nod to start for the first time since the Tonga game. Other than my first Test, the game against Australia was the only one in my career that I played totally by instinct.

We were so fired up because of the New Zealand debacle; we were desperate to prove we were actually a better team than we had appeared that day and the complacent Aussie comments in the media only poured petrol on the fires.

Of course, a key moment in the game was the dismissal of the Australian blindside flanker, David Cody, for punching our openside, Gareth Roberts. Yet believe it or not, and I cannot explain it to this day, I didn't realise he had gone. What I was doing or thinking about at the time, I don't know, but it wasn't until I arrived back in Cardiff after the World Cup that I discovered Cody had been red-carded. The only possible reason I can offer is that I was just so consumed by adrenalin that my mind was elsewhere. I can't stress what a monumental process it was building ourselves up to go out there and save a bit of face for our country after the humiliation of the semi-final.

After the final whistle when I got back to the dressing-room, I cried uncontrollably for what seemed like ages and got terrible stick from some of the boys for doing so. And the grandstand finish probably didn't help on that score. I gave Adrian Hadley the scoring pass for him to touch down for a late try right next to the left-wing corner flag and then Paul Thorburn slotted a wondrous conversion from the touchline to win it for us.

You had to take your hat off to him for executing such a difficult kick in such trying circumstances, but I always fancied him to get it, I honestly did.

It is possible to criticise Thorburn for his lack of pace and the fact that he wasn't the most evasive runner in the world, but one thing in which you couldn't find fault with him was his reliability. Yes, he may have lacked flair and imagination, but he would never drop a high ball, he would never miss touch and you would always back him when he aimed for goal. What's more, nobody trained harder. He also had a great professional attitude that I respected hugely.

There was a comical footnote to that game against Australia, though. As I cried out of pure pent-up emotion afterwards, Tony Gray came across to me and said in all sincerity, 'Don't worry, Ringo, you weren't that bad'!

How would I sum up the first-ever World Cup from Wales's point of view? Well, we were behind in organisation, power and athleticism, particularly up front, compared to the other top teams, and New Zealand especially were light years ahead. I would place France on their day in the top bracket as well. Who knows how we would have coped against them in the semi-final. I think the result may have been slightly closer but not a great deal because we would still not have been able to match their power and athleticism. The play-off win against the Wallabies had been all well and good, but they weren't the real Australia and they played most of the match with 14 men, even if I didn't realise it at the time!

What we did masked the reality of where we were. The public had clearly had the wool pulled over their eyes, judging by the great reception they gave us when we returned. But the players knew the truth; the New Zealand game had made sure of that. Though what was on the horizon did nothing to encourage a reality check among the general public.

5

TRIPLE CROWN, THEN BLACKOUT

When our team manager at the 1987 World Cup, the incomparable Clive Rowlands, was asked where Wales would go following our 49–6 semi-final drubbing against New Zealand, he famously declared, 'Back to beating England.'

His words were to prove somewhat prophetic as, apart from a forgettable one-sided 46–0 romp against the USA in Cardiff that November, our next match was indeed against the old enemy at Twickenham. The last time a Wales side won at Twickenham was 6 February 1988, a full 18 years ago now.

That cold day at Headquarters is one of the most memorable of my career, not just for the victory but also for the shenanigans that went on in London that evening, which I will come to. I recall former assistant coach Scott Johnson, the wise-cracking Aussie, announcing that Wales's plan when they arrived at Twickenham in 2006 would be to run the English all over the park. Well, that was no different to what we intended to do in 1988, except we managed to do it successfully, thanks to a back line that contained four outside-halfs and a pack which, it must be said, was the dominant force.

I recall Staff Jones, my mate at Pontypool, where I was playing at the time, had a huge game against England prop Jeff Probyn. The papers were talking about how Probyn had a unique scrummaging technique and was going to destroy us in the set-piece, but on the day I felt he was inconsequential.

There was all manner of uproar in the Welsh press when Paul Thorburn was left out of the side and, as I've said, I'm convinced that our chat with coach Tony Gray during the World Cup about Thorburn's lack of pace had played a part in it.

I was happy with the inclusion of Anthony Clement, a player who, along with me, Jonathan Davies and Bleddyn Bowen, had grown up playing at number 10. And, in my opinion, the right- and left-footed kicking options that Bleddyn and I offered gave us a lovely balance in midfield. There was a sackful of skill, pace and rugby intelligence in that back division and the two tries we scored through my old school pal Adrian Hadley were real beauties.

The Thorburn apologists argued that we were naive to go into the game without a recognised goalkicker, but when I was called in to replace John Devereux, who broke a finger at the start of Test week, there was no doubt in my mind that I would take on that responsibility. I did my reputation no good on that front, though, as I missed both conversions of Hadley's tries, albeit from narrow angles wide out on the left wing. The other three points in our 11–3 victory came from a Jonathan Davies drop goal.

We were becoming increasingly more confident under the leadership of Gray. The wounds of that infamous New Zealand World Cup drubbing were still a little tender, but at the end of the day we knew we weren't playing the All Blacks in the Five Nations and so we could have a good crack at being the big fish in a smaller pond.

I still hear from journalists who want to talk about the last time Wales beat England at Twickenham and they are always taken aback when I tell them we went there totally confident of victory. Personally, I know I did. To me, they didn't have any real threat in their back division.

I saw Nigel Melville as a basic and limited scrum-half who was never going to dictate anything and although fly-half Les Cusworth was a brilliant player for Leicester whom I admire enormously, he was clearly under orders that day to kick a large percentage of ball away, which is precisely what he did. Will Carling and Kevin Simms were in the centre, but Carling was still raw and again didn't represent any huge problem for us. He was a top bloke, mind you, even though he would go on to become something of a hate figure in Wales in later years. He was seen as toffee-nosed by a lot of Welsh fans, but in reality he was very down to earth and fun-loving. We got on well and the fact that his dad, Bill, used to play for Cardiff was a talking point between us.

To top it all off, their captain, Mike Harrison, was on the wing, miles away from the thick of it, and although he had great pace, we knew England had to get the ball to him first. All the papers had written us off, but we really fancied ourselves.

Yet the day as a whole would prove to be a strange one for me. I did something that would come back to haunt me for many years as we strolled around on the Twickenham grass before the match. For some reason I was being followed by a photographer at that stage of the day, who had singled me out rather than any of the other lads. I was trying to fix my thoughts on the game and just wanted to be on my own, but this guy wasn't having any of it, so I thought I would give him a daft picture in the hope that it would satisfy him and he would buzz off. I turned around, bent my knees, stuck up my hands and made a silly face.

Big mistake. I may have made my point to the snapper, but all it meant was, from that day on, whenever I stepped out of line in any way or did something silly, the snap was used to make the whole thing appear ten times worse. It only serves to make me look a total clown and I hate it. My rush of blood in front of that photographer is something I seriously regret.

England had this idea in their heads that they were going to bomb new cap Tony Clement with high balls, a typically predictable tactic when there's a new full-back in town, but their kicks were too often badly placed and Tony dealt with them every time, with the rest of the backs supporting him by getting behind him and giving him options.

We scored the first try from just such a situation with Cusworth putting a high one up to Clement and us running it back at him to put Adrian Hadley in after some lovely early passing along the back line.

The second was similar, but it began when Jonathan Davies went on an arcing run over to the blindside. Jonathan exposed their back-row forward, Mick 'the Munch' Skinner, that day and spent most of the match winding him up, shouting in his cheeky high-pitched Trimsaran tones, 'Mickey, Mickey, which way am I going, then, Mickey?'

Skinner was cumbersome that day and had no idea how to deal with our angles. He spent most of the game eyeballing Jonathan, looking like he was ready to kill him. It was an ongoing exchange that would come to the boil after the game, of which more later.

Yet nobody was ever going to worry Jonathan in those days: the little man was truly in his pomp in the union game. He had so much confidence in his own ability that it seeped through to the rest of us. He was fearless and fortunately most of us in the back line were on his wavelength. Jonathan was one of the most elusive fly-halfs in the history of the game and, at his peak, his acceleration off the mark was frightening. Everyone respected him as a potential match-winning genius.

Credit to the coach Tony Gray, though, for giving him the licence to play like that. Had Jonathan still been in the 15-man code a couple of years later, I'm sure Ron Waldron would have passed out at some of the things he tried.

Yet I suppose it was Hadley's day because of his try double. Adrian was one of the most laid-back people I have ever played with, but he had real power and pace, even if it was mostly in a direct line. He was one of the best finishers I have ever seen and he had a change of pace combined with a swerve that most could never boast.

Adrian could also kick it a long way, as well as chip and catch, and there were few people who ever got the better of his defence in a one-on-one situation. What's more, the older he got, the more physical he became, which opened the door to a rugby league opportunity for him.

We left the field on an incredible high that day not knowing events were about to take a wilder turn. We headed to the after-match function in the Hilton Hotel in central London and it wasn't long before that man Glenn Webbe came within an inch of triggering what could have been an almighty brawl between the opposing sides. Glenn had brought a little novelty clapping box with him and planted it on the table. It was one of those things that give out a rent-a-crowd burst of applause at the pull of a cord, with loud shouts of 'bravo' and 'more, more' thrown in for extra effect.

'Webby, what are you playing at?' I asked.

'It's got to be done,' he replied, 'I'm waiting for Mike Harrison to make his speech.'

Harrison was a nice enough fellow, though a fairly bland Yorkshireman. He set the tone early on when he tried to crack a joke which went down like a lead balloon. Webby's timing, though, was impeccable.

In the hush of the room, he pulled his cord and the air was filled with fake applause. He did it once, he did it twice, and by that time Mickey Skinner was looking daggers across at us. When Webby did it the third time, Skinner stormed over and tried to smash the box to smithereens on the table only to find the plastic too tough to break.

By this time, there was a bit of a stir being created and people were looking over. Skinner, incensed at his inability to break Webby's box, picked it up and slung it into a carafe of wine. When Webby pulled it out and wiped it, he discovered that the sound effect had been ruined by the wine. He wasn't happy at all, feeling that he had been belittled in public by Skinner.

The two of them started eye-balling each other. I could see Webby pointing Skinner outside and seemingly challenging him to a scrap. That worried me, more because I know how handy Webby is in a ruck and he would probably have got the better of Skinner despite the difference in size.

Next thing, we were out in the foyer of the hotel: me, Webby and Skinner, with about four other England players. I was really starting to fear it was about to go off. Then Webby, brilliantly taking the sting out of the situation while saving his face at the same time, said to Skinner, 'Right, I hear you are handy as an arm-wrestler. Let's go.'

He planted his elbow on a nearby table and, while Skinner looked taken aback, he agreed to the challenge. Webby demolished him – twice.

The Englishman took it fair and square, but later I could see him getting more and more drunk and before long he had put a gateau in the face of our flanker, Rowland Phillips. That was when I could see things degenerating and suggested to Webby that we filter away. Mike Hall and Ieuan Evans joined us and just as we were about to jump in a taxi, Staff Jones came bounding up the pavement, wanting to tag along with us. There was no way I could refuse him, even though it meant we would have to get two taxis, and so off the five of us went to Stringfellows.

We successfully jumped a huge queue in to the club, though we were stunned by the bouncers when we said we were the Welsh rugby team. 'Ah, you're with the Jonathan Davies party, are you?' they asked.

'Yes,' we said, having no idea Jonathan had made any arrangements. He had been a guest on Terry Wogan's chat show that week, so we assumed he had been given tickets to the club by someone he had met in London at the time. In we went, but we found ourselves feeling uncomfortable in a roped-off VIP section with no sign of Jonathan or any of the rest of the team. We were standing, a bit like spare parts in our dicky bows, feeling like everyone was looking at us and wondering who the hell we were.

We decided not to touch any of the free champagne and instead dispatched Staff to the bar to get a round of beers in. While he was getting served, these four absolutely gorgeous top-class women strolled in and before long we got chatting, with Mike Hall exercising his Cambridge University graduate confidence and

Webby his gift of the gab. Next thing I know, the champagne is indeed flowing and we are well on our way with these four girls, one for each of us, and making out as if we're a group of rich playboys ready to show them a good time.

Then, out of the corner of my eye, I spot Staff shuffling at the bar, which was literally about 40 yards away. I turned my attention back to the girls and next thing I heard was Staff, with his Ynysybwl ex-miner's accent, shout across the room at the top of his voice with his hands cupped around his mouth, 'Boys, boys, it's £8 a bloody half!'

I wanted the floor to open up and swallow me. Needless to say, moments later the girls were making their excuses and slipping away. Webby, gutted that the progress he had been making with his patter had been ruined, looked at me and said, 'What did you bring him for?'

'He's my mate,' I said weakly.

However, that wasn't the end of it. Half an hour or so later, Staff had wandered off somewhere and the four of us, fuelled by a couple more beers, started to feel comfortable and confident again. Just then, Webby spotted the four girls again and decided to re-open talks. We began chatting and the conversation started flowing freely between us.

I stuck my arm around Webby's shoulder, my legs aching from the day's game, then, as Webby was talking nine to the dozen with the girls, Staff suddenly sticks his head between us both and says, 'Boys, where's the shitter?' Webby's face was a picture as the girls once again gradually filed away.

Then it was on to the Grosvenor Hotel, where London Welsh were having their usual post-match ball. By now, I was half-cut. About ten minutes after walking into the ballroom, I got talking to a girl in a lovely long dress. We snuck off down a corridor and clambered into a broom cupboard for some privacy, but when I returned I was too drunk to notice that I had managed to get black soot all over my face and my white sleeves and had to slope off, embarrassed, to clean myself up.

At the end of the night, we finally returned to the Hilton where we finished off the celebrations with yet more drinks in the company of Rob Andrew and Will Carling. It had been one hell of a day. Victory for Wales against England at Twickenham happened to me once, and boy did I make the most of it.

But the swagger of the 1988 campaign didn't end there by any means. Next up were Scotland at the Arms Park. The manner of our display in a thrilling victory had people harking back to the golden '70s all over again.

The Scots were 7–0 up after five minutes when they scored a try almost straight from the kick-off through their flanker Finlay Calder, who would captain the British Lions in Australia the following year. It was a frustrating score that came after I had made a try-saving tackle on their centre, Scott Hastings, only for us to make a mess of a lineout and concede the ball at the tail which enabled Calder to get in.

It was the first half, though, that had really set pulses racing, which meant that when we went in at half-time the crowd was still buzzing. We had scored two sublime tries in the first forty minutes. The first from Ieuan Evans came courtesy of classic play by our back line. We sent Thorburn up the middle on a decoy run and then from a set-piece play we called 'Bridgend', lovely quick hands among us all with an early ball by me to Ieuan, set him off on a mesmerising series of sidesteps. That was a real strength of Ieuan's game: he was right up in the class of Gerald Davies on that score. When he went over, I was elated – but I was also accidentally smashed out of the celebrations by a Scottish defender running backwards, which made me look a right fool.

Later on, Jonathan scored what I consider to be one of the best Wales tries of all time. It seemed as if there was absolutely nothing on as he received the ball on the back foot as we tried to construct an attack, but his wondrous eye for an opportunity saw him slide the ball along the floor with a grubber kick through the narrowest of gaps, with his electric pace enabling him to run through and ground for a try.

Yet we were not in front until the final ten minutes, when Jonathan dropped two goals from distance to swing the game our way. A crucial Ian Watkins score followed by a Thorburn penalty allowed Jonathan to win it for us, 25–20.

The match against Ireland for the Triple Crown was an altogether dourer affair. Fair play to Thorburn; his three penalties kicked us to a 12–9 win, but the nature of the game didn't surprise me – it was Lansdowne Road, after all. The ground used to affect us all, but me in particular. It was the most intimidating atmosphere I ever played in. It was the one away ground on the Five Nations circuit where the crowd was right on top of you. At the other grounds where the crowds were set back it felt like the game was less enclosed, which made it feel as though you had more time on the ball.

I always made mistakes there that I would never have done elsewhere. I knew I was a player with a high skill level and so it used to leave me tearing my hair out when I dropped a straightforward pass for no other reason than the atmosphere was getting to me. This game was no exception – I dropped a pass at one stage when under no pressure, which was something I had almost never done in my career.

Whilst our performance took the edge off the celebrations at winning the Triple Crown, our thoughts were all very much on the opportunity we now had to win the Grand Slam with a home match against France to finish the campaign.

But it was as if the gods were against us that day. For a start, the weather was appalling: wet and windy and so unlike the last weekend of the championship in late March – certainly nothing like the hot and sunny day that saw Wales clinch the Slam against Ireland in 2005. It's always a bit silly to blame the weather in hindsight because it is the same for both sides, but it really did knock us out of our stride. It so stymied us from playing to our strengths of spinning the ball wide – we were never going to dominate sides up front and it really hindered our performance.

I recall we were running out of time at 10–3 down when Ieuan went on one of his mazy runs. He chipped the ball up over their defence and practically ran into touch to get around the last man and try to ground the ball over the try-line, but I had supported from the inside. I almost had time to scoop the ball up and dive over the line myself but could see out of the corner of my eye how desperate Ieuan was to score the try and he was already diving full length. I just went to dive to assist the touchdown and make sure of the score, but I touched the ball first, of that I have no doubt.

Thorburn kicked the conversion and we got to within a point, but it was not to be. We were never going to score in the little time we had left that day under those conditions.

Afterwards, Ieuan and I went up to be interviewed by the BBC's Des Lynam. He wanted to clear up who had scored the try, as several TV replays had proven inconclusive. I got a £20 note out live on camera and said it was Ieuan's try – but that he had paid me £20 to say it! At the end of it all, I had let him officially claim the try, but I have always known deep down that it was mine: I definitely got the first touch on that ball.

We were sick at the end of that game. I just knew we would have won on a dry day and the fact that we had got so close against a team that had been World Cup finalists the year before just added to the sense of a glorious missed opportunity.

I'm convinced in 1988 we were a Grand Slam team that never was. We weren't too dissimilar to the 2005 team, though they did what we couldn't do. We deserve credit for beating England and Ireland, two teams who wanted revenge after we had beaten them in the 1987 World Cup, on their own patches. If only we had been able to slide across the roof and keep out the elements like they can today.

They were heady days indeed; a time when I was getting more recognition in my everyday life than ever. I was forever being collared by blokes who wanted to talk rugby when out in town, and women were practically throwing themselves at me. I enjoyed that part of it – I am only human! – but there was also a need to deal with jealous types as well, of which I had a few. I think the social side of things is far more controlled these days: when the Wales team goes out, they more often than not seem to have somewhere cordoned off, or a VIP bar where they can cut themselves off.

Although we didn't know it at the time, the Triple Crown was to mark something of the end of an era for us. From that moment on, Welsh rugby embarked on a downward spiral lasting the best part of a decade – and it began on our two-Test tour of New Zealand that summer. I looked at myself in the mirror after we had lost the second Test 54–9 to the All Blacks at Auckland's Eden Park that summer. I asked myself whether I had given it my all in the two matches we had played against them given the sheer savagery of the hidings they had given us. My answer was an emphatic yes. My body ached all over and I could barely even lift myself off my seat in the dressing-room. I had done all I could. It had just been that we had taken two wallopings off the best team on the planet. And the scary thing was they seemed to have got better since thrashing us 49–6 in the World Cup semi-final the year before. The matches had been a non-stop succession of waves and waves of ruthless black-shirted power that smashed us to pieces. I had quite simply never encountered anything like it on a rugby field. Nor did I ever again.

Our forwards were demolished by athletic giants who set new standards for players in that department, with the Whetton brothers, Alan and Gary, as well as the back-row threats of Wayne Shelford and Michael Jones, to the fore.

They spent a lot of the time hammering into our midfield and we had no answer at all. They would then create quick ruck ball with our midfield defence squashed flat at the bottom of a pile-up and then spread it wide for easy overlap run-ins.

I remember I played at full-back in the second Test out there. I couldn't believe it at the team announcement when they read my name out in that position. I had hardly ever played there in my career and it was not a position I enjoyed. I remembered being horribly caught out of position in one game for Cardiff against Bath.

In the first Test, I remember they kicked off, the ball curved around towards their second row, Murray Pierce, who controlled it then smashed into us to set up a ruck. In the blink of an eye, Grant Fox put up a towering up-and-under. I caught it as it headed towards the join of the crossbar and post, and sliced a kick to touch as Michael Jones smashed into me. That gave the All Blacks a lineout about a metre from our line and, before you knew it, they were over for a try. New Zealand were just so proficient in everything they did.

One time I was stuck at the bottom of a ruck, trying to cling on to the ball, and the noise in there was phenomenal. There were eight forwards all chipping in with comments about what they were going to do, all constructive. If you'd got on the wrong side, they would have kicked the living daylights out of you; if not, they would leave you alone. The loudest of them all was the scrum-half Bruce Deans, who was a superbly confident operator. Then they had a classic fly-half/inside-centre partnership in Fox and Warwick Taylor.

I learnt so much from the way Taylor played on that tour. He was a player who could take the ball eyeball-to-eyeball and make a decision about what he was going to do in the blink of an eye. In the back line, he had John Kirwan coming in from the blindside wing; Smokin' Joe Stanley coming from a wide angle and just smashing into us; John Gallagher, who was the flattest, widest-angled full-back you could meet, who used to just run straight lines; and then there was Terry Wright on the far side, who was Rolls-Royce as well. Yes, their forwards were winning the ball constantly, which made it easier for them, but Warwick Taylor's decision making helped me realise that from that moment on I wanted to be a specialist in that position of second five-eighth or inside-centre. What he did was an education.

He could run, he could step, he could roll passes off either hand, long or short; he could offload soft balls to flankers or centres, he had it all. Taylor is the one stand-out player in my experience of the sport who I thought could take the game to a whole new level and I tried to model my own game on his from that time on.

Unfortunately for us, we had guys out in New Zealand who threw in the towel.

I was disappointed in Tony Gray's coaching. I felt, by this stage, he had gone too far with his relaxed approach, with players calling the shots on tactics. I thought he was allowing Jonathan, in particular, to influence him too much. Jonathan had argued that the problem at the heart of all our failings was the threat of the Kiwi full-back John Gallagher, who was cutting us to ribbons out wide, but I felt he was missing the point. Jonathan wanted the centres to mark man for man and for him to then be able to run around the back of them to cut off Gallagher. In my opinion, it was wrong, but Gray went along with it.

The tour went so badly that Tony was sacked and none of the admittedly few positives that were to be had were taken out of the whole thing. Tony shouldn't have got the boot; instead we should have had an open forum where people threw in their ideas – and the WRU should have backed us, considering we had not long finished third at the World Cup and won the Triple Crown. All of the players and coaches and the management should have gone in to see the WRU, but all that happened was Tony Gray submitted a report.

Jonathan was particularly vociferous about wanting to consult with the people in authority within the union, but he got nowhere. Maybe it would have been wrong for him to have done it alone anyway. The upshot was that he got more and more frustrated. The 15–9 defeat to Romania that December proved to be the straw that broke the camel's back and he moved to rugby league.

At the time, I couldn't blame anyone for going to the 13-man code, though it was a huge decision to make: the assumption was that there would never be a way back; nobody knew union would turn professional before too long. Jonathan made a brilliant success of it, doing so much for rugby league. I can remember getting excited about watching the game on television at the time he was up north.

I ended up missing the Romania game because I was dropped as a disciplinary measure for missing a training session. The reason: I almost went to rugby league myself, having been offered to sign for Wigan – although all I said to the press at the time was that I had mixed up the days. That was half true because the Barbarians were playing matches over here at the time in which I was involved and their training sessions were intermingled with Wales's, which did confuse someone like me.

My head was everywhere over my proposed move north, but in the end I pulled out of it at the very last minute. Wigan had told me they wanted a fly-half-cum-centre and had offered me £95,000 tax free for the rest of that year and the following three years, with £50,000 of that up front. I was also offered a house to live in for free for three months. On top of all this, there was the regular wage. If I played in the first team and they won, I could pick up a £270 bonus. Even if I played in the second team, it was £130 on top of the basic salary. It was tempting, to say the least.

The top man at Wigan was Maurice Lindsay, although I never met him throughout the negotiations – I was told you only met him when you signed on the dotted line. Instead I dealt with an antiques dealer by the name of Jack Robinson.

I was supposed to sign on the Tuesday of the week leading up to the Romania game on 10 December, but I had a sleepless night on the Monday and rang to say I was pulling out of the deal. I lost my bottle completely after thinking about the rights and wrongs of going. Deep down I was worried about whether I would have the pace to become a big hit in the game. I just had too many doubts and in my heart of hearts I remained a rugby union player who wanted to get into the coaching side of the 15-man code when I finished playing. Being ostracised from union was something that terrified me as much as the money on offer from league excited me. When I pulled out, Wigan signed Frano Botica.

On one occasion, I had even gone to meet a delegation from Hull Kingston Rovers in a little Italian restaurant on Cardiff's St

Mary's Street with David Bishop. Bish walked out of there with a large cheque in his hand, which he was still showing people all crumpled up a month later. Rovers wanted the both of us to go, but Bish signed and I didn't, even though Bish presumably had promised them he would try to persuade me. He insisted from the outset that he wanted his deal to be worth £10,000 more than mine, but when I went up to Rovers, I was offered the same salary as him but with a BMW 3-Series thrown in, so it turned out that I would have been on more than Bish all along. But it was irrelevant in the end because the truth is I was never really going to go: I just went up there for the intrigue.

The Wigan offer in 1988 was not their first either. I was picked up from my mother's house once in a Rolls-Royce by a South Wales businessman called Dai Harris, who was in the demolition business back in the mid-'80s. He took me to Wigan to talk about a deal, but they only offered me £60,000 tax free over three years, which simply wasn't worth my while for all the sacrifices I would have had to make. On that occasion, I had a little fitness run-out with two of the big Wigan players of the time, Joe Lydon and Andy Goodway. Both had recently been sent off and were brought in for extra training on a Sunday. I kicked goals and did some sprints, and I can remember going flat out over 70 yards and having Lydon cruise past me looking like he was going at three-quarter pace. I was practically dipping for the tape to beat Goodway, who was a prop/second row, and I wasn't happy about that at all.

However, concerning my no-show for Wales training, I was actually in an office in Pontypool doing my day job of the time with a children's charity when I got the telephone call. I genuinely had got the days mixed up. When I turned up hours later, one of the selectors, Rod Morgan, and the new coach, John Ryan, called me over and said they just couldn't let the matter go and were going to have to make an example of me by putting me out of the team. I couldn't complain, I suppose, although I have always suspected that in some ways they were grateful to have been given a way out of the problem they had in accommodating Mike Hall in the team. He had played in the Varsity match that week and because of that had put himself down the pecking order, but with Glenn Webbe covering up the pain of a dead leg just so he didn't give them the easy option of replacing him with Hall, I eventually gave them their get out.

It was to prove the start of a depressing month for me because against Pontypridd on Boxing Day I picked up that second serious knee injury, which forced me to miss the 1989 Five Nations, as well as most of the rest of the club season.

As I have mentioned, my injury in turn put the mockers on any chance I had of becoming a British Lion on the tour to Australia that summer. That effectively meant being a Lion was a box I was never going to get to tick. The time for me to have joined the British Lions squad would have been 1986 when I was really at my peak, but the planned trip to South Africa had been cancelled. It had always been my dream to play for the Lions, but, to be honest, I didn't dwell on it at the time.

These days, the build-up to a Lions tour starts in excess of 12 months before the squad is announced, but back then I know I personally never thought that far ahead: I just focused on the next game I was due to play. In any case, I was tipped off early by Clive Rowlands, the Lions team manager in 1989, that I wasn't going to go because he said my dodgy knee would not stand up to the hard ground out there. I was galled, however, that Mike Hall went and won selection for the first Test. In my view, I was better than him! I would love to have played in the centre with Jerry Guscott on that trip – I reckon we could have been a dynamite partnership. But we'll never know now.

It was once again a period of frustration for me, but, although I didn't get to Australia that summer, I did make it to the southern hemisphere to play rugby: to South Africa, to be precise. I didn't get what would have been a treasured Lions cap, but there were reasons to be cheerful nonetheless – 35,000 reasons actually.

6

REBEL TOUR – AND A BAGFUL OF CASH!

It's easy to forget these days just what an emotive pair of words South Africa used to be when it came to sport. The exile of their rugby team from the world order during the days of apartheid was fully justified, but the fact remains that for the sheer absence of the team, the sport was all the poorer for many years. Certainly their non-participation in the inaugural World Cup in New Zealand and Australia in 1987 diminished the quality of the tournament.

When the chance to tour the country as part of a world squad to celebrate the South African Rugby Union's centenary year came my way in the summer of 1989, I was immediately interested. Not just because having been there before for the Western Province centenary celebrations six years earlier I knew what a great place it was to go and play but also because I agreed a payment of £35,000 for my trouble; this in the days when the game was still amateur. If the fact that money had changed hands ever leaked out, I would never have played rugby union again, at least not until the game went professional in 1995.

The money was being put up by the South Africans, but the ones who did most to put in place all the arrangements concerning the depositing of the money in Luxembourg and the tax concession were the southern hemisphere players that were involved, who seemed more streetwise and experienced in this sort of thing.

The fee was not enough to set me up for life by any means, but in those days it was a hell of an incentive and there were certainly plenty of things I knew I could do with money like that.

Ten Welsh players joined the tour in all – me, Mike Hall, Phil Davies, Paul Turner, Paul Thorburn, David Pickering, Robert Jones, Anthony Clement, Bob Norster and Phil John – which was an enormous representation from one country for what was supposed to be a world squad, and it caused all manner of political controversy within the Welsh game. Quite apart from the usual condemnation from anti-apartheid groups, which predictably extended to political parties and even local authorities, our going also sparked the resignations of WRU secretary David East and president Clive Rowlands.

Clive came back after he had cooled down from storming out of a meeting of the general committee, but East, who was regarded as a fine administrator, was unfortunately lost to the game.

The problems the tour caused within the WRU were not so much centred around the delicate issue of apartheid but the fact that the union appeared to have been sidestepped in the making of our arrangements.

The truth was the WRU eventually paid the price for sitting on the fence over the matter in the first place. It had tried hopelessly to find a middle path between the apartheid campaigners and the Welsh clubs, who were keen to maintain links with South Africa and had voted in favour of doing so some years earlier. The clubs' argument was that the policy of apartheid was best influenced by maintaining contact rather than through isolation. Though when push came to shove, the union's stance was to pass on the invitations, officially leaving it to us to make the hard decision while claiming the governing body hoped we didn't go. After beginning with a half-cocked approach to the affair, further down the line there was uproar that the WRU didn't have a record of a concrete chain of events in the aftermath. Only in Wales . . .

The first I heard about the tour was when I received a letter from the WRU inviting me to take part in what was an official tour. Originally, five Welsh players had been invited as part of what would be a world squad, which, it was hoped, would be selected from all the major unions around the world. Those five were me,

Robert Jones, Bob Norster, John Devereux, who later pulled out to be replaced by Anthony Clement, and Phil Davies.

At one stage, it seemed like the tour would fall through because the Aussies weren't happy that every last detail had been taken care of, but soon everything was hunky-dory again. That pleased me no end, and not just because of the £35,000: I had brought back particularly fond memories from South Africa and was anxious to return to the country. I had only received something like £700 for taking part back then, but it had been brilliant.

The world team in 1983 was arguably the most amazing side I had ever played in. The front row comprised the two great New Zealand props John Ashworth and Gary Knight, with the Englishman Peter Wheeler at hooker. The second rows were John Perkins and the young Gary Whetton, and we had back-row guys like the Kiwi Mark Shaw and the Frenchman Marc Cecillion.

Knight and Ashworth would go off together after every training session to do 100 metre sprints. Ashworth – the guy who allegedly stamped on JPR Williams' head in a tour match at Bridgend in 1978 – always beat Knight, but Knight's obsession became to one day beat Ashworth. It reminded me of that scene in *Rocky III* when Rocky is running on the beach against his old foe Apollo Creed.

There were more towering New Zealanders in the backs, names like Bernie Fraser and Stu Wilson, who would later write a book together entitled *Ebony and Ivory*, first published in 1984. In the book, they wrote some extremely complimentary things about me, which gave me an enormous boost. In the words of Fraser:

In the World XV at the Western Province centenary was a Welshman named Mark Ring. He was a dream of a player, a back with so much skill, teaming up with New Zealanders and French in free-flow rugby and loving it.

And Wilson:

> Ring was the perfect example of what we have been saying [that rugby should be more of a 15-man game]. It is a tragedy of rugby that such players are not allowed to express their skill for the enjoyment of the crowds when they come to the international arena.

Praise indeed coming from two such legends of the game.

The only disappointment for me during that 1983 tour was that I popped my rib cartilage in the first match against Natal and so didn't have the chance to push for a place in the team for the Tests. The frustrating thing was that I had more or less received a warning about the circumstances in which I picked up the injury from my pal Pablo Rees, with whom I played at Cardiff and who was out there at the time playing for Durban Collegians. Pablo said there would be some rough stuff when my back was turned, and I had let this information go over my head and was hammered from behind and fell awkwardly on the ball, which did the damage.

I gained an insight into Fraser's competitive nature and fierce will to win in that game. On one occasion, he was done for pace on the outside by this winger and he stopped him the only way he could by chopping him down football-style. He would do anything other than let an opponent get the better of him. The crowd went ballistic, but Fraser didn't care less. Just to slow the attacking team down even more, he then went and picked the ball up and threw it behind the advertisement hoardings. Thankfully, the referee was inexperienced and didn't have a clue what to do, so let the game carry on.

I stayed on tour despite the injury and I nearly got in for the Tests, but not quite, after receiving acupuncture for the first time.

I shared a room with Stu Wilson on the tour, who was captain of the party. His professionalism was ahead of its time and it just amazed someone like me, a fresh-faced young kid barely out of his teens. There were other characters on the tour, like the New Zealand centre, Steve Pokere, who was a Mormon. He was always trying to persuade me to go to places like museums when all I wanted to do was have a drink with the boys!

I ended up teaming up with two Irish boys, Willie Duggan and Jonny Murphy, who were great characters and certainly on that tour were heavy drinkers. Jonny had been a promising footballer in his younger days. He'd been on Arsenal's books alongside Liam Brady and Jonny was reputed to be the better player of the two, but for some reason he turned down the chance to join the Gunners and went to work for his family's undertaker business! Each to their own, I suppose.

By the time it came for the Welsh contingent to leave for the 1989 expedition, we were all with the Wales squad at a training camp in Aberystwyth. Everything was arranged for us. We would finish the three-day camp, then at Aberaeron Rugby Club board helicopters which would ferry us to Heathrow airport.

It was highly embarrassing for the WRU that ten Welshmen eventually went out there. Precisely how that came about I don't know, but I would guess it was down to the fact that replacements had been lined up for each of the original five that were due to go in case we pulled out. I also know there were figures on the WRU at the time who had good connections with South Africa and they might well have played a part in making arrangements. All along, it felt as if we were part of yet another WRU blunder, even if it had been brought about by the players themselves.

As the camp ended at Aberystwyth, we got the impression that Robert Jones was going to pull out after a heart-to-heart chat with Clive Rowlands, who was his father-in-law. That worried us because if Clive was against it, we were convinced we were running the risk of being ostracised from the game on our return since he was WRU president then. Robert did go on tour in the end – I think he even boarded the helicopter without Clive knowing.

When our Wales party landed in Africa, we got all the dregs of the kit because we had arrived late. I remember Phil John was like a man possessed, grabbing whatever he could lay his hands on. I also recall Thorburn taking a rather more serious approach to it all than the rest of us, certainly more serious than me. In my view, it was a great expedition to be a part of and getting a place in the team for the two Tests against the Springboks would be a bonus, but Thorburn appeared desperate to make the cut for the Tests. Every time a session finished, he would ask Australian coach Bob Templeton for extra balls so he could go out and do extra training, while none of the other boys even thought about it.

Thorburn had brought his missus with him on tour and he would have her standing behind the posts, catching the balls and getting them back to him, as he took shots at goal. It was as if the pair of them were on a joint mission to deliver the message that he had to be involved for the Test matches. She was a lovely girl, don't get me wrong, but she would come back from his sessions talking about what a great strike rate Paul had produced and quoting this statistic and that.

I didn't make the Test team for either of the games. My way to a place in the centre was barred by two outstanding Frenchmen, Philippe Sella and Denis Charvet, so I couldn't have too many complaints. Although I did figure in the other tour matches against Natal, Northern Transvaal and a South African Development XV. It was only Mike Hall and Bob Norster out of the ten of us who got to start a Test, with Hall playing on the wing in the first Test at Cape Town's Newlands ground and Norster at lock for the second encounter at Johannesburg's Ellis Park, although he was replaced by Phil Davies when he came off injured.

We lost both clashes – 20–19 and 22–16 respectively – but from what I recall they were full-blooded matches and at the end of the series there was very much the feeling that the Boks had been pushed all the way by the tourists and that they were possibly not the force they had been in the past.

What struck me about the Boks was the sheer pace at which they played the game: it was incredible. The game at Ellis Park was particularly rapid, yet when I went out onto the field in the warm-up, I was struck by how fast the track was. It immediately got you in the mood to stretch your legs.

It wasn't totally surprising that as a group we failed to win more nods because us Welsh boys had arrived on tour late and as such had fallen behind the others in the preparations. Yet I was just happy to be on the tour – and if there were times when I got a little bit frustrated, all I had to do was think about what my bank account would look like on my return home. It was a relaxed and sociable tour for me and I was being paid a king's ransom for going. It didn't get much better.

While there was obvious disquiet back in the UK about the apartheid issue, we never really encountered any serious dissent in South Africa. The one thing I do recall is that on a couple of occasions we would be on the bus going to or coming from training and we would all of a sudden do a frantic U-turn as we passed through a township where the road ahead was blocked by fires.

During the tour, there were scheduled training sessions with the kids in the black townships to raise the issue of apartheid and how it was affecting the population and I hope we made a difference on some level on that score. I had no regrets whatsoever about being involved in the tour.

When we returned from the southern hemisphere, the flak truly began to fly, with the WRU claiming to have been left in the dark over a range of issues to do with the trip. Who had been the liaison man that persuaded each of us to go? Why had our travel arrangements not been made through the WRU? Why had ten players gone when originally it was supposed to be five? Who arranged a meeting, understood to have taken place between the players and two unknown men from South Africa? Was there any truth in rumours we had been paid to play? All were questions being raised in the press and it seemed every Tom, Dick and Harry were having their say.

The matter took an incredibly long time to go away because the WRU ordered the late Vernon Pugh, who would become chairman of the body and was a respected man of law, to conduct an inquiry into the affair. The investigation arguably lost credibility because there was no obligation on anybody's part to contribute because it had no legal authority. It therefore relied on voluntary testimony and could never have hoped to leave no stone unturned. Just to complete the disaffection, its findings were promptly placed in the shredder by East's successor, Denis Evans, and were never officially made public, not even to the general committee, which caused yet more ructions.

Inevitably, the report was leaked to the media. It identified Paul Thorburn, the Neath and Wales full-back, as the chief player go-between in the dealings with SARFU to get Welsh players on board. It reported that all the players denied receiving payment. The Pugh report also claimed to have unearthed evidence that two players had transferred money from Luxembourg to bank accounts in the UK. On this issue in its conclusion, the report noted that nothing could be proved satisfactorily either way.

I remember Vernon Pugh asking me point-blank in my interview whether I had received payment for going to South Africa. I just smiled and said no, but there was a look between us that made it clear we both knew I was lying.

The political ramifications of the tour meant little to me as a player. Don't get me wrong, I deplore racism of any kind, but I have always been firmly of the opinion that sport and politics should not mix. Some will say that's a convenient and shallow way of looking at things, but I make no apologies, it's just the way I approach it. When these sorts of offers came along, I just couldn't attune my mind to think of them as anything other than great rugby opportunities. For me, the memories of that 1989 tour are not political or racial ones; they are rugby ones.

After I had returned from South Africa, there were black people whom I regarded as friends who refused to acknowledge me, but I guess that was just a cross I had to bear and it didn't last forever. I was just sent to Coventry for a period so they could make their point. It was particularly an issue for a lot of the black guys I knew from drinking in the docks area of Cardiff, which made me uncomfortable. I would invariably be with my pal Glenn Webbe, who is black and who didn't hold a grudge against me at all, so I would be all right.

Glenn was very supportive and admitted that if he had been invited on that tour, he would have gone, and it wasn't as if he didn't know the realities of apartheid. He had toured South Africa with Welsh Youth and had had bananas thrown at him from the crowd. More often than not, though, Glenn would rise above the abuse by picking the bananas up off the field and eating them there and then. For his dignity in the face of such sickening taunts, he became a hero among the black rugby followers out there.

The tax on the fee was all paid and the loot, as was later discovered by Mr Pugh, was paid into an account in Luxembourg. I was instructed that if I wanted any of it, I would have to make the demand two days earlier to allow time for the transaction to go through, then I would have to get a train to London to an address where I would meet a South African businessman and he would hand over any money in cash. For a fair while, I was nipping back and forth to London and getting my hands on wads of cash and living the life of Riley, going to nightclubs and just generally enjoying myself. My bank manager knew about the money as well and so allowed me a whopping overdraft.

I had parted with some of the cash straight away, mind you: £12,500 of it, to be precise, which I put down on a house in Splott that I bought for £45,000. Unfortunately, because of an untimely crash in the housing market in the early '90s, I ended up selling it for around the same price four years later. That outlay on the house left me with about £23,000 and I squandered every penny of it on nothing in particular. And £8,000 of it had to go in one lump when one day, out of the blue, I received a telephone call from my bank manager.

'Look, I know you've got that money stashed away in another account,' he said, 'but you've run up an overdraft of £8,000 and you really need to sort it out.' That £8,000 had been pissed up against the wall and I had nothing to show for it.

I told him I would make the necessary arrangements and that in a couple of days, I would be there to give him the £8,000 needed to clear the overdraft. I got on the phone and two days later there I was, getting off the train at Paddington station, hungover from a night on the town, on the way to the highly secret source of my South African money. I took the Tube to the office in the City armed with a Tesco carrier bag in which to conceal the money.

I left the office, the bag now containing a puzzle book I had bought at Cardiff station that morning, a copy of the *Western Mail* and a pen, along with £8,000 in cash. On the train back, I got talking to a guy opposite me and then nodded off to sleep only to be woken by him tapping me on the shoulder as we stopped at Newport station.

'Your stop next,' he reminded me. I stuck my thumb up at him and then realised my stupidity: I had fallen sound asleep with £8,000 in a plastic bag down at my feet on the train. I quickly checked – it was all still in there, thank God. My puzzle book was there too!

In my relief, I slumped back in the chair and began daydreaming all the way back to Cardiff. When we pulled into the station, I got off the train, unbelievably leaving the bag and its contents under my seat. Thankfully, I realised straight away as I walked out onto the platform. I hopped back on and retrieved it.

By this time, around mid-afternoon, I thought it would be best if I got the money to the bank as soon as possible. Typically, that didn't happen.

About a week earlier, I had put on a bet at a bookie's called J.M. Charles on Carlisle Street in Splott. It was one of those Goliath bets where there are eight horses involved and there are hundreds of 10p bets riding on different outcomes.

I had fallen out with Martin Daly over something at the time and one of the horses running was called Martin's Friend, so I put one on that. I was also trying to get international tickets for a girl called Val whom I met in a café in Cwm near Ebbw Vale and she couldn't decide whether or not to come down to Cardiff for the game – there was a horse running called Val's Dilemma! There were a couple of other coincidence bets and I made up the others with horses that I genuinely fancied. When I called in to the bookie's that afternoon, I was told I had narrowly missed out on an incredible win of almost £70,000 as four of the horses had come in and the other four had all very narrowly missed out. To make it worse, the bookmaker gleefully pointed out the small print on the betting slip that said there would be no payouts exceeding £10,000 anyway. That was it, I was determined to have my revenge and with all this money on me I knew I had the perfect opportunity.

'I'm going to teach these bastards a lesson,' I muttered under my breath as I put a £100 straight forecast on the dogs – number one to beat six – followed by a series of £50 reverse forecasts. Before I knew it, I had lost £700 of my £8,000 and it was clear I wasn't, in fact, teaching anyone a lesson. I then took a bus from Splott up to the centre of town towards my bank.

By this time, it was turning into the strangest of days. For some reason, a comical incident that occurred as the bus wound its way towards the city centre sticks in my mind. I remember one of the local drinkers coming out of the Fleurs, a local sports club in Splott. He boarded the bus and when asked by the driver where he was going, the man replied, 'Down my nana's.' I sat trying to stifle my laughter in my seat near the front.

I was still deeply disturbed about my earlier luck in the bookie's, which meant there was no hope for me when I got off the bus in town and saw the dreaded arrow which points the way into the Les Croupiers casino on Cardiff's busy St Mary's Street. There was never any possibility of me walking past it and straight to the bank, so up the long staircase I went with the hope of winning back the £700 I had managed to lose since returning from London dominating my thoughts.

When I had been in the casino before with more than £100 in my pocket, I was never prepared to lose more than that sum in one outing. This time, though, the amount of money I had was frightening, even for an experienced punter like me. Saying that, I did on one occasion have a win of about £3,000 in Les Croupiers. That, though, was very much a one-off – and it had, at the end of the day, been a win.

By about 8.30 p.m. that evening, I had been playing roulette for some hours and decided to have a count-up. I was £3,500 down. Still, there was no other thought in my mind than betting chips: I had gone past the stage where I was seeing notes. In other words, I was out of control. I was so gutted at having lost £3,500 that I was now mentally prepared to lose the lot. I had resolved that I was going home either with more money than I had arrived with or just my bus fare home.

The hours went on and the next thing I knew I was sitting at a roulette table all on my own with a load of Asian people watching my every punt. And I was definitely keeping them entertained because by then I was betting bundles of chips at every spin. I was acting like a lunatic. It eventually reached a point where I had no more notes left in my Tesco bag: all I had was a stack of chips which I had been dropping into my bag every time I had a win.

My £8,000, I thought to myself, had gone. Even though I had plenty of chips, I had no idea of their value and I was stone-cold convinced it wouldn't be anywhere near £8,000. At 4 a.m. the following morning, it was time for Les Croupiers to close. They called time, giving me three more spins, all of which I lost, which did nothing for my mood.

I was taken to a private room where I was told that the staff needed to count out all the chips and for a short while I was suspicious about what they were doing. Soon my thoughts turned to how much I had actually lost, though, and my heart began pounding.

Then I was given the value of my chips – £8,010! After all I had been through, after a marathon gambling session in which I feared I had squandered £8,000, I was actually £10 up. I stumbled down the stairs, gave a taxi driver a tenner and said, 'Get me home.'

The next morning, I went straight to the bank, avoiding St Mary's Street, and finally paid in the money.

Despite the fact I had finished up on my money, that episode was a big turning point for me and gambling, and I have certainly never let myself get into that sort of situation since. I still love a bet, in fact I bet almost every day, but I am always in control. There is a long history of gambling in my family and I first learnt to bet through my grandparents. There were bookies all over Splott and I remember on Saturdays if ever I was over at my grandparents, my granddad would be moaning at me for wanting to watch different sports on *Grandstand* because he always wanted the racing on the other channels. My grandmother would send me over to the bookie's to do sixpence bets for her at times and Dad loves the horses as well; it's only my mother, brother and sister who aren't interested.

These days, I can go a run of days without a bet. I don't think you could call it an addiction and I wouldn't say it is out of control by any means. I never bet with what I don't have, only with what I have spare, and I have never borrowed to bet.

I enjoy watching the racing even when I haven't got a bet riding on it because I have a little book where I commit pieces of information about the horses in that race for future reference and I buy the *Racing Post* every day. It's not worth me thinking about the amount I have lost down the years and I know gambling is something you can never really win at, but I am the type of person who will always have a bet if there is a bit of loose change in my pocket.

I remember David Bishop's uncle had a dog called Dexter Bish which was running in a race as a big outsider. There were another two dogs going in the same race whose names I cannot recall but they were linked to Bish in some way. It was the last race of the day at Bristol and I had £19.17 in my pocket, so I put that on a straight tricast and all three came in at 8–1, 6–1 and 11–2. The bookie's couldn't pay me there and then. They gave me £700-odd quid and a cheque for £3,000 that could be cashed at any Coral's. That is always the way I have operated with betting. It is the excitement of betting that keeps me hooked, it's just the type of person I am. I can't sit at home doing nothing, I have always got to be doing something.

If my partner Lisa sends me down the shop to get some food, I cannot go past the bookie's without popping in and having a couple of little bets, anything that will get my heart pumping that little bit faster.

I have always been the same in my attitude to playing sport: it's always been important for me to take chances. When the 1991 World Cup approached with new coach Alan Davies in charge, I found out that I wasn't the only one in the Welsh rugby fraternity willing to chance my arm. However, as some truly dark days with Wales approached, there was one chance I simply wasn't prepared to take.

7

BRIBERY – AND DARK DAYS
UNDER RON MANAGER

It was the week leading up to the final game of the 1990 Five Nations Championship, an away game against Ireland at Lansdowne Road in which both teams would be desperately bidding to avoid the wooden spoon – and Wales the ignominy of a first-ever whitewash.

We had been through a dreadful season under coach John Ryan and then Neath coach Ron Waldron, who was brought in after we were thumped 34–6 by England at Twickenham, conceding four tries to them at Headquarters for the first time since 1921. We were a disgrace that day and the worst moment was arguably when Will Carling barged through what seemed like 20 pathetic Welsh tackles to score a try in the corner. Swansea wing Mark Titley was the last to lay a finger on him and Mark just crumpled meekly to the floor under the England captain, who was hardly a battering ram.

There was another incident that I suppose summed up the yawning gulf that had somehow developed in two short years between the two sides. Rory Underwood dived into the corner despite a great attempt to stop him by Ieuan Evans. It just so happened that Underwood ended up sitting upright with the ball in his hand after he had grounded it and, as Ieuan's back was to him, he decided to bounce the ball off the back of his head.

The way I saw it he was making a mockery of Ieuan, and I stormed over to him in a rage. I was absolutely fuming mad. I'm not proud of it, but I gave him a mouthful of abuse and delivered my insults with real venom close up to his face. It was the kind of action that is brought on in the heat of a sporting battle, though there's no excuse for it whatsoever.

Fortunately, the rubbish I spouted was water off a duck's back to Underwood. Instead of reacting, he just gave me a smug smile and jogged off to take deserved plaudits from the crowd. What's more, if my verbals had upset him, he got his revenge in the best possible way: by scoring a lovely interception try later on to rub even more salt into our gaping wounds.

Our forwards had been utterly caned by the England pack, which included the great second-row pair of Wade Dooley and Paul Ackford, as well as others like hooker Brian Moore and a back-row axis of Mike Teague, Mick Skinner and Peter Winterbottom.

As a side, we were on our knees.

I remember in the hotel the night before the game, one of the team was having pints of Guinness sent up to his room, which said it all about the type of outfit we were. I can remember thinking to myself, 'That's our guy there and he's on the piss the night before the game.' No wonder we were humiliated.

It was a huge blow to go to Twickenham and get a beating like that because two years earlier we had triumphed there 11–3 on the first leg of our Triple Crown. It was hard to believe how the ground could have shifted so markedly in that time.

The following Sunday, a devastated Ryan announced his resignation to the press after realising that he was probably never going to get anything more out of us. He had no choice, really, after the woeful nature of our display.

The Twickenham defeat came after a 29–19 beating by France at home in the championship opener, a game best remembered for the first-half sending-off of the Pontypool captain, Kevin Moseley, for stamping on the French wing Marc Andrieu. Moseley received a ban of 33 weeks for his misdemeanour. We had tried to hang in there, but they grabbed five tries by the end and, down to fourteen men, we were blowing hard.

Waldron took charge for the first time as we welcomed Scotland to Cardiff for the third leg of the championship, but he got nowhere trying to trigger change as we lost to the Scots 13–9 despite arguably being the better side. Craig Chalmers proved the difference that day, kicking three penalty goals for the Scots, although we undoubtedly scored the try of the match through wing Arthur Emyr.

Waldron kept picking me for the team, but I don't know why because the pair of us never got on. In fact, I had little respect for him as a man-manager or a coach. He will probably be best remembered as the person who came in and tried to bring his club, Neath, with him, heavily favouring the guys who played for the Welsh All Blacks in his selections determined, as he was, to go with what he knew and trusted. Nevertheless, as we prepared to go to Dublin we were still in little better state than disarray.

Just days before the game, while we were still in Cardiff, I received a proposition that I will remember for the rest of my life: I was asked to throw a game for Wales in exchange for money. Allan Bateman referred to this incident in an autobiography he wrote some years ago, but the truth is that it never went as far as Allan actually being offered any money – I know, because I was the guy at the centre of the whole business; the guy who, if I had been so inclined, would have been the one actually receiving and then sharing out the money in the first place. It never came to that, though; nor was there ever any chance that it would.

The approach came from a businessman who said he was representing an organisation from London. I was left in no doubt that the London people were major league: in other words, if you took their money, you had to make damn sure you delivered what they wanted if you valued your knee caps. I was told the name of the fellow heading up the operation in the big smoke, but to safeguard my family I will never reveal it – in fact, I was told at the time by the linkman that if his name ever came out I would find myself in 'serious shit' and, to be honest, that scared the living daylights out of me. It was clear that we were dealing with not just crooks but more or less gangsters. The linkman even relayed a story to me about how someone had crossed him only to receive a visit from a gang wielding baseball bats. What I will say is this Mr Big had a track record in this kind of thing in other sports, racing being one, and now he had decided to try his hand in rugby union to see what pickings could be had there.

When the approach actually came, it was done in such a blasé fashion you would not believe it. 'Would you consider taking part in an attempt to throw an international rugby match?' he said.

'No way,' I replied.

'Look, there's a lot of money involved,' he countered.

'How much are you talking?' I asked, purely out of interest.

'Around £35,000,' came his answer.

I chuckled at the very idea and, rather than just tell him where to go, out of my own curiosity I decided to find out just what he had in mind.

'How the hell is anyone supposed to be able to throw a game of rugby?' I said. I just couldn't see how it would be possible. How could one guy out of fifteen change the course of a game? If I was playing in a world snooker final or tennis at Wimbledon, where I would have been very much master of my own destiny, I could have understood, but a fifteen-man team game? I reasoned the only fellow with half a chance of doing it would be the goalkicker, but even he would never be able to offer any guarantees.

'Look, the £35,000 is yours, you can do with it what you like, but you make damn sure that Wales lose.'

The inference here was clear: I would have to rein in a substantial number of my teammates with offers of some of the money if they would come on board with me and ensure that Wales lost the match. And I suppose I could have pulled it off with enough key decision makers in on it, like the hooker, the number 8 and the scrum-half.

Then the bloke confirmed that that would indeed be the plan. 'If it means your hooker throws the ball in wonky, your kicker misses all his pots at goal, then so be it. Give them some cash and get them on board. Or if you want to keep all the dosh yourself, then you'll have to jump out of the way every time Brendan

Mullins [who would be my opposite number at Lansdowne Road] gets the ball.'

That comment sticks in my mind more than any to this day.

It never came to me doing it, though, because I could never have done it; never in a million years. Thankfully, when I refused point-blank to get involved, the bloke accepted my decision and never leant on me. In fact, it was a short, sharp meeting that took no more than five minutes.

In Ireland, I was rooming with Bateman and one night as we lay awake before going to sleep, I asked him how he would have felt if I had offered him £5,000 to help me throw the game. I brought it up because even though I had laughed off the sinister approach, it had affected me mentally. It was on my mind and I suppose, in a way, I had to share it with someone, but it was a mere mention and just that: there was never any question of Bateman having actually been offered the money.

Eventually, it leaked out to all the boys, but it was best forgotten. Bateman raked it all up again with his book and when the media jumped on it, several of the boys directed journalistic enquiries to me! The story blew up again when the South African cricket captain, Hansie Cronje, was accused of match-fixing and was exposed as a cheat. The press were looking for different people in various sports who had been put in a similar position.

As it happened, we lost the Ireland game anyway, but I'm so pleased that we lost it fair and square. I could never have lived with myself otherwise. With hindsight, despite what was at stake, I am not surprised that such a poor Wales team did lose that clash at Lansdowne Road: it always seemed to be a dour struggle in Dublin. It was never a try-fest, no matter who ended up winning.

The 1990 Five Nations was Wales's first-ever whitewash and the mood around the country was such that we really felt we had heaped shame on everyone. And there was no immediate upturn. Little did Welsh rugby know it at the time but the game was in for many more years of relative misery.

A real low for me under the charge of Waldron was when

we were walloped 36–3 by France in Paris during the 1991 Five Nations. It wasn't just the result and performance but also a pathetic incident that occurred at the after-match function, which was usually a fairly glitzy affair in the French capital. I remember in 1985, the first time I attended one, feeling envious of more established players like Terry Holmes and Gareth Davies because they were taken out by French players like Serge Blanco to these posh sponsors' functions. The next time I went out there I got looked after by Frank Mesnel and Denis Charvet. This time round, however, because the Neath players didn't like wing collars, we were given basic WRU dicky bows and dress shirts. A couple of the boys were really unhappy about it, myself and Ieuan Evans included, and we decided to deliberately disobey the coach's orders and wear the wing collars we always wore at functions of this kind. In short, we were rebelling against Waldron and turned up in all our glory at the dinner, thinking to hell with what he and the Neath boys want.

Waldron came over to our table and as usual I felt he singled me out. He literally picked me up by the collar and dragged me away from the table.

'Wrong shirt,' he said.

'Yeh, wrong fucking coach and all!' I replied under my breath. To this day, I'm not sure whether he heard – probably not, because he may well have detonated if he had. The story was leaked to the *Sunday Mirror* the following day.

I wasn't in the greatest of moods before any of this started as Waldron had upset me the night before at the pre-match analysis session at our hotel. We were sitting down, expecting to see video clips of France and the way they played so we could suss out their patterns and identify their dangermen and where they may be vulnerable. Instead Waldron showed us footage of the 21–21 draw we had been involved in against Ireland at home a fortnight earlier.

In that game, I'd had a kick charged down, which had led to one of Ireland's four tries. Waldron fast-forwarded the action straight to this point and in front of all the lads he turned to me with a grimace on his face and let me have it with both barrels. 'Ring, you city slicker' – which is what he always used to call me – 'you pissed about then like you've pissed about all your career. You piss about like that tomorrow against France and you'll never play for your country again.'

I sat in a daze for the rest of the session. Waldron hadn't seemed to have understood that Neil Jenkins, who was playing just his third game for Wales at fly-half, was taking the ball standing still and putting pressure on me and Scott Gibbs in the centre because his passing wasn't sharp enough. I don't want to lay into Jenks because he was still a very raw player, but Gibbs was as well – he was also playing only his third game – and I was stuck between the two of these guys.

It certainly wasn't all bad for me that day. Earlier on there had been a counter-attack in which the Irish centre Brendan Mullin had hacked the ball deep into our territory. I chased it back on my own – I don't know where the rest of our cover defence was – and I suddenly got the rather harrowing feeling of being all alone with 60,000 people watching what I was going to do next. As the ball bobbled around I could feel the Irish stampede getting closer and closer, then the ball bobbled up into my hands and I swivelled around to my left-hand side. The obvious thing to do was to kick it to safety into touch. But out of the corner of my eye, I could see their winger, the blond pace merchant Simon Geoghegan bearing down the flank and as I was on my left foot I feared I could miscue it straight into his arms, which would have left him with an easy canter to our line.

My next instinct, and I don't know why, was to just stop and stand still in the middle of the pitch. It was amazing but other players seemed to stop still with me.

In the meantime, our players had managed to get behind me and I fed the ball to our scrum-half Chris Bridges, who offloaded it to a Cardiff teammate of mine, winger Steve Ford. Steve then just danced through everybody, passed to our big second row

Phil Davies, now the coach of Llanelli Scarlets, and he gave Neil Jenkins the scoring pass. It was a brilliant counter-attacking try and the whole place went nuts.

Then later, after more slow ball from Jenks, I had that left-footed kick charged down by their openside flanker, Phil Matthews. It took one bounce and then flipped up into the arms of Mullin, who strolled under our posts for a try. One moment I was the hero, the next the villain everybody wanted to slaughter.

After the session had finished, I went back to my room, which I was sharing with Ieuan Evans. I felt totally humiliated. I broke down in tears and was inconsolable. Nothing Ieuan said could make me feel any better.

After composing myself somewhat, I picked up a pen and started writing.

'What are you doing?' Ieuan asked.

'I'm not playing,' I replied.

'Don't be daft!' he said.

'I'm not,' I countered. 'I'm writing a letter to Waldron, I'm pulling out now.'

I finished writing, then barged out of the door and headed down the corridor towards Waldron's room, wearing just a T-shirt and a pair of underpants. Ieuan chased me, him just in his underpants, too. We must have looked a completely comical sight.

'Don't do this,' he shouted.

But I wasn't for turning – until he rugby tackled me just short of Waldron's door. He took the letter from me, scrunched it up and put it in his mouth. I'm sure he'd have swallowed it, too, if he'd had to! He succeeded in calming me down and I never did hand in that letter.

It was no surprise that we were stuffed the next day by the French at Parc des Princes. It was the last game of the 1991 championship and again it was probably no surprise that it marked a record defeat for us in the Five Nations. We could only manage a Paul Thorburn penalty to France's six tries.

Blanco was at his imperious best, scoring a dazzling try against us after just two minutes when he went charging down the wing, kicked ahead and scored from more than 50 yards. As for us, we barely threatened the try-line. In fact at the final whistle, it was probably lost on each and every one of us that we had not crossed the French line in Paris since Dai Richards went over way back in 1983, a truly appalling and unbelievable statistic.

Personally, I was relieved that it was the last time I played under Waldron. He presided over Wales's embarrassing annihilation in Australia that summer, where we lost the Test match 63–6 to the Wallabies in Brisbane – a tour I wasn't selected for – and after that he was gone. And it wasn't before time, in my opinion. I didn't like the way he coached. You had to do everything his way: I felt there was no room for any debate or discussion whatsoever. If there was a scrum on the left-hand side, you had to attack right. Everything seemed regimented and based on the law of averages. It was about going from A to B to C and I felt there was no time at all for any innovation or any opportunity to play the game as you saw it. I was always of the opinion that sometimes you had to go backwards to go forwards. That would be frowned on in today's game, I know, but if you have the vision and you can see something and you know you can create the space, then why not?

I thought the way Ron wanted us to play made it easy for teams to defend against us because it was painfully predictable. If we were to get back to our natural style of play, it was my belief that we needed to do the unexpected occasionally. I don't mean all the time, but at least we had to make opponents fearful of what may come out of the bag every now and then. I tear my hair out even today at the way some teams go through phases and crab across the pitch, looking to wear down the opposition.

It's only now, a hell of a long way down the line, that coaches the world over are beginning to realise that a defence-orientated game is not the way forward. I think they have accepted that they have to start thinking about the unorthodox.

The way Waldron and I parted was typical of our relationship.

On the day of the semi-finals of the Welsh Cup at the National Stadium just before the ill-fated tour to Australia, during which teammates disgraced themselves by scuffling amongst each other at the post-match function, Waldron approached me.

'Look,' he said, 'there's a rumour doing the rounds that you are going to make yourself unavailable for this tour to Australia.'

Now he wasn't all that far off the mark because, to be honest, I was thinking along those lines, largely because I simply couldn't bear the thought of going on tour with the bloke. I wouldn't have called it a deeply personal thing because I didn't view him as a horrible person – if I saw him now, I would like to think we could sit down and have a drink and a chat together – it was just that I didn't rate him as a coach because I felt he was trying to shackle me all the time. My fears at going on that tour were to prove well founded, mind you, not just because of the Test massacre by the Aussies but also the fact that we lost 71–8 to one of their provincial sides, New South Wales; a match in which we leaked an incredible 13 tries. But in response to Waldron's question, I told him in no uncertain terms that I was available to tour.

'Great,' he said.

The following day, he announced the touring party and I had been left out. I had mixed feelings about it, but I was annoyed deep down because I knew I could have stayed behind on my own terms instead of suffering the kick in the guts of non-selection. At least I could console myself with having made myself available to my country. If my country didn't want me, then so be it. I had nothing to reproach myself for. What got to me was that there was no explanation as to why I had been omitted: it was just a straightforward selection and that was that. Possibly Waldron had been hoping I would make it easy for him by making the decision not to play myself. I say that because it would have been surprising if the day before he was due to make his squad announcement he was still undecided about my involvement.

I didn't think too deeply about it at the time. As I never really wanted to go in the first place, I never got down in the mouth about it that summer. Instead I had some time off, and I probably needed it, to be quite honest. I wasn't surprised to hear the horror tales that emerged from the tour and the problems the rest of the squad encountered with the Neath cliques. It had been building towards that for some time.

What really put me off the idea of going to Australia was that I had already experienced a tour under Waldron's leadership when Wales went to Namibia for a two-Test series in the summer of 1990 after our infamous Five Nations whitewash. We won both matches, though the fact that we could only manage 18–9 and 34–30 victories against what was a Third World rugby nation said it all about the mess we were in at the time. There was also a raft of withdrawals from the squad – ten altogether – before we left.

Thorburn's kicking was the difference in the 18–9 Test victory, while in the second game we let them back into it by conceding a late flurry of points, having led 30–15.

It was a tour to forget and one that was never going to live long in the memories of Wales supporters. The only excuse we could possibly offer was that the heat was as intense as any of us had ever played in.

I was actually asked to captain the side in one of the midweek games, but I was soon regretting that decision when a couple of days before the game against one of their provincial sides, a free day for the squad, I was with a few of the others in the hotel bar relaxing with a beer or two.

All of a sudden, Waldron appeared. He didn't speak to anyone else, but instead looked straight at me and said, 'Get in the lift and get up to bed!'

It was evening time but nowhere near late enough for him to be able to argue that it was high time we got our heads down.

'You're joking,' I said.

'Fordy [Steve Ford], take him up to bed,' he replied.

I was dumbstruck. He wanted Steve Ford, one of my Cardiff teammates, to escort me up to bed. Waldron took my beer off me as we got up and basically frogmarched me to the lift, with an embarrassed Fordy doing as he was told and straggling along by the side of us.

I walked through the doors of the lift and as they were about to close, I said, 'Ron, this is ridiculous.'

'Listen,' he said, 'you're captaining your country in a few days' time. There's a lot of people back home who think that's ridiculous!'

And with those words the doors closed, leaving me totally bemused. He'd had the last word, as usual, and as I stood there in disbelief, Fordy began to laugh. I didn't see the funny side.

However, that was not the only time that a lift sticks in my mind from that trip. One evening, I had gotten myself fairly drunk and when I woke up the next morning, I couldn't be bothered going down for breakfast, so asked my room-mate, Ian Bucket, the former Swansea prop, to wake me up in time for training. Ian forgot and the inevitable happened – I slept through. When I woke up with a start and realised, I feared immediately that I would be sent home and began thinking how I could cover myself.

I went downstairs to reception and told the concierge what had happened and said that I needed his help to get me out of trouble, promising two stand tickets for the second Test match if he agreed to play ball. He asked me what I wanted him to do and I told him that I would tell Waldron that I had missed training because I was stuck in the lift – I needed him to verify it when Waldron checked out my story, as he was certain to do.

At first, the concierge said he wouldn't be able to do it because an incident like that had to be recorded in a logbook and people would have to be called out to fix the problem. But my silver tongue sprang into action and I eventually managed to persuade him to help me.

When Waldron returned from training, he immediately wanted to know what had happened. Then, sure enough, came the threat that I would be sent home unless my excuse was a genuine one. So I told him I had been stuck in the lift.

'Oh, you were, were you?' he replied, clearly not believing me for one moment. When they checked it with reception, of course, the incident was all recorded in black and white and that was the end of the matter. I was in the clear.

In my view, Waldron seemed to favour Neath players on several occasions. On that tour, we had a prop called Jeremy Pugh in the squad, who, at times, appeared to me to be getting special treatment from Waldron.

What made it worse is that I never had a lot of time for Pugh, or 'Piggy' Pugh as we used to call him, because in our eyes he bore more than a passing resemblance – it was a nickname that used to drive him nuts. Once on tour in New Zealand in 1988, Pugh did something to his eye in one of the matches and reappeared after treatment wearing an eyepatch like some battered and bruised hero. I decided to have some fun by cutting out a piece of one of the table napkins and sticking it across the eye of this decoration boar that was on the wall of the place where we were having our after-match meal. When Pugh spotted it, there was a chorus of laughter and sniggering, but he wasn't happy about it and started having a go at me. It even got to the stage where there was a bit of pushing and shoving, but then Glenn Webbe stepped in to play the peacemaker.

'Come on, lads, we're all in it together, we're supposed to be teammates,' said Webby. 'Now, come on, let's all shake hands and have no more of this nonsense.'

So Pugh and I shook hands, then Pugh went to shake Webby's hands only to be met with a flat forked hand in the shape of a pig's trotter!

I felt that Waldron had never really gelled with a lot of the boys because of his approach to training. I remember him bringing in a new fitness guru, a chap by the name of Alan Roper, who was a veteran marathon runner. From then on, training became about running, running and more running. I remember on a Thursday night before one clash against Ireland, we had a training session at Swansea's St Helen's ground – Waldron moved us down there to train away from Cardiff as one of his first little changes. This particular time, though, we turned up at St Helen's, where the floodlights were on and the big green pitch was all ready for us to go through our moves and get a good feel for the ball two days before an important Test match. Instead we were dragged across the Mumbles Road outside the ground to the big wide pavements that run parallel to Swansea Bay and forced to run between the lamp posts!

After a murderously hard session, we went back across the road, showered and went home without so much as going within five yards of a rugby ball. To me, anyway, it summed up the whole regime.

One of the few people who seemed to have Waldron's card marked was my great pal Webby, the winger who made his name with Bridgend. I remember Ron telling Webby that Ieuan would be getting the right-wing's jersey and as such Webby should go back to Bridgend and tell the club to start playing him on the left wing.

'Ron, I'll play anywhere for Wales, I'll even play tight-head prop – but when I do, I'll play it like a right winger!' Webby replied.

Webby and I were great pals in those days; we still are. I remember the Wales team went to the Gower peninsula, a beautiful spot, for a training camp this one occasion. We had been strictly paired off to share rooms with people who would be playing close to us on the pitch to foster good understandings and, as such, I was in with the centre Mike Hall. As we were unpacking our cases, Webby burst into the room and told Hall to sling his hook.

'I'm sharing with him,' he said, and off Mike went. Webby didn't give a stuff about who was supposed to be in with who.

In the end, Waldron's health let him down. He suffered a blood clot in one of his lungs after returning from the debacle in Australia and he was forced to quit – although it's highly unlikely he would have been allowed to carry on, even if he had been fit.

As for the bribe, I quickly forgot about it. There were other pressing matters, not least the approach of the 1991 World Cup, where we would be under the almost suffocating pressure of playing in front of our own fans. But at least I felt there was now a coach in charge who believed in me – and was willing to base his whole strategy around what I could offer.

8

WORLD CUP 1991

By the time the disastrous 1991 Five Nations campaign had finished, bookmakers had lengthened Wales's odds of winning that year's World Cup, jointly hosted by the home unions, from 66-1 to 125-1. They say the bookies don't often get it wrong; I guess that once again rang true in our case, even though we would be playing our three pool matches against Western Samoa, Argentina and Australia at Cardiff Arms Park.

Having finished third in the inaugural tournament in 1987, we were one of the seeds, but for us expectations were as low as they would ever get. That said, to retain a shred of pride, the general consensus was that we had to at least reach the last eight.

Of course, our task was not made easy by the make-up of our qualifying group. Australia were the favourites to lift the trophy in some quarters and their team, led by coach Bob Dwyer, did go on to do just that, so we were not tipped to get any change out of them whatsoever. Then we had two non-seeds who were about as strong for non-seeds as you could get. There was Argentina, who, despite having lost their legendary fly-half Hugo Porta, who was by then 40, were still a rock-solid rugby nation with a long tradition who could hold their own against the top sides in the world, and Western Samoa. Even now, those two words strike a chill down the spine of many a diehard Welsh rugby fan.

Their status as a South Sea island with a population of just 160,000, far less than the population of Cardiff at the time, masked the fact that they actually had sixteen New Zealand-based players in their ranks and two who plied their trade in Australia. Wales had beaten Western Samoa 28–6 in Cardiff in 1988, but it was clear that they had since used the then lax laws in the game about players switching national allegiance to their advantage. Names like Frank Bunce, Stephen Bachop, Brian Lima and Pat Lam, all of Kiwi descent, went on to become household names on the Test circuit with Western Samoa and later Samoa. So even though this was the country's first experience of the World Cup, it was clear the team were going to take a bit of beating.

The appointment as coach of Alan Davies, who had been in charge of Nottingham as well as England A and the England Under-21s previously, rekindled my enthusiasm for the game, particularly as he gave me my first chance to play fly-half at international level, which was something I had always wanted to do.

I remember when Alan first took over, Bob Norster took me with Cardiff and Wales fly-half David Evans to meet him at the airport because for some reason that was what Alan wanted. In the car on the way back, Alan turned around and asked who should play fly-half for Wales or, more to the point, who wanted to do so? David said he didn't mind where he played, but straight away I said I wanted to wear the number 10 jersey. That's the way the situation was dealt with. I think Alan was looking for that kind of positive attitude, someone who was going to put his hand up and say, 'I'm your man. Take a chance on me.' So they moved us around, making David a centre and me a fly-half.

We didn't have long to wait for our first outing because in the first week of September, we welcomed France to Cardiff for a warm-up game that was also meant to celebrate the new £400,000 Arms Park floodlights. It was Alan's first match in charge and it was a vastly improved all-round display from us. We won far more of our own ball and I was basically given a free rein to play it as I saw it in the pivotal role.

The final score, 22–9 – Wales having lost to a French outfit once again inspired by the irrepressible Serge Blanco – did us little justice, but I was massively encouraged a day or so later when a letter arrived through my door from Alan Davies congratulating me on my display and saying it was a great start. I couldn't have been more eager in my anticipation to play for my country on home soil in my favourite position in what was now becoming the most important tournament in the world game.

Just a few weeks later, though, we were out on our ears after a thrashing at the hands of Australia. Worse still, when I returned to my house and listened to the messages on my answering machine. I was left dumbstruck. There were dozens of poisonous remarks from members of the public, people I didn't know from Adam, screaming the most hurtful abuse down the line at me and telling me to retire because they couldn't take any more. The gist of it was 'do us all a favour and retire, for God's sake' accompanied by effing and blinding and the most appalling language. How they got hold of my number, I don't know; I suppose in those days we weren't as detached from people as many international sportspeople are now. I was still just an ordinary guy about town, living in Splott, the suburb of Cardiff where I had grown up, so I guess there were ways.

The abuse cut me to the quick. It was an example of just how high feelings were running. I could understand how passionate the fans were about seeing Wales do well and how our failure was driving everyone nuts, but there was no excuse for that type of behaviour and typically none of the callers had the guts to leave their names.

Some might say I should have been above such claptrap and ignored it, but in truth I was already having doubts about carrying on and this just tipped me over the edge. I would defy anyone who has ever had to listen to that type of abuse not to feel similarly, particularly as some of the messages contained some extremely nasty threats, which I would have been quite entitled to pass on to the police.

The tournament got off to a horrific start for us, as we lost 16–13 to Western Samoa. Even though they were actually a very strong side because of their Kiwi contingent, there was no use in pointing to that as an excuse: they were Western Samoa, end of story. For us to lose to them at home in a World Cup opener was unforgivable. Even now, it is remembered, if that's the right way to describe it, as one of the darkest results in the history of the Wales team. It's right up there alongside the 96–13 defeat in South Africa in 1998, when half the stadium at Loftus Versveld was laughing at us by the end.

The build-up to the tournament was totally ruined for me as just a month before the October start it was decided I needed an operation on my right knee. The problem was wear and tear on the cartilage because of years of over-compensating on that leg after having wrecked the ligaments in the left one earlier in my career. There was no choice at the time: I had to have the surgery because I had displaced cartilage after the French game. Subsequently, that month for me was all about a race against time. I spent the whole of the run-up to the competition at the Penoyre House rehabilitation centre in Brecon, a place the WRU used at the time, recovering on the treatment table.

My knee was holding up by the time the World Cup came around. I wore a protective support around it and never had any trouble with it. The key problem was that I had spent the preparation to the competition sitting on my arse without being able to do any running. At the time, I was very into my running and I really needed to be getting some air into my lungs to get me sharp.

Even though I wasn't fit aerobically to play at my peak, Alan Davies made it quite clear to me that he didn't much care. Adrian Davies, the Cardiff fly-half, was the only other number 10, but Alan suggested to me in private that he would prefer it if I played even though I was battling with my fitness. It would seem that Alan just didn't rate Adrian as highly as me. That's the way things go in rugby and sport in general.

Despite the presence of so many obviously dangerous players in the Western Samoan team, we were accused afterwards of having underestimated them and then paid the price for complacency. I really don't think that had much to do with the defeat. The real problem for us was that we just didn't have the ability or the presence of mind as a team to get the ball away from their hit men in the midfield. We were actually dominant in the scrum, but they messed up our lineout altogether. Most important of all, they were a yard and a half faster to the ball in all departments and tigerish in everything they did.

In midfield, Frank Bunce was their main man and I was trying to roll passes across him using Arthur Emyr as a decoy runner. The problem we had was Mike Hall. The former Cardiff and British Lions centre, now a pundit for BBC Wales, had all the time he should have needed, in my view, to get the ball out to Ieuan Evans or Anthony Clement, who were pacey runners that could have won the game for us out wide; however, Mike couldn't seem to take a pass and give it away quickly enough when he was under pressure, so he kept getting smashed to pieces and we were getting nowhere.

We were never really in the game until a late rally when I helped put Ieuan over in the corner for a try, but it was too late.

I'll hold my hand up in that I missed a few key shots at goal that day, which you could say ultimately proved the difference, but the bottom line was that they were too good for us up front even though they were hanging on in the scrum.

The aftermath of the game is a blur, but I do recall the sense of shock that swept the nation. 'Rock Bottom' screamed the headline of the *Western Mail* on the Monday morning after the match, with their chief rugby writer, John Kennedy, noting that Welsh rugby was 'tottering on the brink of the abyss of the final humiliation'. It's hard to know what words he could have chosen to hammer home the message any harder.

Even the great Gareth Edwards didn't mince his words, saying that had what looked a perfectly good try by Robert Jones not been disallowed and Wales won, it would only have papered over the cracks.

We had now only won two of our last thirteen matches at the Arms Park and had just become the first IRB nation to fall prey to one of the so-called lesser nations in the history of the World Cup. An indication of what the victory meant to the Samoans, though, was their captain Peter Fatialofa's description of the day as the greatest of his life.

The following Wednesday evening, we had to face Argentina and we did manage to get ourselves back on track in some shape or form by registering a hard-fought 16–7 success. I thought we played OK and I remember we were reasonably pleased as a team, even though we had hardly brought the house down with anything we had done under the floodlights.

Then followed a total drubbing at the hands of the Aussies. We had hardly any possession and we were absolutely smashed in every department. In truth, we were never really in the game. It was obviously a must-win situation for us and, believe it or not, we went into it genuinely believing we could win. Yes, the odds were massively stacked against us and on paper we had no right to believe we could get within 20 points of them, but when you are playing in a World Cup on home soil, you subconsciously believe you can win a game like that. In fact, throughout my entire career, there has only ever been one instance when I have taken a field genuinely not believing we stood a cat's chance in hell of winning. That was on the 1988 tour to New Zealand when we were unfortunate enough to face what was probably one of the most fearsome outfits in the history of All Black rugby. They had beaten us in the semi-final of the World Cup on their soil six months earlier and when we went back, you couldn't help but think that you had no chance of winning. But I had never felt like that at any other time.

With hindsight, though, maybe I should have been more realistic about that Aussie game, especially considering the state of some of our preparation. The day before, we were training at the army base right next to the old Severn Bridge, where England often used to train when they were due to play us in Cardiff. I remember that Alan Davies had the idea of a move along a back line where I would line up at inside-centre. The plan was for me to receive the ball from whomever stood at fly-half and then hold up the ball and deliver it late with a disguised pass to our wing, Arthur Emyr, who would come crashing through from the blindside wing as the fly-half made a looping dummy run. It may sound complicated; it wasn't. But that didn't matter because this day on the training ground we didn't have a chance of executing it for one good reason. I took the ball from David Evans, who was the fly-half for the move, and I held it and held it and held it, just waiting for Arthur to appear. No sign of him, though. I looked around and there he was practising his golf swing on the pitch, completely and uncharacteristically oblivious to the move. He was in another world while we were supposed to be honing our moves in the last training session before facing Australia. It was shambolic.

It was typical of what lay around the corner for poor Arthur because the next day in the match against the Wallabies, long after the result had been put beyond doubt, we were launching an attack desperately trying to conjure a consolation try. Arthur suddenly received the ball in a bit of space and decided, for reasons best known to himself, to attempt a drop goal even though three points would have been irrelevant to our cause. He miscued it terribly, however, with the ball squirting along the floor underneath the posts in a way that neatly summed up the entire 38–3 trouncing for us.

I liked Arthur, though; in fact, he was the salt of the earth and when he later went on to become head of sport at BBC Wales, he offered me a contract as a pundit.

With hindsight, it was perhaps no surprise that Australia hammered us, but for all the pain and frustration that came with the defeat, it was those horrible messages on my answering machine that were to prove the finishing of me. I was only 29 years old, young by any standards to be calling it quits at international level, even taking into account the continuing trouble I had experienced with my knees. When I look back, I realise the decision was brought on by a build-up of despair and desperation at the whole experience of playing for Wales in the previous two years or so.

I'd been through the Ron Waldron era and all that it had brought with it: virtually two successive whitewashes only prevented by a home draw against Ireland, the bully-boy tactics I felt Waldron employed with me, and the humiliating incidents in the bar in Namibia and after the French match at the function. Now there was all this to contend with: the anguish of a nation, the realisation that as a rugby force we were bottom of the pile and the dreadful thought that some of the public believed I was more or less solely responsible.

For all that, when I look back I feel I should have given it another season; maybe I should have allowed myself to go through a good pre-season period of fitness and conditioning the following summer and given it another crack with Wales. But I'm afraid it wasn't really a time for logical thinking on my part and, as I say, the flak flying in my direction had a deep impact on my mindset.

I remember when I was first starting out in the game, I used to pick up the papers and I was almost always flavour of the month. If I wasn't man of the match, I was picking up a player of the year award. I was spoken about in glowing terms as the next big thing. Sometimes I would even finish a game and know deep down that I hadn't played as well as I could have, yet still I would be reading compliments about my contribution. Later in my career, I was panned by the critics far more often, but it was the opposite then: so many times I felt I had done all right only to read a wave of negative remarks.

Knowing what I now know, I would tell aspiring players not to read their own press and to make up their own minds about their performance. I have seen international players become almost obsessed with the way they are portrayed in the media; so much so that it dominates their mood when they should only be thinking with a cool head about their own game. Worse, it leads to paranoia; players see shadows that aren't there and they subsequently alienate journalists who then only end up giving them worse press because they think they have a bad attitude. It's a bit of a vicious circle.

Perhaps if I had kept a cool head I would have won more Wales caps, yet I was by no means finished as a player altogether. I stayed on at Cardiff for the rest of that season, which I loved. I would play whenever I could get the blue-and-black shirt on. Internationals today play less for their clubs and regions. A punishing modern-day schedule is to blame for that, as is a more professional approach to the game, to be fair; but I still think there have been players down the years who have been too slow to pull on their club jerseys.

I would play for Wales in the Five Nations and then even if we had just one week's break before the next game, or a month, I would be itching to play for Cardiff or Pontypool in between. The pity was in those games I was more often than not rubbish, largely because I just couldn't get my head right despite my keenness to play. Turning out for Wales was always such a massive adrenalin rush that playing for your club a week later felt like a comedown and, as difficult as this is to describe, I just couldn't get myself feeling right inside. I can never remember playing well in one of these games, making mistake after mistake, and it happened time and time again, even though at the start of the week leading up to them I would try desperately hard to get my head right.

I didn't have to contend with that problem after the World Cup, though: from then on, it would be club rugby only.

9

BASEBALL AND BISHOP

Where I come from in Cardiff, if you grow up playing sport and have an eye for a ball, it is inevitable that you will play baseball. The sport has its own niche in the history of the city and has been played for more than a century by men and women on the parks of the capital. It has had its own characters as well. I could list blokes I've played with who have phenomenal hitting power, bowling pace or catching ability, yet as sporting personalities remained largely unknown other than to those directly involved in the game.

I played from a young age right through to adulthood when I became a dual Welsh international, winning four baseball caps at a time when I was far better known for rugby. Baseball became my summer sport. Although I had played cricket as a youngster in the local leagues for Morgannwg, the same team as my dad, I used to find the day too long: you would have 45 overs a side, starting at 2 p.m., and not finish until 8.30 p.m. sometimes. Quite frankly, by the end I found the whole thing boring. Baseball was more my thing. It was shorter, sharper and faster. That said I would consider one of my most thrilling moments playing sport to have taken place on a cricket field.

I was working for Companies House and playing for the Department of Trade and Industry team in the Welsh Civil Service Cup final. We were up against the DVLA at Gowerton Cricket Club in a 40-over match and rarely have I been involved in a situation where we snatched victory from the jaws of defeat in quite such dramatic fashion. The DVLA had in their ranks a guy who had played a bit for the Wales Minor Counties team and, to be honest, it was a bit naughty on their part because this fellow clearly didn't belong at our level. He opened the batting and the bowling, which I thought was really sad, and when we batted first, he quickly rattled through our top order.

I went in to bat at about eight or nine and managed to scramble eleven or twelve runs, but we were skittled for 111 and so ate our tea believing we had more or less lost the game. We were convinced of our defeat when their star man helped them to sixty without loss, but by that time I was really frustrated with the whole day. I was also fielding on the boundary furthest from the pavilion and was desperate for a pee.

As there was nobody around, I decided to quickly relieve myself there and then, but it was just my luck that their main man sent a steepling catch my way as I was in full flow. There was nothing I could do but put up an optimistic hand and hope the ball stuck – it did, and that sparked a revival.

Wickets fell at regular intervals after that and we also managed to tie down their run rate. By the time they reached the last over, they needed two runs to win with four wickets remaining, which is where my intervention came into play. On three separate occasions in that final over, their batsmen nudged the ball to me at cover and every time they tried to get a quick single to claim the draw, only for me to knock the stumps over with direct hits using my baseball throwing arm. It was mayhem. When our bowler claimed the final wicket, we clinched an incredible victory. I'll never forget it.

I always found playing cricket easy after baseball, not least picking up the ball and throwing it because you had a smooth role rather than the bobbling and bouncing park pitches we'd had to contend with.

I won my first Wales cap against England at the Newport Civil Service ground in the annual match between the two countries in June 1984. David Bishop was also in the team. I was the fourth-ever rugby union international to represent my country at baseball: Bish made his debut a year earlier before he was capped in rugby, and Viv Huzzey and Jack Wetter achieved the honour in 1908 and 1920 respectively. I'm proud of that, immensely proud.

Baseball in its British park form rather than the New York Yankees game most people refer to is probably unknown across vast areas of the UK – for example, I'm not aware that it is played at all in London in any organised capacity – though it requires bravery, skill, strength, speed and intelligence, which is why I will always cherish having made it to the top of my particular tree in the game.

When I won my first cap, I was clean bowled for a duck (when a good ball strikes your body with you making no contact with the bat) by a fellow called Jeff Linge who was extremely quick. He just whipped it right across my midriff when my intention had been to dab the ball down on the offside and run to get my eye in, but I made the fatal error of changing my mind at the last moment and trying to steer the ball around the corner. The rest is history, as they say. I remember thinking, 'So, this is what international baseball is all about.'

The irony was that the anticlimactic nature of my international baseball debut mirrored my first rugby appearance against England a year earlier. I never had the chance to bat again that day because we won by an innings and 16 runs, but I did do something that at least left me with the feeling that I had made a contribution. I used to field at long stop, which is basically the area behind the backstop and either side of him, with the bowler giving you signals about what type of line he intends to bowl down. It's a difficult position to play because you find yourself dealing with all the thick and thin edges off the bat and because you play on a public park, you have the added challenge of often having to deal with a ball bobbling along a far from smooth surface. You also need a good throwing arm at long stop because sometimes you would be required to throw from way behind the batsman right to the other end of the diamond at base two.

Anyway, it came to the last play of the match against England and the guy on the pegs had a thin edge which span away, but I managed to storm in from long stop, dive full length and catch it about an inch off the floor. At least that was some consolation for my batting shocker.

My second cap in July 1986 at Cardiff's Roath Park was a happier occasion for me. I plundered seventeen runs out of the 106 we scored in our solitary innings and finished the game with no fewer than five catches to my name to win the BBC's man of the match award.

I sometimes wonder how I made the Wales team, mind you. There used to be a bit of corruption at the trials each year, with bowlers from the same club looking after their own batsmen, trying to make them look good. Bish, who was an Old Illtydians teammate, told me one year he would bowl a half-pace ball at my off-peg that would be ripe for smacking away. When I got to the pegs, feeling relaxed and confident, he whistled one past my nose which felt like the fastest ball he had ever bowled. I looked up . . . he was laughing.

However, like rugby, it is the experiences I enjoyed and the friends I made playing baseball that are as important to me now as any actual statistical achievement. In 1991, just a few months before the start of the rugby World Cup, having moved by then from the Old Illtydians club to a side called Grange Albion, I was picked again for Wales against England up at Liverpool's Edinburgh Park. At the time, the then Liverpool manager Graeme Souness was signing Dean Saunders and Mark Wright and they were both staying in the same hotel as us, the Adelphi, in the middle of town. They would prove to be not the first Liverpool players we would bump into that weekend.

The night before our game, we were in the wine bar next door to the hotel and spotted John Barnes, also at Anfield at the time, at a table on his own. There were lots of people from Cardiff in there who had come up to watch the baseball, many of whom were keen footballers as well who played for local sides, and inevitably it wasn't long before one of our followers went over to speak to Barnes.

To my amazement, I was told minutes later that Barnes wanted a chat with me. I didn't need a second invitation because he was a player I admired enormously and at that time he was really in his prime as one of the biggest names in the game. We had about a 15-minute chat over a glass of wine and I was astonished by his knowledge of Welsh rugby and of my own exploits in the game. He told me about the banter he would have with Ian Rush every time Wales played England in the Five Nations and how the Liverpool boys all took an avid interest in the tournament when it came around every year.

It surprised me no end that he even knew who I was, to be honest, and I was incredibly flattered when he complimented me on my style of play, saying he liked the way I was always prepared to try something different. I have since grown suspicious of his great knowledge of rugby and it has crossed my mind that one of our guys filled Barnes in on Wales and Mark Ring beforehand and that I was the victim of a well-worked wind-up! All I can say is that if I was, I'm still unaware of it to this day.

We stayed out drinking all night, with Bish, as usual, the instigator. I would never have done that before a rugby international, but baseball to me was always far more of a leisure sport. I make no apologies for the fact that I never took it as seriously as my rugby, even though I was as proud as anyone to represent my country in the sport. We never lacked motivation ahead of a game and on this occasion while David Bishop was at the forefront of the previous evening's revelry, once we got into the dressing-rooms, he turned into a madman, pumped up beyond belief, making sure we beat the English. He was the greatest motivator I ever came across in sport: as soon as he pulls on a jersey which is red featuring three feathers, the passion and emotion that flows out of him is all-consuming and it tends to rub off on everyone.

When Bish went into that mode, I was suddenly filled with guilt

Leicester Tigers, 1960. Dad is in the middle of the back row.

Me as captain of St Albans Primary rugby football team. My brother Paul is
in the back row on the far right.

With the Cardiff Schools team after beating Bridgend Under-11s. John Actie, who was later wrongly convicted for the murder of Cardiff prostitute Lynette White, is second from right, with me next to our captain Paul James. (*Western Mail and Echo*)

With the famous Dewar Shield as an Under-15 Cardiff Schoolboy.

at the prospect of letting myself down, having had too much to drink. The bottom line was I was representing my country and I had been pissed the night before . . . but then I quickly realised that Bish, the man whose emotion had made me feel this way, had been the main instigator of the drinking!

We won that day by six men holding, or by six wickets in cricketing terms, with me scoring twelve and a duck in what would be my last baseball international for Wales.

There is one experience I went through as a result of baseball, however, that I wouldn't wish on my worst enemy. We were playing at a park called Llandaff Fields in Cardiff one evening and during the course of the game, I received a hefty blow right where it hurts the most, the ball thudding into my privates as I went for a catch while fielding on base three, my late reaction coming because I had been daydreaming in the hot weather. I went down like a sack of potatoes but recovered enough to finish the game and then go for a couple of pints of Brains Dark in a nearby pub with the boys afterwards.

As I supped my pint, I began to feel a bit queasy and it wasn't long before I was doubled up in agony with a pain in my stomach. It was then that one of the lads suggested I get it checked out. He ran me to a nearby hospital and I hadn't been there long before I was lying on a bed being sick. I told the doctors what had happened and was dispatched to another hospital, where I soon had tubes attached to my groin after having developed an enormous haematoma.

The doctors let me go after one night's stay, but I had to go back there every Monday for a fair while to be checked over. I soon struck up a bit of a rapport with another guy who was going in for the same kind of treatment after being kicked in the same area by an animal while on safari (I don't know which was worse!).

On what was about my third visit to the hospital, one of the doctors took me into a private room and gave me some news that floored me.

'You've got cancer,' he said.

I went cold. 'No, no, it can't be,' I cried, absolutely devastated.

The doctor left me to my own devices for a minute and a short time later one of his colleagues entred the room.

'Look, Mark,' he said, 'there has been a terrible mistake. You have been mixed up with your pal.'

It turned out that the guy who had been dealt the blow on safari was the one with the cancer and not me. You can imagine my emotions at that stage; they were a mixture of unbridled relief, anger and confusion.

'You can take this further if you want,' he said, meaning that I would be quite within my rights to launch an official complaint, but in all honesty I was just glad to get out of there and forget the whole thing. To this day, I have never again seen the chap who had become my temporary mate and I sincerely hope he made a full recovery.

While I just wanted to forget about what was a truly awful moment, it has unfortunately scarred me psychologically. I have a huge mental problem with my private parts these days. I know there will be people who will chuckle at that, but it's a genuine and unpleasant thing for me to deal with. I have been to the doctors three times to have myself fully checked out and if I get the slightest twinge in the groin area it sets me off worrying. Sometimes I'll have a little feel around that region while in the bath, as all men do, and I'll think I have found some lump or other that shouldn't be there when in reality it is nothing harmful and nothing everyone else hasn't got. I've never been right since that experience in that hospital room and I've told my doctor all about it, admitting that the problem is as likely in my head as anywhere else.

Each time I've been to the doctor's, I've been checked out and it's been found that there is nothing wrong with me which has given a massive temporary confidence boost, but each time I've ended up having the same worries return to my mind.

*   *   *

When I got back into the baseball as a young man, having played it so much at school, I initially went to play for the St Peter's club in Cardiff. Many of my mates from rugby began playing baseball for Old Illtydians, with Kenny Poole, Pablo Rees, Terry Holmes and Brendan Macaloon, all ex-Cardiff players, Bish and even footballer David Giles, who played for Wales as well as the four Welsh clubs Cardiff, Swansea, Wrexham and Newport (now a Conference South club) getting involved. We all joined more established pure baseballers: fellows like Kevin Trevett, a brilliant sportsman who died in a work accident at a tragically young age.

Old Illtydians did well. We climbed the leagues quickly and won the Welsh Brewers Cup in 1988 against a team called Caerau, from a tough suburb in the west of the city, in a game that was televised and attracted a huge crowd to Roath Park.

Later, one or two of our boys moved on to pastures new and I decided to join Grange Albion, one of the oldest and most competitive teams in the sport in Cardiff. I learned a lot of tricks of the trade from some of their old campaigners, even though it was quite late in the day for me and I had already been capped.

For example, there was one piece of gamesmanship I saw in my time at Grange Albion that would have been worth remembering for the future. There was a batsman holding base one with his team short of players left in, who was edging off his base, trying to get around and get back to support the few batsmen remaining and keep the innings going. The bowler, Sean Simmonds, had the ball in his hand at the time ready to bowl the next ball and he walked back in his box and suddenly turned round and mimicked having bowled the ball without actually releasing it.

To make it look realistic, the backstop clapped his hands together up in the air as if he had caught the ball. It completely fooled the batsman into thinking he had bowled. Then when the batsman realised he'd been duped and tried to abort his run to base two and get back to base one, the bowler would fire the ball in for the dismissal.

Some of the sledging was legendary. It was ten times worse

than anything they go on about in cricket. And I have to say that sometimes a lot of it was really personal, which is where the ability to be tough when required and look after yourself came in to baseball. As I said earlier, a lot of the boys who played were hard nuts with football backgrounds who would remember one another from footy matches when there might have been a nasty foul or two, and often these things would spill over into personal vendettas during the match.

This type of environment was, of course, right up Bish's street and it was through baseball that we became close pals. Bish is friends with the Welsh international footballer Craig Bellamy: they're from the same part of Cardiff and Bish was even best man at his wedding last summer. I know the pair of them go back a long way. The Bellamy family have a baseball background as well.

What can I say about Bish? The first time I saw him play rugby was at the Cardiff Schools Under-11 seven-a-side competition and he was astonishingly good. I was a couple of years younger than him and followed his career closely as we went up through the age groups. Bish has always been a bit of a wild boy; he has always tried to make the best of any situation and always tries to have a good time. He was the youngest player ever to go on tour with Cardiff when he travelled with them in the late '70s.

The natural thing to assume was that with the talent he had and being a home-town boy, he would go on to enjoy a long and distinguished career with the Blue and Blacks, but it never happened because he blotted his copybook with the club. Bish has always been handy with his fists; he's always been tough and he will admit that in his younger days he would get embroiled in street fights and sometimes actually go looking for trouble.

He was once responsible for the most almighty brawl at a baseball match between Old Illtydians and Grange Albion. Our Old Illtydians team included me, Bish, Kevin Trevett, and the former Cardiff rugby player Brendan Macaloon, and there were always all manner of wind-ups going on. A week or so earlier, I had played in a charity football match with Bish down at Neath Rugby Club and the fellow who had made the speech at the end of the game remarked how good it was that the 17 sporting celebrities who had been named in the programme for the day had all actually turned up to support the cause. Bish's name wasn't in the programme, for some reason, and Glenn Webbe piped up with, 'Yeah, and one celeb's turned up today and his name wasn't even in the programme!'

I immediately feared how Bish would react because I knew he hated being embarrassed in any way. He was seething, though he did nothing at the time.

I made the mistake of mentioning it to Kevin Trevett and it made its way back to Macaloon, who brought it up on the day of this baseball game against Grange Albion, foolishly winding Bish up about the matter. When I arrived to play, Bish pinned me up against the wall.

'What have you been saying?' he snarled. 'Have you been shit-stirring?'

I managed to save my skin with a few meek words, but Macaloon just wouldn't let it drop all afternoon, every now and again making digs about Bish not having had his name in the programme for this game. After Bish was clean bowled, he made his way to the calling box, but Macaloon continued to wind him up from the bench.

Then all of a sudden, Bish ran over to him in the middle of the game, jumped on him and tried to knock his block off. The whole of the Old Illtydians side jumped in, to the astonishment of the Grange Albion team, and after the mêlée dispersed, Bish and Macaloon started heading off to the dressing-room to sort it out with their fists.

That was when a chap called Kenny Poole, who used to run the side and was really well respected, stepped in and negotiated with the both of them.

Before we knew it, the game had restarted and Bish was bowling out of his skin and Macaloon was stopping everything at backstop, which resulted in us winning comfortably. It transpired that Kenny had told Bish that Macaloon thought he could handle anything he bowled, and told Macaloon that Bish thought he was too fast for him at backstop. Both had played like lunatics just to prove a point to one another. It was brilliant psychology from Kenny, who prevented what could have been a nasty punch-up that both men would have regretted.

It was perhaps a shame that Kenny wasn't around when Bish and I ran into trouble one night in a Cardiff club. It had generally been a quiet evening; in fact, I think it was a Sunday and we were at a place on St Mary's Street in the centre of Cardiff. There was an attractive girl in there who was sitting on her own and I started talking to her, not knowing that she was with a Somalian guy. I also didn't know that there were a good few of this fellow's mates in the club at the time as well.

While Bish was in the toilet, this guy came up to me with his pint glass and rested it on my cheek as if to threaten that he was considering smashing the thing in my face if I carried on talking to his girl. When Bish came out of the toilet and saw what was happening, he came over and landed an absolute haymaker in this bloke's face without any warning whatsoever. After a delayed reaction, the like of which you see on TV, the Somali dropped to the floor.

In no time, the bouncers had come over, just as a group of this guy's friends rushed to get at us. Two of them got through the cordon and went for Bish one after the other. Bish hit the first one with a left hook, flush between the eyes; the second one got a right hook to his jaw that knocked him backwards and over a chair. Bish had knocked three blokes out cold and I was just standing there open-mouthed. I have never been a fighter.

The bouncers ushered us out of a back entrance at the side of nearby Cardiff Market as the police sirens wailed. Bish turned to me as we made good our escape and said, 'Where the hell were you when I needed you?'

'It all happened so fast for me, David,' I said, as if butter wouldn't melt in my mouth!

Incidents like these tend to get exaggerated in real life when told among friends down the pub of an evening, but I kid you not I have told it here exactly as it was; it was like something out of a film. Bish had a Welsh vest for boxing and has always been handy, yet in all my days of seeing blokes come to blows, I have never seen such a pair of fast fists. And every punch he threw was right on the button.

Bish would stand toe to toe with anybody. And he would never waste punches. But there is another side to David Bishop. I know that for everything his record says he has done, for every punch he has thrown, he has a heart of gold deep underneath. He can be very polite and respectful; for example, when he used to come to my house when we were younger, he would always call my dad Mr Ring.

Bish has also always been the type to stand his ground no matter who confronts him. Even when he went on that tour with the Cardiff senior team he wouldn't take any crap from the older players who tried their best to control him. On one occasion, they gave him the club koala bear, which had been at the Arms Park since 1947 when the touring Australia team had left it there. They told Bish on the tour bus one day that as he was the baby of the tour, it was his role to carry this bear around with him until they relieved him of the duty. As soon as they turned their backs, Bish ripped the head, arms and legs off the bear and threw the scraps of stuffing and material out of the window. Most of the senior players thought it hilarious, but the Cardiff committee men were not in the slightest bit amused about this young whipper-snapper showing such contempt for a part of their heritage. That was Bish, though; he didn't give a toss.

We always had a healthy respect for one another through sport and through our families, and I stress again there were so many times when Bish could be the perfect gentleman. It says it all about the respect I had for him that I went up to train with Ebbw Vale after they were the first club to give him a chance in senior rugby. You always knew that at that time Ebbw Vale didn't really have much about them – but with David Bishop in their team, they always had a chance. That was the aura of the man.

It wasn't long before Pontypool spotted him, though; they had their scouts all over that part of the world, looking out for talent, and the rest is history. Everyone knows what he achieved at Pontypool and there is a compelling argument to suggest that in his pomp with the club he was the best scrum-half in the world – except that people never saw him play on the biggest stage consistently because he was never selected for Wales, apart from the one time against Australia in a 28–9 defeat in Cardiff in November 1984.

I remember when we ran onto the field that day – it was only my second cap – Bish literally picked me up and threw me with the sheer elation and motivation for what lay ahead pumping through him. He was so fired up to finally be playing for his country. I don't think he did himself many favours that day because if anything he was too motivated. He didn't pass the ball to the back line enough and played as if he genuinely believed he could beat the Wallabies on his own, but not even the great Bish was ever going to do that because that Australia team was a great one. The inspirational David Campese was their star man as they clinched a Home Unions Grand Slam.

Enough has been said down the years about what a travesty it is that Bish didn't win more Welsh caps. In fact, you still hear people on radio phone-ins talk as if he is still the greatest exponent of scrum-half play they ever saw. In my mind, at the time of his peak, there was indeed nobody to touch him, certainly not in Wales.

I recall reading an article in a national newspaper back in the '80s where Clive Rowlands was extolling the virtues of Robert Jones as a great scrum-half, arguing that he was the man to take Wales to the next level and make the number 9 shirt his own. I laughed because only a week or so earlier, Pontypool had played Swansea and Bish had thrown Robert around like a rag doll, once even picking him up with one hand and slinging him over the touchline. Don't get me wrong, Robert is a great friend of mine and he was a wonderfully gifted player who had a fantastic career, but he wasn't David Bishop.

Yes, Robert's pass was probably quicker and arguably more technically proficient but that didn't mean he bought you any more time because Bishop kept marauding back rows at bay through his sheer presence. They knew they could not afford to make too quick a decision to charge a fly-half because Bish could undo them with one barnstorming, powerful surge up the middle. Bish could kick the ball huge distances with both feet, he could drop goals with both feet and his vision in front of a pack of forwards was unrivalled.

As soon as he put the ball into a scrum, he would be looking over to see what the opposition back row were up to. He had a brilliant rapport with his own back row, always knowing when to keep the ball in and go for a double drive, or get it out quickly and spread it to the backs. His physicality was menacing, but he also had a sublime rugby brain that created total and constant pressure for the opposition.

Bish's exclusion from Wales duty was wrong and it was probably a lot to do with the selectors at the time, who didn't seem able to see beyond Bish's wild lawless streak. For politics to deny our country the services of such a great player was a crying shame.

I am always loathe to label players the greatest of all time and I have always struggled to split Bish and Terry Holmes in the pantheon of great scrum-halfs. In my era, they were the top dogs and I had bundles of respect for them. They were both effective in their own way. If you broke down each department of skill and judged them, then Bish would edge it. But if you looked at the mental side of things as well, Terry would come more into it because he undoubtedly had the better temperament.

One of the reasons I finished with baseball in the end was because my throwing arm gave up on me due to the number of operations I had had because of rugby injuries. I keep some treasured memories of my time playing the sport and I will always be proud to be able to call myself a dual Welsh sporting international. Bish could boast the same and I'm eternally glad that I had at least one full season playing rugby alongside the great man.

10

INVINCIBLE POOLER – ALMOST!

I caused a bit of a sensation when I quit Cardiff to join Pontypool in the summer of 1987, but I don't regret the move for a moment. To many rugby fans, Mark Ring will always be synonymous with Cardiff and, sure, I have always considered them my club, but Pontypool occupies a precious place in my heart, particularly my first spell there during the 1987–88 season when it is no exaggeration to say we were among the best club sides in Britain and definitely the best in Wales.

We finished top of the old Merit Table that season and we won the unofficial *Western Mail* Club Championship based on the percentage of wins clubs took from their own fixture lists, and some were harder than others. My only regret is that we didn't do the treble by winning the Welsh Cup as well. We should have done but were beaten in the semi-final at Cardiff Arms Park by probably the second-strongest side that season: Neath. The team's record by the time we wrapped up the season was Played 47, Won 45, Lost 2. Not bad by anyone's standards and, incredibly, we finished with a 100 per cent away record, not counting that semi-final.

On a personal note, things couldn't have gone much better. I topped the scoring chart with 357 points from 32 matches, which included 14 tries, 59 conversions, 47 penalties and 14 drop goals, beating Bish into second place for good measure.

Pontypool was for years seen as the prime example of a tough, no-nonsense Gwent valleys club, the kind of place to which the English teams used to dread going; the famous Pontypool front row of the '70s – Tony Faulkner, Bobby Windsor and Graham Price – had most to do with that reputation.

The club spawned so many other top-class and hard-as-nails players down the years. I suppose I wasn't the type of player anyone would have expected to join Pontypool and I know there were plenty who thought such a so-called city slicker with all the self-confidence in the world did not belong at a place like Pontypool Park. And to a certain extent, I can understand that.

The legendary former Pontypool player and coach Ray Prosser strolled over to me at one of my first training sessions at the club and said, 'What are you doing here, son? This is a valleys club.'

I simply told him that I had become disillusioned at Cardiff; I had seen players brought in from outside the club and given jobs and cars and generally looked after in a way that I had never been. I told him that I felt I wasn't getting the same opportunities and I felt a bit taken for granted. I was vulnerable because of the way I felt at the club: I believed those in power thought I would always be there, no matter what, and that they would never have to push any boats out to keep me. At the time, I was working at Companies House in Cardiff, earning peanuts, and I was fed up of other guys being handed a better deal on a plate, being given jobs as sales reps or with breweries.

'A shepherd hath no honour in his own land,' Prosser replied simply.

It was a bit cryptic, I'll grant you, but it was clear to me straight away that he knew exactly what I meant. I have often thought about those words in terms of the way I feel I have been treated by my home-town club down the years.

David Bishop was a big influence in getting me to Pontypool; wherever he went – like when he was at Ebbw Vale – he would telephone me to try to entice me to go there with him. He knew from our early days that I could play at fly-half and that circumstances at Cardiff just before I left were not allowing that to happen, so he began badgering me to link up with him at Pontypool and become his half-back partner, and as inconceivable as it might have seemed at one stage that I would move to Pooler, I began to give it serious consideration. I was a Wales international and I wasn't even taking home £100 a week from my job, so I began to think about leaving and finding a club that would help me out work-wise, and help me get on in the world and make some decent money for once.

I so very nearly ended up at London Welsh before I decided on Pontypool. I actually told Cardiff that was where I was heading when I left. I had been to London to meet with one of the Exiles' board members, Denis Horgan, who was a good friend of my dad's. Denis had always said to go and see him if ever I fancied going to London. He took me all around and showed me what was what before asking what I wanted to do for a living. I told him I didn't know. The club were then really professional in their response, giving me a form on which was a series of questions, where I had to mark from one to six whether I liked various things or disliked them. You know the type of thing: like a lot, don't mind, dislike intensely . . . At the end of it, they put me into the bracket of wanting to work with people and told me they would look for an opportunity in the leisure industry. That suited me just fine.

Before all this, they had taken me down to the Thames and shown me this beautiful house where I could live if I joined them. It was next door to a house owned by the singer Midge Ure, so that was very appealing.

They also decided I needed to get some qualifications to work my way up in the leisure industry and so said they would arrange for me to enrol on a course at what was then the South West London Institute. The college would allow me to basically condense a three-year course into one year because the man in charge was a friend of Denis Horgan's. After completing the course, I would have been qualified to run my own leisure centre.

All this very much appealed to me, but I was concerned about being out of the public eye in Wales – the fact that I might have been out of sight, out of mind in terms of the selectors. However, that wasn't at first enough to put me off and I had more or less agreed the terms when I came back and took the telephone call from Bish. He had got wind of the fact that I was about to go to London Welsh.

'Come training with Pontypool,' he urged.

They were the last team on earth I wanted to play for because they had a reputation for being a forward-orientated team who played nine-man rugby. Bish was persistent, though. He told me about this brilliant run up a hill at Pontypool Park that the players called the Grotto and said that I would find it a real challenge. That was enough: I agreed to go to training just to test myself on that run. To be honest, it half killed me. It didn't help that before we even ran over the Grotto we had endured punishing sprint runs that reduced the legs to jelly.

The Grotto was two huge climbs followed by a run through the park and I came in about sixth or seventh, which I would have been happy with if one of the props hadn't passed me on the home straight. When I went back to the old training shed, club stalwarts Bobby Windsor, Ivor Taylor, Ray Prosser, Goff Davies and Bish were all sitting there. They must have struck at the right moment as I was on a high after finishing a tough session because when they put it to me about partnering Bish at fly-half I was suddenly sold on the idea and agreed.

In terms of my career outside rugby, it was probably the worst thing I ever did because the London Welsh thing was such a good opportunity for me to get something in my locker outside of playing that could help me get on. But rugby-wise going to Pooler was probably the best thing I ever did because the way we played that season was nothing short of devastating.

What a team we were. In the front row, we had the likes of Staff Jones, Mike Crowley, Steve Jones and Graham Price, who was still going strong at the time. Our second rows were Hadyn Morton, Richard Goody and Kevin Moseley, although after Moseley was injured early in the season Eddie Butler came out of retirement to play second row and did a blinding job there. There was the amazing pocket battleship Chris Huish at blindside flanker, with the brilliant Mark Brown on the openside, and Frank Jacas at number 8.

Behind the scrum, Bish and I controlled at half-back, with Roger Bidgood and Keith Orrell in the centre and Pablo Rees at full-back. We could pick from Sean White, Sean Hanson, Steve Watkins and Alan Glasson on the wings. Bobby Windsor was head coach – I was very fond of Bobby – and Goff Davies was in charge of the backs.

We had a lot of fun along the way, even though it was a long, hard season. Graham Price was on his way down at the time and was not the scrummaging force of old, but Pricey was still very fit and would never let an opposition team dominate us. Sometimes he would drop a scrum after coming under pressure and referees would think it couldn't possibly be Pricey at fault because of his reputation and award us the penalty!

Bish was basically the one that kept the forwards going because his presence at the base of our pack was phenomenal; in fact, he was like an extra forward himself.

My link-up with him at half-back was as good as I ever imagined because Bish had so much trust and faith in me. In times past, Bish had clearly not had that trust in his number 10 because Pontypool were a renowned nine-man outfit who would use their pack to soften up teams, with Bish keeping them on the front foot with box kick after box kick.

We played all the top English clubs, going to Gloucester, say, on a Tuesday night to face a packed Shed, to Coventry, who at the time were a powerful side, to Bath and even to Munster, the current European champions. And we beat them all; in fact, we were unbeaten away from home the entire season (not counting that cup semi-final on neutral ground against Neath) and that is some achievement.

We lost the second game of the season at home to Bridgend, which was a real jolt. We had been 15–0 up and I was playing against my best friend, Martin Daly, who was at centre. I remember scoring a try after working a double dummy scissors, going over under the posts. We were cruising, but we lost 24–15. The absence of Bish through injury was perhaps the deciding factor.

Bish gave me a rollicking afterwards, claiming I'd been the one who had cost Pooler the match and saying that I had tried to overplay things instead of putting my boot to the ball and keeping things in front of the pack, but I wasn't having any of it. I'd scored 15 points and I simply asked him what more he expected me to do.

Yet ultimately that and the Neath cup game were the only times we lost during the entire season. We played Neath three times that year and beat them twice, so we were gutted they got the better of us in the biggest game of them all.

Again, we had taken what looked like a comfortable lead that day, going 9–0 up at half-time, having scored one of the tries of the season from our own 22. I had sat in the pocket, looking like I was just going to clear, and when the flanker came tearing at me from a scrum, I jinked past him and made a half break. I sent our full-back, Pablo Rees, scorching through a gap up the middle and the ball was sent out along the line for the wing Sean Hanson to canter home in the left-hand corner.

In the end, though, the wind played its part because after half-time it turned around and we lost it 20–9, playing into the elements, with Thorburn banging goals over from long distance. Ultimately, I believed Hanson cost us the game because he stepped in off his wing when Bish had the inside covered and drifted off his man for Neath's clinching try. I told him so afterwards as well and we almost ended up fighting about it.

It hurt like hell that we weren't going to have our big day out in the final, especially as we had come through some momentous matches to get that far – none more so than our 29–18 win against Swansea at Pontypool Park in the third round. We went 11–0 down early on and came back to win 29–18, with Bish landing two incredible penalties from long range and out of thick mud to turn the match our way. After the final whistle, Bish insisted we both applaud the thousands of fans on the bank and when we went over to that side of the pitch, he lifted my arm up and the cries of 'Pooler, Pooler' made the hairs on the back of my neck stand on end.

However, it was Neath who were the up-and-coming pretenders to our throne and when they came to Pontypool that season, there was real anticipation: they were seen as the only side really capable of giving us a game. In the end, we got a controversial 16–13 win amid accusations that one of the linesmen had cheated to cost Neath the spoils.

Steve O'Donaghue, the ex-Pontypool hooker who helped Bobby Windsor coach the side and did a lot of business with Bobby, ended up running the line on the one side. It was the last minute of the match and we were behind and chasing the game in injury-time. We knocked the ball into the corner and Sean White, our right winger, gave chase. As the Neath wing, Alan Edmonds, and Paul Thorburn tried to clear the danger, there seemed to be all manner of confusion over whether O'Donaghue had flagged for a lineout. If he had, referee Gareth Simmons hadn't spotted it, but clearly Thorburn and Edmonds were confused about something.

It all ended with Thorburn losing his footing and Sean White gathering the ball and making it over the line for the winning try.

What happened with O'Donaghue's flag was the hot issue after the game, though. The Neath contingent were in uproar, but it didn't matter. The referee hadn't seen it and that was that. The only consolation Neath could cling onto was that we still had to go to their place to play them before the end of the season – but when we went to The Gnoll, we beat them 13–9.

Despite the trust I say Bish and I had in one another, we did have our moments, and the night we played Gloucester away sticks in my mind more than any other. By this time, we had strung a lot of wins together and had so much belief that we never thought we were going to lose a game; at times in some matches, it felt as though we were actually toying with the opposition in the sense that every person in the team believed it was only a matter of time before we closed it out in our favour.

The other factor was Bish's motivational team talks before each game. He would be like a warrior going into battle to save the town of Pontypool, but it worked because he used to get everyone walking out onto the pitch feeling ten feet tall. I've never been one for silly over-motivated warm-ups; if someone started rolling their sleeves up and punching walls and head-butting doors, I would always be thinking, 'You do what works for you, mate, but it's not for me.' There was something different about that kind of thing when Bish was doing it. It wasn't so much what he said, it was his persona and his own self-confidence that would rub off on everyone else. David Bishop could not be beaten this afternoon, tonight, or whenever. And if he couldn't be beaten, you couldn't be beaten because he was in your team.

When we met up to travel to the Gloucester game, we only had 14 players. That may sound hard to believe, but that was what it was like in those amateur days, especially for games on midweek nights when people may have had work commitments. Things were laid-back at Pontypool, though, and before long we had worked out a solution: we were going to pick up a fellow called Adrian Parry, or Bill Sykes, as he was known to the locals, a man renowned in the area for his colourful escapades. He was a winger and agreed to play when we turned up on his doorstep out of the blue.

When we ran out for the game, we had fifteen players and no substitutes, a situation you would never have in a million years these days, friendly or no friendly, though back then you were only allowed two substitutes anyway. As usual there was a volatile atmosphere at Gloucester and it soon began to have an effect on the standard of our play. Then I caught a ball behind our posts after they missed a penalty and was faced with a decision.

Me being me, instead of banging the ball into touch and settling things down, I tried to dance my way out of trouble. I got as far as the 22, where I was upended and sent to the bottom of a ruck, where I gave away another penalty – this time in an easier position – which Gloucester knocked over with ease. Bish went bonkers.

'You bloody idiot!' he roared at me. 'We've got a game to win here and you'd better get a grip. Me and you are responsible, so start putting that ball in front of the forwards and let's start getting this game won.' This, incidentally, is a politer version of what actually came from his mouth.

A few moments later, Gloucester had another penalty. They missed it. Bish caught the ball and tried to dance his way out of our 22 only to be knocked down and concede a penalty which they got from a far easier position! I just looked at him, shrugged my shoulders and smiled. This time he smiled, but then followed up with, 'Hey, now let's me and you start knuckling down!'

That's just what we did and we ended up claiming a famous win; however, it took us until the last minute of the game and it was down to the unlikeliest of heroes. As we desperately chased the result, I decided to put a Hail Mary kick into the left-wing corner behind the goal-line and hope for the best. A collection of Pooler and Gloucester shirts tried to claim it and it bounced off a couple of heads and shoulders before it fell to a guy wearing our red, black and white, who nestled it in his midriff and fell on the floor for the winning try.

I ran over in elation not quite sure who had got the touchdown, but then the hero stood up and began walking back with the ball. It was Bill Sykes.

That was not the only time I tasted glory on English soil with Pontypool. One of the proudest games from my own personal point of view was at Coventry, who, as I have already said, were far more of a force then than they are now. A Midlands-based referee blew us off the park that evening: he was so one-eyed it was incredible.

Our pack were on their knees, even though I had done everything I could to nurse them through by playing the percentages and kicking the ball to the corners whenever I could. It came to the last play of the game and they had just kicked a penalty to go in front 9–7 and our captain, Steve Jones, turned to me and said, 'What do you think we should do next?'

I told him that I would kick the restart deep into their corner and that our flanker, Mark Brown, who had lightning pace, had to chase to put pressure on them like his life depended on it. 'They'll probably slice a clearance kick into touch,' I added, 'then we'll have a two-man lineout. The ball can be passed back to me and I'll drop the winning goal!'

And that is exactly what happened – to the last detail. It was as if I had mystic powers. I had called it spot on, with me applying the finishing touch by planting a kick through the posts from about 35 metres, my second drop goal of the evening. Steve Jones still talks to this day about how the action unfolded exactly as I had suggested.

As I came off the pitch that night, I couldn't resist making a gesture or two to the home crowd, who had given us a lot of anti-Welsh stick all evening, although when the referee spotted what I was doing, he promptly frogmarched me off the pitch. But I didn't care.

Shortly afterwards, I was on cloud nine when the great Ray Prosser told me that he had never witnessed a better fly-half display. I recalled something else he had said to me just before the first game I played for Pontypool. As I walked up to the gates of the ground, Pross had called me over. 'Son, let's have a word,' he'd barked.

'What's up, Pross?' I'd asked.

He pointed to his leg and said, 'Just remember what that's for.'

It put me off a little bit because right away it was as if I was being told that the forwards did the main job at Pooler and my role was just to keep it in front of them with my boot and not try anything fancy. Thankfully that didn't happen because we expanded our game and I'm chuffed that someone like Pross ended up having some admiration for me as the season progressed. At the time, he described Bish and me as the best half-back pairing in the world. Coming from someone like him, it really meant something.

Our away win at Munster that season – something that is all but unheard of these days – was another game where we snatched victory from the jaws of defeat. Their centre, Michael Kiernan, thought he had won them the game with a late drop goal, but he milked the plaudits of the crowd for too long and wandered out of position as we went to restart. I nudged the ball along the ground into the gap where Kiernan should have been, got to it just as it bobbled up and volleyed it into the hands of Roger Bidgood, who cantered in for the match-winning try amid total silence at Limerick's Thomond Park. Some of the things we pulled off that year were remarkable.

I have fond memories of my antics away from the rugby field during my time with Pontypool that season as well. I couldn't drive at the time, so the club began paying for me to have driving lessons, though I wasn't the best in the world and failed my test three or four times. I even turned to Rowland Phillips, who everybody said looked like me, and asked if he would take my test for me!

Rowland owed me one at the time because of a favour I'd done for him a few years earlier, but it never came to Rowland actually doing the test for me: common sense, for once, prevailed.

It's a wonder I ever passed at all, mind you, given what Bobby Windsor put me through one day. He had given me a job as a sales rep with his chemical business while I was with Pontypool and needed me to go down to Cwmbran to do some work at Welsh Water. I was still learning to drive at the time, so he insisted I take his Vauxhall Cavalier, with him in the passenger seat, to give me some extra practice.

'How else are you going to learn?' he said, as he tossed me the keys.

Well, we went down there with the car jumping all over the road – how I didn't crash I will never know. By the time we reached Welsh Water, my nerves were so shot I couldn't work.

I put my driving woes down to the fact that the club was trying the fast-track route to me passing the test and I was subsequently putting myself under too much pressure instead of taking it one step at a time. The solution was for Pontypool to give me a driver – Bish!

Now, he already knew I wasn't the handiest behind the wheel. One night a few years earlier, I had gone with Bish to watch him play for Pooler and as we drove up from Cardiff we were hopelessly late; he was never going to make kick-off. As we hit the Pontypool traffic heading to the match, I was waving frantically at cars, shouting at them, 'Get over, get over! David Bishop's in here and he's late for the game.'

Pooler started with 14 men and Bish ended up jumping out of the car and running the rest of the way to the ground down the side of the road. He left me to manoeuvre his car as best I could into a lay-by, so I chugged it over to the side of the road and left it dreadfully crooked. As I got out to stroll the rest of the way to Pontypool Park, who should be driving the car behind us? The Wales coach of the time, the late John Bevan, that's who. Goodness knows what he made of the pair of us clowns, not to mention Bish arriving late for the game.

That was by no means our only scrape in a car. Bish once drove us home from training at Pontypool and for some reason reacted late to a big grassed roundabout at the top of Malpas Road, the hill that leads from Newport up towards Cwmbran. Before we knew it, we were sitting in the car in the middle of the roundabout. When we reversed onto the road, we were smacked by another car making its way around the island.

As if by magic, the flashing blue light appeared and a policeman clambered out of his Panda car. He came to the passenger's side and when I rolled down the window, very much fearing the worst, he simply took all our details and then asked if the car was OK to drive.

'I think so,' I said.

'Well, I'd get on your way quickly, if I were you,' he replied, 'because these people are trying to claim you reversed around the roundabout!'

All I can guess is that the officer might have been a Pontypool supporter. It was just one of those reckless things I was happy to go along with in my younger days. I'm fully aware that we or another motorist could have paid a higher price.

One day Bobby sent me and Bish down to a chemical company in Cardiff to do a bit of business and off I set in my shirt and tie with my samples box and my briefcase.

'Go round the back, up the iron staircase and you'll find a guy who knows me. He'll do some business with you,' said Bobby.

The aim was to try and sell him my oil-dispersal granules, but it didn't quite go to plan. After going up the iron staircase and into the room, there was this old guy wearing half-moon spectacles with his head buried in some paperwork.

He looked up. 'Can I help you?' he said tersely.

'I'm representing Bobby Windsor,' I said. 'I've come down because he asked me to get in touch to see if you'd buy some of these oil-dispersal granules.'

'This is Curran Oils,' he said with total disgust, 'we make the bloody things.'

Just as I was about to apologise and explain that there had obviously been some crossed wires, Bish walked up from behind me, went straight over to the guy, grabbed him by his tie and half yanked him over his table.

'Look here, you,' he said, 'don't you ever talk down to my mate again!'

'Bish, Bish, please,' I said. He calmed down and we left with no harm done.

Another time, Bobby sent me up to a place called Doncaster's in Blaenavon where they manufactured Rolls-Royce engines for aeroplanes. 'Go and see Lyn Cowells,' he said. 'He's a regular at Pontypool and he knows me. He'll probably know you as well. See if you can get in there.'

At reception, I asked the lady behind the desk for Lyn Cowells, who I didn't know from Adam. I told her not to worry that I didn't have an appointment because Lyn and I were 'like that', crossing my fingers and holding them up in front of me.

'Me, Lyn and Bobby are old rugby pals,' I said, remembering what Bobby had told me about him being a Pontypool regular. 'We're always drinking in the club together.'

Two minutes later, the receptionist returned and said, 'You do realise Lyn is a she!'

Bobby had tucked me up again; I couldn't get out of there quick enough.

Bobby was a real character, but I began to realise that on occasion he was using me to try and get in with people he didn't know. Before I started with him, I was taken around for a week and shown the ropes by Glenn Webbe, who worked in the same line for Steve O'Donaghue. We went to a British Tissues factory down near Maesteg one day and Glenn told me what I was about to witness would be the hard sell. Glenn told me that he had spent ages talking to this guy, known as 'Old Ted', about rugby but that he never bought a thing from him. 'If I could only get him to buy a couple of boxes of wood filler, even if it's only to get rid of me,' said Glenn.

When we arrived, Webby asked for Old Ted but was told he had recently passed away.

'I don't believe it,' Webby replied. 'When I tried to sell him some wood filler, the last thing Ted said to me was that he would buy it over his dead body!'

* * *

You may wonder why I left Pontypool after that glorious 1987–88 season. Well, Bish was leaving for rugby league and Pablo Rees, another great friend of mine from Cardiff, was also going, so I felt a bit left on my own. I had rather hastily spoken out in the press against Cardiff when I'd left them a year earlier, criticising them for the reasons I have already outlined, so I had to write a letter to the club seeking permission to return.

Pontypool were good about me going – I sensed they were just pleased to have had me there for one season – but it was not the end of my Pontypool days: I would return there for the start of the 1993-94 season. When I left for the second time, however, the circumstances were far more acrimonious, resulting in a totally unjustified stain on my character that I don't believe I have fully scrubbed away to this day.

11

YOU THIEF!

I had never envisaged going back to Pontypool when I did, two-thirds of the way through the 1992–93 season, making my return in a 38–30 defeat away to Swansea.

I left Cardiff for reasons similar to those that had forced me out back in 1987: I just didn't feel appreciated there. That may sound big-headed, but it wasn't as if I craved any special treatment; I just wanted Alex Evans, the Arms Park coach at the time, to understand what I could offer the team.

In the period up to my departure after Christmas 1992, I had missed just two games for Cardiff all season, but my relationship with Evans had always been uneasy. When he first arrived, I remember he called me in and said he wanted me to play an Andy Slack type of role at the club. My ears pricked up, but then Evans explained that the Australian Slack had played a key role in bringing through the great Wallaby centre partnership of Tim Horan and Jason Little and that was what he saw me doing at Cardiff.

I understood what he was saying to mean that in essence I was to develop younger players to take my place as I was verging on being over the hill. I felt like he was virtually putting me out to grass. I am convinced that he had been misled by others into making a rash judgement and it led me to suspect that somebody had been filling his head with derogatory remarks about me. I admit I didn't have the spring of earlier years, but I felt I had so much more to give, and I was looking for more support than appeared to be given.

The galling thing for me was that I was told by my pal Mike Rayer that after I had left a meeting was called to try and shed light on why the Cardiff wingers' tries had dried up. Mike, who I would trust implicitly to play a straight bat with me on something like this, made it clear that it had become obvious that my absence was a key reason. He said footage of the tries they had scored before I left almost always involved me. By the end of the session, it was apparent what the common denominator was, although when Evans asked the team for their thoughts on what was going wrong, none of them had had the guts to say so.

I was chuffed to hear that I was missed and hoped that Evans had been taught a lesson for letting me go. He needed to understand the influence I'd had on the team. When I went back to Pooler in the new year, I was of course bursting to make Cardiff regret letting me go.

Pontypool were in a bit of trouble and were in danger of relegation because a lot of players had left around that time and I'd like to think I played a key part in keeping them up, with victory against arch-rivals Newport at their Rodney Parade ground a particularly sweet moment.

I also tried to instigate a move towards a more professional approach at Pooler. I wrote a letter to the club's committee saying that they should look at appointing a director of rugby and examine the organisation of the whole set-up. The game was moving on and Pooler were being left behind. They had never been regarded as a fashionable and forward-thinking club in the first place. But my views were totally ignored. It meant that the following season, for which I was appointed club captain, was a real struggle. Pooler simply hadn't done anything to take themselves forward off the field, and on it our squad was threadbare in terms of proven ability. We had a lot of youngsters in the squad who, while promising, were not really ready for the harsh realities of the top end of the senior game. The warning signs were there when we shipped 74 points away to Bridgend in our first game of the season, but again we did just enough to survive.

I was certainly coming to the end of the road. My knees were playing up and all the knocks and bumps I had sustained in rugby since I started playing at the age of seven seemed to be coming back to haunt me, which is what tends to happen with the advancing years. I had definitely lost a yard of pace as well.

It was hard work, to say the least, and we struggled all the way through, but I managed to attract a few new players, such as old Cardiff teammates Paul Armstrong and Matthew de Maid, and I'd like to think that under my guidance our young squad blossomed. Still it's amazing how the atmosphere at a club can change when results are not going your way and how the search for a scapegoat can quickly develop.

On 15 October 1994 Pontypool began a run of seven straight league defeats – which included an embarrassing 22–11 reverse at home to minnows Dunvant – as we went down 24–17 to Gwent rivals Abertillery, also at Pontypool Park. Lo and behold by January 1995, I was public enemy number one among some of the influential members of the club's committee.

At this time, I was accused of having stolen money from a club account used to save funds for an end-of-season tour. There was less money in the account than officials at the club imagined and so they pointed their fingers at me. I found myself in the position of being accused because I was one of the signatories of the account, but I was guilty of no more than failing to raise enough money for the tour.

At the time, I was working as a fund-raiser for a children's charity as well, so was pretty well versed in what it took to organise large-scale functions. However, in our efforts to raise money we suffered some heavy losses because fund-raisers we put in place didn't work out as we had hoped. For a start, we didn't make as much as we had expected from our international ticket allocation, which was no fault of mine. We had taken money out of the account to buy the tickets on the understanding that we could sell them to a third party, who would subsequently sell them on as part of a hospitality package for a tidy profit, take a cut and give the rest of that profit back to us – it sounds complex, but we were doing nothing outside of what all clubs used to do at the time. We were let down by our contact, though, and never made a penny on the whole thing.

We also staged a fund-raising event out in the old Savvas Club in Usk, which was a fairly out-of-the-way place that had a reputation for bringing in big names from the entertainment world. Unfortunately, the night was a flop because nobody supported it and we ended up losing a significant amount of money.

Before I knew what was happening, I was being told that the powers that be felt I was guilty of this crime and as a consequence I could no longer consider myself a Pontypool player.

I was appalled at being branded a thief. I've many faults, but anyone who really knows me will tell you that stealing is totally against my character. Yes, I once took a few vegetables as a naive youngster from a stall when I was blind drunk in central Cardiff but that hardly amounts to me being labelled a genuine thief. All I can say is that the accusations Pontypool threw my way were totally false and unforgivable. I certainly found out who my friends were in the aftermath.

The greatest injustice is that I have never had the chance to defend myself. At the time, I called my solicitor to investigate what kind of case I had for defamation of character. He was quite prepared to take the case on, telling me that I had every chance of pursuing a successful claim. Pontypool did not make their reasons for dismissing me public either, which just led to a welter of rumours. The details of the accusation they were levelling at me were always going to do the rounds of the small world that is Welsh rugby anyway.

In the end, though, I spoke to Alex Evans at Cardiff about resuming my playing career and he said he would have me back on the condition that I dropped any dispute I had with Pontypool. He said he didn't want the distraction interfering with what I did for Cardiff, or the club itself to be in danger of becoming embroiled in the row. For that reason, I decided against taking the case any further.

As I have said, the accusation has left a stain on my character for years and I'm fully aware that even now there are probably people who have doubts about me because of it. Deep down I have always thought that the reason certain Pontypool board members wanted me out was because my game had gone and I could not do the things I had been capable of during my first spell with the club. I am convinced they must have heard a rumour that money was missing from the account because of something underhand on my part and then persuaded themselves it was genuine. The irony was that I had seen the beer kitty being abused on countless occasions at Pooler, with proceeds left at the end of a night going straight into the pocket of whomever could get their hands on it, though I can say categorically that I never got involved in any of that. To be accused of such a serious theft was horrifying for me. What I found unacceptable was that the Pontypool committee believed that I was capable of it.

The only person who backed me publicly was Bobby Windsor and that was typical because we went back a long way. Bobby was one person who knew my character. 'I was not at the meeting which decided to get rid of him and it was certainly not my decision. I disagree with it,' Bobby told the *Western Mail* at the time. And tellingly he continued, 'If we were top of the league, there would not be any problems at Pontypool RFC.'

Bobby knew the score and when I told him what had gone on, he resigned. Nobody else backed me, which disappointed me enormously. Instead, people put other considerations first and were quite happy for me to be hung out to dry with my reputation severely damaged. It was all over the newspapers that Mark Ring had been 'sacked in mysterious circumstances' because for legal reasons nobody could come out and say that I had been labelled a thief. I was devastated by the whole business.

I had done my best for the better part of two seasons to drag

Pooler up the league, even though they were still stuck in the Dark Ages and were trying to get by with little more than a bunch of kids.

If nothing else, it was a very sad end to my association with Pontypool. I still love the club and will always love the Pontypool supporters, but I hate the people I hold responsible for the whole affair. I will forever be disappointed in them for not believing in me.

It saddens me to see where a once great club like Pontypool is now, languishing in Division One East of a revamped Welsh structure, playing against sides like Ystrad Rhondda and Newport Saracens. With all due respect to those clubs, such games would have been seen as classic David and Goliath matches only a few years ago rather than bread-and-butter league games. Yet I am not altogether surprised. From the time of my pleas that more professionalism should be injected into the place, Pontypool have appeared complacent about so many things. It resulted in them allowing their clubhouse to go and once that happens, as I found to my cost at West Hartlepool, of which more later, the soul of the club goes with it.

Their chairman, Jeff Taylor, resigned his post in the summer of 2006 saying the club was 'racked with divisiveness from top to bottom'. Again, how sad. Perhaps the real crux of the problem is that in the good old days Pontypool was always run by old stalwarts like Bobby Windsor and Ray Prosser, people who knew the game inside out and had the club very much in their hearts. The club's current position is proof they have been mismanaged, so in many ways they have only themselves to blame, though I would never gloat about Pooler's situation. I still love the club despite the way I was treated in my second spell there. I'm sorry to say that I cannot see any quick return for them to the Welsh Premiership. People will say Pooler are the classic victims of the move to regionalism, with fans' interest dropping off because they realise the club can now never aspire to the heights of previous seasons. Yes, there's something in that, but Pooler's problems run far deeper. I wish them nothing but success and prosperity in the future, but I think it's unlikely.

When I left Pooler for the second time, I was in my twilight years as a player, but in truth the '90s were far from the best chapter of my career.

12

HEADING TOWARDS THE END

By the time the '90s homed into view, Cardiff as a team were on the wane after the glory days of Welsh Cup success that had characterised the '80s. There is no doubt the early years of the decade were a period of relative decline for Cardiff and we endured some lean times in terms of results. We had a lot of raw players and little quality, and a number of our senior players retired within a few years of one another, though it wasn't long before the era of Australian coach Alex Evans began, with him taking charge in 1990.

I've respect for Alex as a coach and his track record at club and international level speaks for itself. He is a shrewd thinker who knows what he wants and his first course of action at Cardiff was to take us back to basics. We did drills that focused on communication, we looked at mauling techniques and concentrated on retaining the ball through multiple phases, and we gradually became more competitive. But nothing could ever alter the fact that when he had arrived, he had talked about me playing that Andy Slack role.

After being sacked by Pontypool following one and a half seasons with them, I had to write a letter to Evans asking to come back to the club in the early months of 1995. In a way, I'm surprised he gave me the time of day because, as I have already mentioned, from day one it seemed to me as if he had listened to derogatory remarks about me and made up his mind I was a bad influence.

Adrian Davies, the outside-half at Cardiff at the time, the man

I had kept out of the Wales team at the 1991 World Cup, was, I believe, uncomfortable with my presence in the centre during my final spell at the club. I was just too big a personality too close to him. I think the bottom line was that he didn't feel secure about his own position or in his own decision making with somebody like me on his shoulder. Adrian wanted to be the controller, which he was, and I genuinely didn't want to step on his toes. It was just that I did not believe he was capable of exerting the required level of control and for that reason I couldn't hold back on becoming tactically involved because I wanted to get games won.

It transpired that I began making decisions from the midfield and I suspected that Adrian used to go back to his pal Mike Hall, who was a senior player and later a captain, and complain about it. The defining moment of this situation – and I'm fast-forwarding a bit here – was when we played in the inaugural Heineken Cup final against Toulouse in January 1996. At the time, Andy Moore, who also played for Wales, was scrum-half. What a player he was! I know Rob Howley went on record with his grievances about being kept out of the side, but in my opinion Moore was simply the better player at that time, even though Howley went on to do great things.

In the first half, we were destroyed by the running angles of the French and also by their sorcerer of a fly-half, Christophe Deylaud, who spent much of the 40 minutes laughing at us. In short, Toulouse had way too much nous for us.

Now, I knew from experience that to trouble French sides you had to gain their respect and as the half-time whistle approached, we had got nowhere near doing so. We used to have a set-play move called 'Thumper' after the nickname of one of our coaches, Alan Phillips, the former Cardiff and Wales hooker, who is now team manager with the Wales squad. It demanded that if we had a scrum on the right-hand side of the field just in or around our own 22 metre area, the fly-half would stand in the pocket to clear the line but the ball would be moved straight to me at inside-centre. I would then move a flat pass through for Mike Rayer to make a break using a variety of other decoys to hopefully confuse the French.

Yes, it was a risk, but it was a risk I felt we had to take if we were going to change the course of the game and make Toulouse believe we were not afraid to try the unorthodox. As well as hopefully gaining us some ground, I knew it would play with their minds and it was a crucial time as half-time approached. I started screaming, 'Thumper' at Andy Moore, but Adrian Davies was having none of it.

'Don't you dare! Don't you dare!' he cried. And Andy Moore listened to him and threw the pass out, Adrian cleared the lines and we went in at the interval having given Toulouse nothing to think about whatsoever.

When we got to the dressing-room, Terry Holmes, who by then had taken over from Alex Evans, pulled me off, telling me that he thought my legs had gone, and put Jonathan Davies on in my place in the centre, even though he had barely played that position in senior rugby in his life.

I have since watched the video of the Toulouse game and, in my opinion, my legs hadn't gone at all. We had just been cut up by a brilliant French side to which we had no answer. Speed of thought had outdone us, not anything that was or wasn't in our legs. Worse still, I knew when I had called moves like Thumper before, they had ended up winning us games.

One time against Swansea at the Arms Park, we were trailing by three points with minutes to go and had a scrum deep in our own 22. I had a feeling that if we put a box kick down the throat of Mark Titley, the Swansea wing, he might fumble it, so I made the call and that is exactly what happened. We swept up field, won a penalty and went for the try, rather than the three points that would have tied the game. We got it, too, through our own winger, Steve Ford, and snatched a victory we hadn't looked like getting moments before.

I don't want to sound like I'm blowing my own trumpet, but

the situation was all about having a feel for the game, which is what I believe I had. I don't think either Adrian Davies or Mike Hall would have called that move in a million years.

Alex Evans making a snap judgement about me was not the only example of me being disappointed with the behaviour of an individual towards me at Cardiff in my later years at the club. In 1992, I had wanted to become captain of Cardiff, though originally the decision seemed to be between Mike Rayer and Mike Hall. Rayer is a lifelong friend for whom I have enormous respect and fondness. Hall? Well, it's different with him. We get on well now and, yes, I do have time for him – Mike used to speak well of me every now and again in his role as a regular pundit for BBC Wales and I'm thankful to him for that – but I've never had that much regard for his abilities as a player and I've more or less told him as much to his face. I used to call him Wales's first agoraphobic three-quarter because I thought he always seemed to run into contact rather than space. But back to the captaincy issue. As I have said, it was between Rayer and Hall. I approached Rayer and said, 'Mikey, I want you to know you've got my vote.'

For years at Cardiff, those who threw their hat into the ring to be skipper would have to win votes from teammates in a ballot if they were to get the job. Like a politician running for parliament, you had to stand and hope you had enough popularity to land the job. But what Mike said to me left me taken aback.

'There's no vote these days, Alex is just picking who he wants.' Apparently, you could put your name forward, but it was to be the coach's decision from now on and nobody else's. 'And in any case, I'm pulling out,' Mike continued. 'Alex has indicated to me that the full-back position is unsuitable for a captain because it is not in the thick of the game.'

I made my decision quickly. 'Mikey, if you're not putting your name forward, then I am.'

I then approached Mike Hall and told him I was going to tell Alex that I wanted to be considered for the captaincy. I won't hide from saying it: it was a job I had always coveted. Hall then replied that he had no idea I wanted the job and that if he had known, he would never have sought it himself in the first place. I was left with the impression (rightly or wrongly) that he would not stand for it if I was going to.

When I went to see Alex the next day to tell him I wanted the job, he said, 'Well, you know Mike Hall wants it, too.'

I said I knew, and then he asked me to talk to him about the direction I would take the role. When I'd finished, Alex said something that raised my eyebrows. First of all, he said, it was Mike Hall who had been the one who'd suggested to him that full-back was not a position from which Mike Rayer should be captaining the team. When I told him I was under the impression that Mike Hall wouldn't stand against me, Alex said it was news to him. He told me Hall had been with him that very morning, emphasising that he still wanted the job. I was stunned and confused. Hall had gone on holiday that day for a couple of weeks, but the next morning, you've guessed it, he was named captain of Cardiff RFC.

There was no ballot. Alex Evans picked him, and I'm convinced his mind was made up that Hall would do the job before I even went in to see him. I felt I had just been made to look foolish in trying to state my case.

I wasn't the only one who had his nose put out of joint at Cardiff though. I saw the same happen to Jonathan Davies when he returned to rugby union and the club after six years in rugby league amid a media frenzy in November 1995. Such was the fuss surrounding the return of the prodigal son that our home game with Aberavon was switched to a Sunday to accommodate a live transmission by BBC Wales, with Jonathan fitting in at full-back in the absence of Rayer, who was out with a broken leg at the time.

It turned out to be a rather embarrassing anticlimax for Jonathan through no fault of his own: I scored three tries that day and there were suggestions I upstaged him. That was wrong because none of the scores were that great; I was just getting on the end of moves and being in the right place at the right time. In fact Jonathan was frozen out by his own teammates. All I wanted to do that day was get the ball in space and roll some flat passes for Jonathan to burst into the line, but I hardly got the ball myself because all that seemed to happen was that Adrian Davies continually missed me out to Mike Hall, who consistently crashed into the Aberavon defence like he always did and set up rucks. We won 57–9 after cutting loose later on, but, with all due respect, that was more down to the weakness of the visitors than anything else.

Jonathan never stood a chance that day and I was disappointed when he included me later in naming the group that had frozen him out. Nothing could have been further from the truth and I have since told him so and I think he has accepted my version of the events. I knew how Jonathan felt because he was seen as a threat to other people's places in the side, just as I had been. It was as if some players had made their minds up to teach him a lesson, to give him the message loud and clear that he may have been the returning superstar but Cardiff RFC was about other players now.

For my part, I was delighted to have Jonathan on board: we went back a long way and he was a great, great friend of mine. Maybe he genuinely did think I was involved in his being left out of all the moves that day, but I hope I have put the record straight now.

As for Hall, well, when he came to Cardiff from Bridgend, he was treated like a hero by the club's hierarchy and didn't play for six weeks for no apparent reason, which I could never quite understand. He used to laugh it off when I called him an agoraphobic centre who just wanted to put the ball under his arm and run into people. He had skin as thick as a rhino.

When I went back to Pontypool for the second time in 1993, we played Cardiff and a fight broke out. I decided to take my frustrations out on Mike Hall, but as I went over to him the Cardiff wing Simon Hill grabbed my arms behind my back and gave Hall the chance to land a good couple of punches on me. So he got one over on me that day as well! We had a laugh about it after the game, but deep down I was angry.

When Alex Evans came back to Cardiff for his second spell in the 1992–93 season, he was not as effective because, from my point of view, he tried to do everything himself. He dropped me for the first time in my career in favour of Colin Laity, who was strong and robust but in my opinion of limited ability.

Alex sent me down to Rumney to play for the Rags, but I just couldn't be bothered, so, without telling him, I went to watch my local team, St Albans, in a cup game against Llanelli at Stradey Park. It was coming up to Christmas time and my lodger at the time, Sean Casey, who was a market trader, managed to get hold of some leftover Father Christmas hats, so I went down there with Christmas looming and sold them outside the ground with a mate for £2 each. We had a cracking day and made a few quid into the bargain.

And that was it for me at Cardiff for the time being. I went off to Pontypool, although I would later return to play under Evans. When that happened, I hoped he had learned his lesson about what I could offer the side, but he was still pretty unforthcoming with me. He was stubborn.

I was finished at Cardiff after that experience against Toulouse in the Heineken Cup final in January 1996. Terry Holmes telling me my legs had gone at half-time had a huge effect on me. I thought if Terry Holmes had said it, then it must be right, even though I now disagree. Saying that, though, I suppose Terry did have a point.

Even though I tried to play on when I became a coach with West Hartlepool and Penzance, I was a pale shadow of my former self. It was a sad way for me to end my Cardiff career at the age of 33. I felt I could have continued at the Arms Park for another couple of years if I had been given the chance to play fly-half; I could have sat back and controlled games from that position without having to worry about lightning quick centres running at me, but it wasn't to be and it was time to move on. My life was about to go through a major upheaval.

13

OH, ELLIE

Ellie, you're breathing well
And your heart is strong.
Ellie, keep keep fighting on girl, prove the medics wrong.
Some things in life one can't explain,
How a one in twenty thousand chance hurts your tiny frame.

Though your mother's starting to feel the strain,
As they pump more drugs into your brain,
My mind is numb – I feel a cold, cold chill.
Your eyes are closed and your body still.
We're losing you, you're fading fast.
Detach the tubes, set you free at last.

Chorus
Down the rocky road and rough terrain,
Where just six Polaroids remain,
Of a beautiful girl who came into our lives,
Who breathed her last breath in the arms of my wife,
Who brought us love we never thought we'd have:
Ironic thoughts of a day so sad.

In your mother's arms, that's where you belong,
That special bond, a love song.
Friends, family, they've all come along
To give us the strength to carry on,

And when some day our tears run dry,
We're no longer asking those questions why.

Oh, Ellie
Oh, Ellie

How do you put into words the devastation of losing a child?

It's a question posed by so many people who have been touched by such a tragedy: the horrific experience that every parent hopes they never have to go through. Strangely, putting it into words when it happened to me, as I did in the above song, was the one thing I could do, though expressing the way I felt verbally was something I found much harder.

I penned the song in the aftermath of the death on 28 July 1996 of my baby daughter Ellie, and I read a poem, which contained many of the same lines, at her funeral at St Alban's church in Splott, the area of Cardiff where I grew up. Putting my thoughts down on paper has always been something I have found to be a source of comfort in troubled times, even if nothing can ever really repair a part of you after a loss like that.

Ellie's death, at just four days old, occurred during my marriage to Hayley Rose. At the time of the tragedy, it had been around three years since we'd walked down the aisle. I met Hayley through her stepfather, a chap by the name of John Inker, with whom I worked at Companies House. Me, John and Hayley's mother, Carol, are very good friends and still enjoy a drink together now. John used to tell me about Hayley, who was employed in the hairdresser's across the road from where we worked, and I would go past there and say hello from time to time. I was in my mid-20s and at first considered her too young for me: she was a good few years my junior. Nevertheless, she was a very pretty girl and she did leave an impression on me.

Years later, I bumped into her in a nightclub in Cardiff and was struck by how much she had matured. She had made the transition from girl to woman. She had a boyfriend at the time, but we clearly hit it off and, within a year or so, we were engaged to be married.

Our courtship, however, was not always smooth as a result of a woman with whom I'd had a one-night stand before I began my relationship with Hayley. I had thought nothing more of it until she hit me for six outside a club one night with the news that she was pregnant. In my eyes, it had been a bit of fun and I could not bring myself to want anything more to do with her. Furthermore, my parents were staunchly Catholic and I was petrified about what their reaction would be.

When I eventually told my mum and dad about it all, which I remember was a really difficult thing for me to do – I half-expected them to disown me – they were really supportive. But then tragedy struck: the child was stillborn. Days later, I found myself with the mother, her sister and a priest at a burial in Cardiff. It was a hugely difficult time.

This was happening when Hayley arrived on the scene and, looking at my situation, she should have run a mile, but she was so supportive just when I needed her to be. That was one of the reasons why we fell very much in love.

We were married at St Alban's church on 28 August 1993 and were soon getting on with married life. It wasn't long before we agreed the time was right to have children, but for one reason or another we could not conceive for a long time. Eventually, Hayley fell pregnant and when she went into labour in the summer of 1996, we duly headed off to hospital. That was when our tragedy began to unfold.

It didn't take long for the chain of events to begin. The first inkling that something was wrong came when one of the monitors in the hospital room where Hayley was giving birth began to indicate a problem. Naturally, I was concerned, especially since Hayley had been in labour for a long time. The doctors soon decided they would have to hasten the birth.

A midwife began to help Hayley with the labour and everything seemed all right again. The distress our little girl had endured was apparently over. But then all hell broke loose, by which I mean all kinds of panic, the like of which you tend to imagine only happens on television or in films and will never happen to you.

An emergency Caesarean was performed, but it was already too late. The umbilical cord had seemingly ruptured during the attempts to induce the birth. This meant our baby had been starved of oxygen and had suffered massive brain damage.

She was born – and she was beautiful. She looked perfectly healthy to us, but she was whisked off to a special-care unit straight away. It wasn't until a few hours later, by which point Hayley and I were both very distraught, that we saw her again. We were told that the trauma had been caused by Vasa Previa, a particularly cruel and rare condition that can lie undetected until late in pregnancy. Without wishing to blind anyone with medical science, it causes foetal blood vessels from the placenta or the umbilical cord to cross the entrance of the birth canal beneath the baby. If these vessels rupture, as was seemingly the case with Ellie, then there is a high risk it will prove fatal. Unfortunately, the vast majority of Vasa Previa cases are not diagnosed until after the damage has been done. The hospital told us that baby Ellie's condition would be permanently vegetative. They made it clear, in other words, that she would be all but brain-dead.

At that particular stage, I didn't know what we would do: all my beliefs pointed to us bringing up Ellie no matter how bad her condition, but I'd be lying if I said I didn't stop and think about the effect that would have on our lives. But in the end we didn't have the chance to think any more about Ellie's future: having been given all manner of drugs just to keep her alive after the trauma of the birth, Ellie began to have fits.

I started asking questions now, serious questions, and after four days I was told by a consultant that Ellie was not going to make it. He said there was nothing further they could do and it was now only a question of waiting for her to go, which would probably be just a matter of days. They began to wean her off the drugs, and then we had to go through the agony of watching our daughter slowly pass away, becoming weaker and weaker, her tiny little breaths becoming less and less frequent and more of a struggle with each passing hour.

We were put in a special room where I held the baby at stages, though she was in Hayley's arms for most of the time, the bond between mother and child already so strong. When the end came, it was a Saturday night.

I was in denial early in the evening. I remember going out of the hospital to fetch a takeaway curry simply because I wanted it to feel as normal a Saturday night as possible, as if that room, with its television, was our living room at home. I brought the food back and watched the Atlanta Olympics on the box, desperately pretending things were as they would be anywhere else.

Within a few hours, it was clear that Ellie was nearing the very end, as her breaths became more of a struggle. Ellie was in Hayley's arms, but we cuddled together, waiting and waiting, until eventually we knew it was over. Our little daughter, Ellie, had gone. We cried, and cried.

When I managed to compose myself, I went to call one of the doctors, but I was in a different world, consumed by my own grief and already beginning to worry about the effects it would have on Hayley. That was what kept me going in the immediate aftermath, the sense that one of us – me – had a duty to be strong. I knew I had to be supportive for Hayley.

We had great support from the family, and in time we started going to bereavement classes, but there is only so much such 'support' can do for you at a time like that. At the end of the day, it boils down to you yourself having to deal with it, having to somehow find a way of carrying on. We subsequently learned that Vasa Previa is diagnosable through a pre-birth scan, but its rarity means that it is not often looked for. I know the International Vasa Previa Foundation continues to work hard to spread awareness of this condition.

I read out my poem at Ellie's funeral. People said to me afterwards that they were amazed I'd held myself together so well. They were probably all too aware of what an emotional guy I am and, I admit it, I do tend to switch on the waterworks easily, but that day, of all days, I didn't cry, even though my voice probably wobbled on one or two occasions as I read. It's strange when I think about it, but I can only say that my eyes stayed dry out of a sense of duty. It was a day I knew I had to get through, most of all for Hayley's sake, but also because of the enormous number of people who showed up to pay their respects: family, current friends and friends from way back, Cardiff rugby teammates, work colleagues.

We buried Ellie in the babies' resting place in Thornhill and began the difficult process of trying to move on. I would go to Ellie's grave regularly – I still do now, although not as often as I used to – and would wander around the cemetery after spending some time next to my daughter's resting place.

As the weeks and months passed after Ellie's death, Hayley and I both lived up in the North-east, then in Cornwall, because of my rugby commitments. When we returned to Cardiff, we settled first in the Whitchurch district of the city, but eventually moved to the neighbouring suburb of Rhiwbina, where I now live. But we were not happy.

We were still going to bereavement classes, where we were told that six out of ten marriages fail after going through what we had been through, though we were determined it wouldn't happen to us. But I began to go down to the pub a lot and even when I took Hayley with me I would end up talking to my mates for most of the night and, gradually, our relationship deteriorated.

After nine years of marriage, Hayley decided one day that she was leaving. When she did finally go and the door slammed shut, everything we had been through really started to hit me hard, like a delayed grieving process. I stopped drinking altogether for three months and went road-running most days of the week. The weight was falling off and I was beginning to feel in so much better shape for doing it.

Then Christmas arrived and my mates persuaded me to get back down to my local pub, the Butchers Arms in Rhiwbina, and that was where I met my current partner, Lisa. We now have two wonderful children, our little girl Madison and baby son Luca. Lisa is about nine years younger than me, but we are very, very happy.

That's not to stay I will forget the past, though. Whenever I pass the cemetery, I almost always pop in and sit there on the little bench by Ellie's grave. And I always lay flowers if the occasion is appropriate.

I haven't spoken to Hayley for a long while and, even if I did, these days it would be nothing more than a polite 'hello' or 'goodbye'. Ironically, I am still good pals with her stepdad, John, with whom I play five-a-side football every Monday night, and golf. I guess that is the way it will always be now because my life is with Lisa, Maddy and Luca.

Lisa and I aren't married, even though I love her dearly. There is something about the whole rigmarole, fuss and expense of another wedding that doesn't appeal to me, and I can't see how it would change the way I feel. I suppose there is an element of 'once bitten, twice shy', but I cannot envisage ever being with anyone else now. Who knows, we might take the plunge one day, but to date I have been denying Lisa the chance!

It's fantastic for me now to have a little girl and boy. I'd prefer Luca to play football before rugby, and I reckon he might be a decent player if he takes after his old man because I was always very good with the round ball when I was younger – I only ended up concentrating on rugby because of the schools I went to. Yet I would also like the chance to take Luca to mini-rugby on Sunday mornings – I am relatively old at forty-three to be dad to a one-year-old child, and it's on these occasions that I sometimes worry about my age. I just hope that my battered knees hold up long enough for me to be able to run around with him when he is older. I would hate to not be fit enough to be able to show him some of my old tricks and help him in his development.

Whatever the case, I am just thankful that I have Lisa and two amazing children and that I am happy. You can never forget the loss of a child, but you can recover.

14

GOING WEST IN THE NORTH-EAST

By the start of the 1996–97 season, it was clear that my best playing days were behind me, even though I wasn't ready to retire altogether. I had also made up my mind that I wanted to pursue a career in coaching because I saw it as a natural progression for someone like me. Some players are just not cut out for it, even though they think they are – you can spot them a mile off when they try to take on jobs that are too big for them – but when it came to rugby I had always been a thinker as well as a player. I felt I could see things before they happened. What's more, I saw myself as a bit of a strategist. I confided my intentions in Terry Charles, son of the great John Charles, with whom I had played in the Cardiff Rags team some years earlier. Terry was somebody whose opinion I respected enormously. Terry, who is still a PE teacher at Llanishen High School in Cardiff, told me that if I was serious about becoming a coach I had to get away and learn the trade in a different environment from Wales and that was a plan I started to formulate in my mind.

I had been introduced to some of the top people at West Hartlepool at a function at the Belfry golf course, their head honcho being a fellow by the name of Phillip Yuill who had a construction business and was one of the biggest house builders in the North-east. The point of contact was Gareth Williams, the older brother of my former Cardiff teammate Owain Williams, who had built up contacts with the West Hartlepool hierarchy on the after-dinner-speaker circuit. We chatted about the position of coach and I made it clear I was interested.

Just a few weeks later, I received a call from Phillip Yuill, asking me to apply for the job. He made it clear the position would be mine, barring any major mishap. It wasn't long before I was offered the role of director of rugby, which came with a £20,000 tax-free signing-on fee and a £45,000 a year salary for two years. It was a player–coach position in essence, even though I was officially director of rugby, and I saw it as a great opportunity.

The problem West Hartlepool had experienced was that they had been a yo-yo club for too long: winning promotion to the top flight of the English league one season only to be relegated the next. As I took charge, they were back in the Premier Division alongside the Baths and Leicesters of the world and looking very much like they could stay there. The bottom line for me was that this was a chance to coach at the highest level of the English game, something that I could have never turned down in a million years.

The North-east is an area far more renowned for football than rugby, but there was a decent well of players in the region and the nearby universities were great resources.

When I first arrived, West Hartlepool had some fine players in their ranks, even if the squad was far from star-studded. There was the big Scottish number 8, Rob Wainwright, for starters. He would go on to become a British Lion in South Africa in 1997. There was the full-back Tim Stimpson, who also went on to tour with the Lions and ended up moving to Leicester. There were other more than adequate performers, like Andy Blythe, a centre who had just made the England A squad when he sadly suffered a broken neck playing for Northampton, and Mike Shelley, who went on to captain his home city club, Leeds.

My first job on taking up the reins was to try to persuade most of the squad, including the guys mentioned above, to stay with us. It was a task that proved beyond me, though not for any lack of effort on my part but because these were the early days of professionalism in rugby union and players who had shown they had something about them were moving on to lucrative contracts with bigger, and certainly richer, clubs elsewhere. Wainwright left us to go back to Scotland, a move I don't think he had too much choice in because their union was putting him under pressure, and Stimpson went to Leicester for a lot more money.

Another problem we had was that Sir John Hall had taken over at Newcastle. Hall bought out the old Newcastle Gosforth club, pumped his money in and improved the facilities and staff, bringing in Rob Andrew, Dean Ryan and Steve Bates to run the side. They got straight into recruiting players on our patch from Durham and Newcastle universities – at Durham in particular there were some fantastic players – and started to make themselves the number one club in the region. It meant that we at West Hartlepool were slowly being squeezed out of the picture.

Ironically, it was a player based in London whom I missed out on signing that would prove to be the one that got away. I got wind of a guy who was at college in London who was due to come up to Newcastle University, so I went down to Newbury one day to watch him play for an England age-group side against a touring outfit from New Zealand run by the great Sid Going. The player's name was Jonny Wilkinson.

To be honest, I cannot say I was all that impressed with what he did in that game. It was clear he would have a future in the professional game, but at this time he was no more than adequate. Moreover I have always had a thing about left-footed fly-halfs: they just don't do it for me.

I managed to get a number for him and thought we may have a chance of landing him because if he was coming up to the North-east, surely he would want to play for a Premiership side, which West were and Newcastle, at the time, weren't. His schoolmaster at the college just happened to be Steve Bates, though, so Jonny's future was mapped out at Newcastle.

Phillip Yuill told me to do what I could in replacing players and that the average wage I could offer them was around £20,000 a year, although with that they were given free accommodation in a Yuill home, which was a huge attraction to some. I was told to build a young side and that even if we were relegated I would be asked to carry on the work and get us back up.

I was sent any number of player CVs – in fact, I had a bin in my office and had become expert at lobbing them into it from halfway across the office – but I remember seeing one which looked like the most fantastic thing I had ever seen and I invited the guy to train with us immediately. According to his CV, he had played for England Schools, England Colts . . . England just about everything! He was a second row and his size, his weight and his fitness level, which included a marvellous bleep-test result, made me believe we had stumbled across a real gem. 'Who the hell is this guy?' I thought to myself. I was soon to find out.

I have never been so embarrassed for a bloke in my life than when he came to train with us. Despite everything on his CV, he was little more than a weed. He was nowhere near as big as he said; he looked pitiful and his skill levels were non-existent. He looked as though he had barely kicked or passed a rugby ball in his life! I don't know how he had the audacity to turn up. We let him do the training session and then I pulled him aside and said, 'Look, no disrespect, but don't bother coming again, you're not for me, mate.' He took it well and just seemed chuffed to bits that he had been able to train with us.

I heard later that he had tried to the same thing at Sale with Paul Turner, now the coach of Newport Gwent Dragons. Paul told me one team actually signed him without bothering to see him train – I would have loved to have seen their faces.

There was another CV I was keen on. I had received it from a guy claiming he was James du Randt, brother of the famous Springbok prop Os du Randt. The résumé told me that whenever Os was called up by South Africa, this kid took his place in the Orange Free State provincial team. He was 21 years old and supposedly attending York Agricultural College. Except he wasn't: there was, in fact, no such person. It was a bogus CV playing on the name James du Randt, or Jimmy Durante, the singer!

Thankfully, I realised this before I invited him to training, although not before I had telephoned a reporter at the local paper and asked him to do a piece about how we were on the verge of signing this guy. And it went to print as well. He'd made me look a complete mug.

To this day, I don't know who was behind Mr Du Randt, but as Terry Charles always told me, I had to learn by my mistakes – just as I made a mistake when Northampton offered me on loan Grant Sealey and Budge Pountney, who went on to play international rugby with Scotland, and I didn't pursue it because I felt they were being forced upon me and I wanted to make my own decisions! There was something about the name Budge Pountney that put me off, which was ridiculous, I know, but I did learn from the episode and in future whenever I was offered players, I at least took the time to look at them. The frustrating thing was that we were crying out for a player of Pountney's ilk at the time. If he had made half the impact of another Kiwi whom I did bring on board, then we would have been laughing.

Ivan Morgan was a number 8 from Canterbury who at the time used to lead by example. He went off travelling after a while but not before being brilliant for us. The club got him a job in Newcastle, a 40-minute drive away, and he used to be at the gym by 6 a.m. every morning and in the evenings too when he finished work. His dedication was an example to everyone. One day I asked him what motivated him and he just said it was the New Zealand way; he said that if he didn't go to the gym, somebody else would, and they would have the edge on him. It seemed to be an attitude that was just bred into those who played rugby in New Zealand.

However, the club was always up against it because of the player departures. It was typical that I ended up falling out with the guy who did stay, Derek Patterson, who, in my opinion, seemed to think he had a divine right to selection. I just didn't rate him as highly as he seemed to rate himself.

I had to wheel and deal a little bit and ended up taking quite a few promising young Welsh players up with me to plug gaps in the squad, names like Mark Roderick, Chris John and Stephen

John. There was also the then ageing Gerald Cordle and Matthew Silva, who came back to union from rugby league clubs Bradford and Halifax respectively. I believed they could all do a job, and Cordle in particular was a well-known figure who I knew all about from my early Cardiff days.

I was determined to make a success of myself in the North-east and while upping sticks to the other end of the country might have been an issue to others, it certainly wasn't to me. Not only was it a brilliant opportunity, but the money was also great and I had been given a house and a car into the bargain as well.

My move north came literally just as the sport turned professional and my playing career was virtually over, which meant I had missed the opportunity to set myself up financially with the talent I had. I'm not bitter about that at all because that's just the way it went, but when it did come to being offered the chance to do well out of the game financially, even if it was ostensibly as a coach, I wasn't going to hesitate over a thing like moving house. The deal with West was as player–coach but deep down I knew that with the way my knees were, if I managed another season I would be doing well, so all my thoughts started to come from a coach's perspective.

That said, I didn't find it easy to make the transition; not at all. I was used to being a player: I was a fanatical trainer and rugby, to me, had always been about running around outdoors, expressing the ability I had or working towards being in peak condition. All of a sudden at West I was having to spend time in the office sorting out players' contracts, balancing the books and dealing with all the headaches that surround a modern professional team. I couldn't complain about it because these jobs were very much a part of my remit as director of rugby, but I was spending far too large a percentage of my day sitting at a desk for my liking.

Even though the sport itself had gone professional, I felt the way West were operating at the time was semi-professional. They had not reached the stage where they could pay big salaries to players and as such we trained two or three evenings a week as opposed to every day. On top of that, our budget had been frozen because of a dispute between the RFU and the Premier clubs – nothing changes there! – over funding from the television contract with Sky. The clubs had been promised millions of pounds, but we couldn't get our hands on it, which didn't help a club like West Hartlepool one bit. Initially, I think we were due to receive about £750,000 to run the side for a season and though that is peanuts compared to what is needed these days, back then it would have given us a real chance to run a decent side that could compete at that level.

In the event, West didn't survive that year. It turned out to be a straight fight between West and Orrell for relegation – we beat them once and lost once, but we should have won the latter – and we went down after winning only three of our League games all season.

We also managed to turn over Saracens at our place despite the fact that they were setting the agenda for professionalism by using the cash from their backer, Nigel Wray, to bring in players like Michael Lynagh and Thomas Castaignede. That was a particularly satisfying defeat because a team of cameramen from Sky had flown up with Saracens, taking footage of their journey from London, something that was unheard of in rugby union at the time, and here was lowly West Hartlepool spoiling the party by beating them.

There was one other victory, against Bristol at home, that still leaves me feeling mystified. On this particular day, we were forced to put out what I considered to be a weak side, but they played with incredible intensity and pace, the like of which I had not seen from my players before; in fact, I'd seen nothing approaching that level. We had youngsters playing, we had a hooker in the back row, we were badly depleted by injury across the side and we had no strength in depth whatsoever. Yet we were phenomenal. I had never seen – nor did I ever see again – such speed, aggression and commitment from my forwards. They played like men possessed. All I can say is if they had played like that consistently, we would have been mid-table that year without any relegation worries whatsoever.

At the time, I was ecstatic about the win, but to this day I have never discovered what motivated a team to raise its performance like that.

Next for us came the crunch away game against Orrell, the one I mentioned earlier that we should have won. We went into it knowing full well the importance of the game, but we were undone by a freak piece of bad luck before we had even kicked off.

I recall the day for another reason as well – it was the day I came across a young Austin Healey, who was scrum-half for Orrell. I was playing at outside-half for West and by then had been playing senior rugby for nigh on 15 years all over the world, yet Healey was without a shadow of a doubt the mouthiest guy I had ever come across on a rugby field. He chipped away at me all match with personal abuse, the gist of which was how I was an old man who had no business still being on a rugby field. If Healey had shown me he was an exceptional scrum-half, then I could have perhaps accepted the stick a little easier, but as far as I was concerned he was distinctly average.

I admired his ability greatly later in his career and I think there were times when his versatility led to him being badly treated by the England set-up; to me, he was a world-class winger with incredible evasive running skills and at his best he played the kind of role Shane Williams plays for Wales nowadays – in fact, I wouldn't be surprised at all if he was an influence on Shane's earlier career. Yet I wonder just how much his penchant for mouthing off became his undoing over a period of time.

I was annoyed with myself after that game because I rose to Healey's bait and gave him a bit of verbal back. In responding to Healey's criticisms, I convinced myself that I was indeed getting old and that my mental focus on the field of play was waning. As a general rule, I was never one to get involved in that kind of nonsense on a rugby field. When I was younger, I used to concentrate so hard on the field that I hardly ever heard anything like that – except on one occasion, mind you, when I did say something to an opponent during a game which I bitterly regretted afterwards. It was a clear case of me coming up against someone who played my position for the Wales team in a club match and being just that bit too motivated, too wound up.

I was playing for Pontypool against South Wales Police down at the Waterton Cross ground near Bridgend and I was in direct opposition to Bleddyn Bowen, the centre who captained Wales when we won the Triple Crown in 1988. That day, I was desperate to prove myself against Bleddyn, who I have always regarded very highly as a player and a person, and I felt he lacked confidence in his game and that he was a little vulnerable and, to my discredit, when one of my teammates tackled him during the game, I bellowed out, 'Get hold of him, he's bloody rubbish anyway,' and made sure it was more than loud enough for Bleddyn to hear.

What made me feel worse afterwards was that Bleddyn rose above my outburst and resisted the temptation to say anything back. I was embarrassed after the game, feeling that I had let myself down. It wasn't the person I felt I was and I worried about what I could be becoming. David Bishop thought it was fantastic, but not even his reaction could alter my mood.

The freak piece of bad luck that day against Orrell which I mentioned earlier occurred as we were going through what was known as an Auckland Grid warm-up, a complex, structured training exercise that demands good communication and requires players to be totally aware of what is happening around them as they run across each other. I wasn't a fan of this type of preparation for a game, preferring something more traditional, but I suppose the grid was a good way of sharpening up the senses before battle. Unfortunately, our two scrum-halfs, the one starting and the one due to be on the bench, had their senses knocked out of them when they accidentally clashed heads doing this exercise. They knocked themselves spark out, which meant we had to go into the game without a recognised number 9.

It was quite incredible when you consider that out of 22 players warming up by randomly running across each other, it was the two scrum-halfs who collided and the blow was severe enough to put them both out of the game. I had to ask one of our wingers to play in a position that was totally alien to him and with scrum-half such a pivotal role in a rugby team, we found ourselves at sixes and sevens too many times throughout the 80 minutes. Our game was severely disrupted and since I was playing at outside-half, I noticed it more than anybody. It was little wonder we lost in the end.

Yet if the Auckland Grid cost us dearly that day, another form of conditioning we were fortunate enough to experience had the opposite effect. We had managed to get the former British Olympic coach, Frank Dick, on board to take charge of our fitness and his innovation and supreme knowledge of his field enabled a side which was really too raw and inexperienced to compete at that level to become a far tougher proposition for opponents. Frank got our lads fit, and I mean seriously fit.

There was another factor to him becoming involved as well, as he was bringing with him Dr Ekkart Arbeit, who had once been in charge of the East German Olympic team. Arbeit spent a week with us, focusing on maximising physical power to play professional rugby. What intrigued me most was his emphasis on the importance of the 'little muscles' in the human body. Arbeit claimed much of the training being done at the time was too concerned with pumping iron in order to build up big muscles like quads, biceps and calves.

One of the first things Arbeit said in his broken English was that we should try to train like gymnasts. For example, when you watch gymnasts on television at the Olympics, you will see them on the rings or on the horse or the floor holding their bodies in mid-air using just their hands and arms for support. Arbeit stressed to us that the only way they are capable of doing that is because of the attention they pay to building up their core 'little muscles', which he insisted we focus on. What never ceases to amaze me these days is the fitness of top-level footballers, 99 per cent of whom are supreme athletes. Sometimes I smile wryly when I see one do a backflip to celebrate a goal because I always ask myself how many rugby players I know who could do the same. The answer is always none. So just how much agility and natural power do they really have? I could never imagine any rugby player I know running about a pitch for 90 minutes the way the footballers do; they wouldn't have the lung capacity, for starters. So it was no surprise to me to learn that Arbeit had worked with Italy's top Serie A clubs, including Torino and Juventus, before he came to us.

At the time, nobody thought anything of us using Arbeit, even if there were a few eyebrows raised because of unproven earlier allegations about his involvement in a drug-fuelled East German training programme. Although nearly 200 former East German sports coaches and doctors were prosecuted in the late 1980s, Arbeit was not charged and there was no evidence against him.

In the summer of 2003, a storm erupted when Frank brought in Dr Arbeit to work with the heptathlete Denise Lewis. There was widespread condemnation of the link because it was believed Lewis was staining her reputation by working with him, even though the governing body, UK Athletics, had approved the arrangement.

Frank's loyalty to Arbeit also drew criticism, but at the time we didn't really think too much about it. We were just glad to have someone who clearly knew what he was talking about on board to advise us.

It wasn't until the New Zealand conditioning expert Andrew Hore came to Welsh rugby just three or four years ago that there was a move towards concentrating on what Arbeit called the 'core muscles', in other words the smaller muscles around the body, and we started to see a vast improvement in the fitness of the national team. Yet I had spoken at length about Arbeit's philosophy to Terry Cobner and Mostyn Richards at the WRU ten years earlier and they had just pooh-poohed what I had to say.

One thing we did have going for us at West was a number of very promising youngsters; in fact, at one stage we had about eight players in the England Under-21 elite squad. One of those was Liam Botham, the son of cricket legend Ian. After I had left the club, I was quite influential in Liam's move to Cardiff where he had one or two very successful seasons playing on the wing. I remember getting a telephone call from Cardiff chairman Peter Thomas who was pally with Ian Botham, telling me that Botham junior was looking for a chance and asking me what I thought of him as a player, having worked with him previously. I strongly advised Peter to give him a chance. Liam was on a menial contract at West when I was there and he had just chosen rugby over cricket despite taking a load of wickets on his first-team debut for Hampshire. There have been plenty of better rugby players down the years than him, but he was a solid, reliable performer. He also had to cope with the extra pressures that his name brought with it.

I remember shortly before one match at Bristol, a newspaper had paid an ex-girlfriend of his to try to set him up. Liam was about to be married and was approached by the girl, who basically tried to persuade him to sleep with her with the promise that she would say nothing to his fiancée. Liam's answer wasn't what the newspaper was hoping for, insisting instead that he was spoken for. When he later got wind of the set-up, he was fuming, so much so that he might as well have not played that day because his mind was elsewhere. The incident opened my eyes to what it must be like to live under the spotlight. I dare say his father had been through that sort of thing many times over, but it must have been difficult for Liam to cope with, being a young man trying to make his own way in the sporting world.

I found Ian Botham to be a fine bloke. I wouldn't count myself as a personal friend of his, but I have always enjoyed his company and his dedication to his son was without question. I remember one freezing, cold evening we fielded a combination side up at Otley and there were only a handful of hardy souls watching from the dilapidated stand but two of them were Ian Botham and his wife, Kath. They would follow their son to the ends of the earth. I think Beefy appreciated the fact that I was the one who gave Liam his first chance in the game. I used to see him in the clubhouse later in my career at Cardiff having a couple of beers and he was always a pleasure to be around. He was very down to earth.

I was sacked at the end of that season when West got relegated, which was a little different to what they proposed when I first took the job. Phillip Yuill had moved on by that stage and Andy Hindle, the fellow who had been influential in taking me to the club, was now running the show. In the end, though, I suppose I was the architect of my own downfall. I had suggested bringing in someone like the ex-New Zealand flanker Mike Brewer to help me with the coaching, as I knew he was over in Britain at the time doing some work for the Canterbury brand of rugby clothing. It must have stuck in Andy Hindle's mind as Brewer ended up succeeding me. I was just called in one day and told I was out.

The real crux of the matter was that Hindle seemed to want overnight success. I was absolutely choked because for all our struggles in the top division that season we had destroyed teams from the league below us whenever we had met them. This had convinced me that with a bit of development that summer we could have rebuilt ourselves the following season and enjoyed some dominance, albeit at a lower level. I felt we would then have been better prepared to have another crack at the Premiership.

It saddened me that after I left the club they agreed to a ground-sharing arrangement with Hartlepool United Football Club and knocked down the Brierton Road clubhouse and ground for housing development. I had always said once they did that they would lose the heart and soul of the club, and I think I was proved right.

Just a few years earlier, West had enjoyed phenomenal success, attracting big crowds and even managing to bring in the great All Black brothers Alan and Gary Whetton to play for them. Furthermore you could argue it was more of a rugby than a football town, with about eight clubs within its boundaries of which West was the most illustrious. The potential to grow, even with the emergence of Newcastle Falcons down the road, was there. Newcastle just proved to be the demise of the club, however, and West now languish in the North-east Division Two of the English system.

But it was not the end of me, far from it. Almost immediately, I received a telephone call from the agent Mike Burton. I was being offered a very attractive salary to become head coach of Penzance and Newlyn.

15

PIRATES OF PENZANCE

I accepted a £20,000 payout when I left West Hartlepool as I was still under contract, so I felt very fortunate that I was walking straight into another well-paid job, even if it was at the other end of the country.

I took Kevin Moseley, the former Wales lock, with me from West down to Penzance and Newlyn as a coach and I also brought in the prop Martyn Madden, who would later go on to much better things with Llanelli but at the time had allowed his weight to balloon to a level that was preventing him from fulfilling his potential. Martyn was playing the odd game for local sides in Cardiff, but I could still remember watching him play outside-half for the Cardiff Schools Under-11 side and I knew that he had skill and talent if only it could be harnessed properly. In the end, I played a big part in getting him to Llanelli. I rang the Scarlets' team manager Anthony Buchanan with a hearty recommendation and I think Martyn was grateful because by that time he was ready to move from Penzance.

Meanwhile I was more than happy with my lot in Cornwall. Hayley and I had been married for nine years and we were excited at the prospect of a good salary, with a house and a four-wheel drive thrown in for good measure. All this was made possible by Dicky Evans, the Penzance benefactor, who was of Welsh descent but had become a Cornishman through and through. Dicky was a self-made millionaire who ran a business in Kenya, where he was based, exporting fruit and flowers to companies such as Marks and Spencer. He was also a tax exile who was only allowed into the

UK for 90 days a year, so was good enough to invite me out to Kenya when we were agreeing the deal. I stayed in his fantastic house and we played golf, and he promised me that I could have holidays at Hemingway's, his private resort on some island in the Indian Ocean where marlin fishing was the number one pastime.

The club ended up finishing runners-up in Division One in my first season, which was disappointing because promotion as champions had very much been the aim – and the expectation, for some.

By this stage, I had become increasingly disturbed by the behaviour of Dicky. He was passionate about the club, so he would turn up for quite a few of our games, but instead of keeping a low profile and watching from the stand he would be on the touchline spouting off quite vocal criticisms of the team if things were not going to plan. I didn't like it one bit. I felt if anyone was going to dish out rollickings to the players it should be me, and in turn I was prepared to take the heat from Dicky in private if he had any particularly pressing problems.

I was also concerned about further involvement by him in team affairs. He would take me out for meals where we would talk about what we wanted to achieve for the club and he would spell out his ambitions. It even got to the stage where Dicky started dining with my assistant, Kevin Moseley – it wasn't exactly reassuring.

Other developments began to make me feel undermined, too. Not long after I started at Penzance, I got wind that there had been a meeting to which I had not been invited between Dicky and a fellow called Don Rutherford, one of the top English coaching-development gurus, who had been around a long time. Dicky had often tried to use his influence to get the RFU to make Cornwall a proper development region, with a full-blown academy and a professional team that could be fast-tracked to the highest level. He argued, not without some justification, that Cornwall was a great catchment area with a traditional interest in rugby that had as yet gone unexploited. This has more or less happened now with the emergence of the Cornish Pirates team. It was rumoured that Don Rutherford would prefer an Englishman, if possible, to head up the rugby side of things – and Mark Ring wasn't one of those.

Not long after this, Dicky appointed Peter Johnson as assistant director of rugby. Johnson is a lovely fellow and has since written quite a few books on coaching. He had been involved with the Bristol academy and brought a few of their youngsters with him to play for Penzance. His recruitment puzzled me at first, but, again, he had the advantage that he was English. It was clear that Peter, against whom I hold no grudges, was being groomed as my successor.

The final demise of my situation at Penzance, apart from the fact that we lost a few crucial games, which meant we wouldn't be going up, was the fact that I could no longer deliver as a player. Dicky was paying me such a handsome salary because he believed he was getting Mark Ring the player and Mark Ring the coach, but by this stage my knees were in a terrible state and I was way off the pace. One knee was particularly bad – in fact, I think it was worse then than it is now – and I just couldn't handle the twisting and turning of my legs that rugby demanded. I think Dicky had expected me to score three tries, three drop goals and umpteen conversions every game and that didn't happen. Subsequently, he became very critical of me personally while on the sidelines during matches. I didn't hear anything specific that came out of his mouth, and I don't know how I would have reacted if I had, but I could hear his general screaming and balling. Loyal supporters would come up to me in the bar after games, saying, 'You should have heard him on the side having a go at you.' They would outline what he had said about me and other players in fine detail and it left me amazed. After one of our cup games, which we had won but in which we had not played well, he went off for a long walk with Moseley while the rest of the players and I went to shower. Again understandably their closeness made me feel very uncomfortable, but there was nothing I could realistically do about it: Dicky was the boss, he was paying the wages and he was free to behave however he wanted.

Things came to a head when I was called in to the office one day and told I was not being kept on. Dicky was out of the country at the time – Peter Johnson was out of the office as well that day. The news was delivered to me by a club official whose name I can't even remember. And that was it, the end of another adventure in a remote corner of England.

Yes, I was upset, as I had been when I was given my cards at West, but I also felt a touch of relief. For so long working with Dicky had been making me uncomfortable and the situation was only getting worse. In any working environment, the most important thing is that you are comfortable and trust your colleagues, the people in whose company you work day in, day out. You need the confidence that comes with the knowledge that people are backing you and willing to support you at every turn. Without that you don't really have anything.

All I wanted was to be given the backing to go out and translate the confidence I had to my players; self-belief is a commodity that is passed on simply by your everyday demeanour on the training ground and generally just around the place. If in a sporting environment the coach feels down or under pressure from the directors, then that feeling is quickly passed on to the players, who then invariably begin to under-perform. I wanted no part of anything like that and in that sense I was glad to get away, but I would be lying if I said I wasn't disappointed about yet another failed foray into coaching.

I had found myself in two situations, both of which were far from ideal, and probably the biggest lesson I had learned was that trying to be a player and a director of rugby was impossible. It had to be one or the other: if you tried to be jack of all trades, you would end up being master of none.

On the positive side, I had gained a lot of experience; the work I did at West Hartlepool with Dr Ekkart Arbeit being a prime example. It was just a pity that the WRU refused to listen when I offered to talk to them about the benefits of his training techniques. Then again, maybe I shouldn't have been surprised. I had a pretty good idea of what they thought of me at the time – to them I was just Mark Ring, the retired player, who had failed as a coach at West Hartlepool. The Penzance experience did little to enhance my reputation in the coaching world either. It frustrated me to think that people would just make a blanket judgement about me because of my early exit from both jobs without having any understanding of the circumstances in which I had found myself. I was embarrassed by it all and my time in England had definitely tainted my mood, though I have to accept that it is just the way it works in rugby.

How right Terry Charles was in telling me that I had to go away and learn by my mistakes. I had made plenty of them, but I was older and wiser, and I had increased my bank of knowledge considerably. If nothing else, I had given coaching a go; I had at least backed myself and my own ability in both situations and spent time at the sharp end. It was an apprenticeship for me and that's the way I always look at it.

I am always wary when I see sportspeople retire and walk straight into the top end of the game as a coach. OK, so West Hartlepool were in the English Premiership when I took over, but the job itself was never going to be one that would appeal to big-name coaches already established because there just weren't the resources to work with there. It needed somebody like me, who was ready to accept the challenge and in the process make a name for himself in the world of coaching. Saying all this, I am not one of these people who likes to trot out the phrase 'great players don't necessarily make great coaches'. There are exceptions, of course, but if you have played international rugby, I think you are bound to stand a far better chance of being a successful coach. I would advise any sportsperson considering a career in the coaching world to serve their time at a lower level or to at least take on a job where they have it all to prove, where the circumstances are going to test their mettle to the limit.

The one other sour taste left in my mouth with regard to Penzance was Moseley. I had originally offered him the opportunity down there. He had taken charge of West briefly after I was booted out, although he was on his way when Mike Brewer arrived there, and then at Penzance it was the same: he and Peter Johnson took charge.

I think Moseley is still down there. I had given him his first chance in the professional world, but when I had to leave Cornwall, I got the impression that he didn't really care two hoots where I went from there.

Whatever happened in the South-west, it was time for me to head back to Wales; more specifically to the club which had always been my club: Cardiff RFC.

16

A CAPITAL MESS

I took a big wage cut to go back to Cardiff to work for the club's Capital Rugby community development scheme while also being backs coach to Terry Holmes.

It was the start of 1998–99, a landmark season for Cardiff because we had been taken into a series of friendlies with English clubs, along with Swansea, following a dispute with the Welsh Rugby Union. The two clubs – dubbed the 'rebel clubs' – were desperate to improve the standard of competition in the league and felt the old-fashioned WRU had failed to react to changing circumstances. Swansea and Cardiff had expensive squads to finance in the new professional era and were desperate to offer a better product to their supporters.

After a rip-roaring start to the matches against the English sides, we were left floundering as somewhat depleted teams began to come over from the other side of the Severn Bridge. This lessened the impact of any victories, not to mention the attractiveness of the fixtures to the supporters. By the following season, the two clubs were back in the Welsh leagues, though.

However, this had little effect on me or my job. My working week would be divided between going around the schools coaching the kids as part of my role with Capital Rugby and training with the Cardiff backs. To begin with, I felt part of a strong staff. I had huge respect for Terry, and Tony Faulkner, one-third of the legendary Pontypool front row of the '70s who was there working as a scrum doctor, along with Hemi Taylor, who was employed as the forwards coach.

The fact that I was earning a relatively low wage didn't bother me unduly either because by this time, after two difficult years in England, I was just glad to be back home. I had been in Wales all summer after leaving Penzance at the tail end of the previous season and had almost immediately been promised this position with Cardiff. It took some months to materialise, but I started in the September of 1998. Then I was up and running: I had my kit bag full of balls, my cones, my pump and my club car, which was important in order to get about as Capital Rugby demanded. I just hoped that the whole Cardiff thing would take off for me. The money and the sponsorship the club had gained seemed to have placed it on a sound footing and I sincerely hoped that I could work there for a good few years. There was only ever one club for me and here I was working for it.

I was no more ambitious than the next man and was prepared to give Terry Holmes my 100 per cent loyalty, but I would be a liar if I said I didn't one day hope to take charge of the club as head coach. I saw my role as an opportunity to bed myself in and take the first step onto the bottom rung of the ladder.

Then Terry Holmes left and it changed everything for me.

To this day, it makes my blood boil when I think how badly I felt Terry was treated by the club. They said he resigned, but I believe that he was left no option but to go and was made a scapegoat for the failings of his players, whose performances let him down unforgivably towards the end of his tenure.

Terry's Waterloo proved to be a semi-final match in the Welsh Cup, a competition in which Cardiff and Swansea both competed despite the fact that they were playing outside the Welsh league system. We were hammered 41–10 by Llanelli at Bridgend's Brewery Field and just four or five days afterwards Terry was gone, even though the situation we found ourselves in was by no means of his making. Terry had not been helped by the make-up of the season.

As I said, it started well enough. One victory we had up at Leicester against a strong Tigers side was simply outstanding and another clash against Richmond at the Madejski Stadium in Reading was one of fantastic quality, even though we lost. Everything was going swimmingly up to Christmas, but then it all unravelled as the English clubs stopped fulfilling their part of the bargain. The matches lost all their intensity: we were winning far too easily against what were little more than development sides and so were totally unprepared for the reality of facing a fired-up Llanelli in the pressure-cooker environment of a Welsh Cup semi-final when, as usual, the world and his wife were baying for Cardiff to lose.

The inevitable happened: we were stuffed despite taking an early 10–0 lead. One of the most jolting features of the match was how the Llanelli prop Phil Booth, an ex-Cardiff Youth player, pushed our British Lion Dai Young all over the park in the scrum. In fact we were battered up front, which nullified the threat from our scrum-half Rob Howley, who spent the entire game on the back foot. The mistakes just snowballed from there.

Terry's departure typically seemed to coincide with the usual round of politics in the game, this time involving the Welsh Rugby Union and Peter Thomas. One minute, it seemed Peter was rebelling against the WRU, going all the way to actually playing outside their jurisdiction. The next, he was back on board, arranging how Cardiff would assimilate into the Welsh game – and be nominated for the Heineken Cup at the expense of Ebbw Vale, who should have claimed the final berth because of their league finish. What sticks in my craw now is that Cardiff Rugby Club was eventually the only element not to suffer for the decision to rebel. It wasn't just Ebbw Vale; there were also many fine referees who, because they had presided over rebel matches, never took charge of games again. As I say, I suffered, too, as Terry did.

I was not surprised to see Lynn Howells, whom I have nothing against whatsoever, take over from Terry. He was a WRU man who would go on to work as assistant to Graham Henry when the Kiwi arrived in Wales in 1998. I telephoned him when he took up office to find out where I stood, fully aware that I could be in trouble. Sure enough, he told me he would be bringing in his own man,

Geraint John, to work with the backs. It was something I accepted without argument: Lynn wouldn't be the first or last to want to go down his own route. For me, it meant that I was left with just my Capital Rugby work – and a reduced annual salary.

I made up the shortfall in the evenings by coaching local clubs, such as my old club St Albans, and in fact I went straight into helping out St Peter's, the little club who famously beat Cardiff in the Welsh Cup in 1993. They were under threat of being relegated from one of the lower divisions, which would not only have reduced their status but also seen their funding from the WRU severely hit. It was thought we would have to win our last four games to survive, though in the end we won three of them, which was enough because the other results fell kindly for us. I played as well as coached and even though it was at lower level and in truth a bit of a sideline for me, I got enormous satisfaction from playing a part in what St Peter's achieved.

I wasn't really upset about my treatment by Cardiff because what happened to me was an inevitable consequence of Terry's removal, but I felt dreadfully sorry for Terry. He was a brilliant man-manager and coach, and I believed he had left partly because Peter Thomas seemed to me to have bowed to pressure from the WRU, who wanted Cardiff back in the fold on their terms and with their man in charge.

There were other changes at the club and later the region of Cardiff Blues – Bob Norster being made a full-time chief executive was one. I have the utmost respect for what Bob achieved as a player and it would be silly to try to make out he didn't have some wonderful times with Cardiff and Wales – I've also no doubt his intentions have been good throughout his playing and non-playing career – it's just that my own personal impression of Bob from playing alongside him and working under him at Cardiff is not favourable.

In my view, one of his mistakes was the appointment of Gary Knowles to take charge of Capital Rugby. Knowles works on the community development side of things with the Blues these days but told everybody that back in the '70s, at the time of its famous front row, he had played for Pontypool. I'm not disputing the fact he wore the jersey, but it seems to me that his achievements at Pooler may have been reasonably limited. Bobby Windsor coached me, I played with Graham Price, and I coached alongside Tony Faulkner and not one of them had a clue who Knowles was when I asked them.

On one occasion, Knowles came out with me to do a session at Stacey Road Primary School in Cardiff with a load of ten- and eleven-year-old kids. I was teaching them how to spin pass a ball. I had worked out for myself the importance of the thumb in spinning the ball, so, say, if you are passing off your right hand, the left thumb should press hard into the ball and spin it downward as you release it. I just found little tips like that worked for the kids because they were things they could easily take on board.

Now, Knowles had come to observe and just as we were about to start the session and I had explained what I wanted the kids to do, I went to give them a practical demonstration, telling them, 'I will spin pass the ball to Mr Knowles and Mr Knowles will spin pass it back to me.' But, to my amazement, Knowles didn't seem to be able to spin pass it. That summed it up for me.

When I finally left, I told him to his face exactly what I thought of him, which wasn't complimentary, I can assure you. I think it upset him, but I didn't give two hoots.

In later years, my work with Capital Rugby in the schools did become mundane – Knowles's presence hardly helped matters – but to begin with I had enjoyed myself. I was trying to teach kids basic core skills, but the challenge was to make it fun and to cater for differing abilities, girls as well as boys. I used to work with different schools over a four to six week period, when I would start with a get-to-know-you session followed by a programme of fun games, where I would try to improve skills and also build a few characters as well, since it was part of a community project, after all. The aim of what we were doing would be to get the children interested enough in rugby for them to carry on playing after we had gone and make it very much a part of their lives. I became frustrated, though, because I had lots of ideas that I was just not allowed to bring to fruition, such as the introduction of coaching videos.

The irony of the whole thing was that because every day I was working out which drills I could do and handling rugby balls almost incessantly, I was finding my own skill level was actually increasing, even though I had finished playing. This only convinced me that what we were doing must be working. I never consulted coaching manuals, whether I was working with the kids or the senior players; I just used to find out what worked through my own trial and error. One example of that was when I was desperately trying to get kids not to run ahead of the passer when they were passing the ball along a line: not easy, especially when you are working with kids of limited ability. So I started telling them to pass to an imaginary man in front of the receiver. This way I managed to get them accelerating to receive the pass, which was what I wanted.

I took that with me and did it with the seniors, taking them right back to basics, and you know what, so many of them needed it. So many still do at the highest level of the game today. I sometimes watch Test matches and the standard of the passing is dreadful, though static kicking from hand is better than it has ever been. That says it all. Passing skills are incredibly remedial among certain teams and in a professional environment that is just not acceptable any more. It's like playing professional football and not being able to pass a ball ten yards in a straight line with your instep.

I've long since left Cardiff and, unless there are radical personnel changes, I cannot see myself ever going back there. Cardiff became Cardiff Blues following the regional revolution that hit Welsh rugby in 2003, but despite a purple patch towards the end of the 2005–06 season, the lack of progress on the playing side at the club has been no real surprise to me.

I like the chairman, Peter Thomas, as a person and I believe he does care passionately about his involvement with the Blues, but

I think he has been ill-advised on some issues down the years and by people who don't really know the game sufficiently. And I am one of those who has suffered because of that.

Peter once said to my dad that there would always be a role for me at Cardiff and while I'm not so naive as to expect that to mean a coaching job for life, no matter what the circumstances, I wish he had fought my corner a little more than he did at times when it was clear to me that someone, somewhere at the club had poured poison in his ear about me.

Cardiff is such an old-school club in so many ways. I have always wondered how many people there are behind the scenes who think you are 'not the type' to be getting on at their club. Peter was initially very pro-Mark Ring, but he has never really promoted me. He has done the opposite with Bob Norster and Dai Young, mind you, backing them to the hilt time and time again down the years through some very lean spells.

I remember about five years ago Adrian Hadley telling me that Dai and Geraint John had agreed to join Bridgend as a coaching team. Adrian was chief executive at the Brewery Field at the time. When it came out in the press that the deal was on the cards, I understand Peter Thomas jumped in and offered Dai a new contract. Again last season when it looked as though Dai might go to Saracens as forwards coach, he ended up pledging his loyalty to the Blues after talks with Peter and Bob.

The single biggest stumbling block for me about Peter Thomas, however, is that I cannot forgive him for what happened to Terry Holmes. I just felt Peter was the one who took us into that rebel situation and he should have done what he has done so many times since with Dai Young: he should have backed Terry unequivocally in public and practically insisted he carry on.

As I've already said, when Lynn Howells told me I was not part of his coaching plans and that Geraint John was to take over the running of the backs, I did not throw my toys out of the pram, though that's not to say I thought it was a good appointment. Geraint is a likeable bloke and I would not want to fall out with him by being critical. He already knows how I feel about his coaching abilities because I have told him directly before, though whatever my opinions are of him as a coach, I do respect him and I will always have time for him.

I will always be a fan of Cardiff and I watch the Blues matches avidly, and a lot of what I saw from them while Geraint – who now works for the Canadian Rugby Union – was in charge of the backs did not, in my personal view, show him in a particularly good light. You just have to look at the likes of the Robinson brothers, Nicky and Jamie, or Rhys Williams and Craig Morgan – I just have not seen these young guys develop in their time at the Arms Park as I always believed they should have done because all of them have so much talent. Their skill levels and evasive running ability did not improve as they could have, but most of all they seemed too often to lack the confidence to go out and express themselves.

I was actually called in to help out with the backs coaching after leaving Capital Rugby and saw it for myself. Nicky Robinson has massive ability but continues to be inconsistent; Jamie, I suppose, has had a nasty knee injury, which has hampered his progress, but I still think there is more in him than we have seen. Craig Morgan has all but gone and now plays his rugby at Bristol. Rhys Williams probably had his worst-ever season in 2005–06, but for a long while he has been down on his luck. He lost his place in the Wales squad and I don't think he'll ever get it back on a regular basis. Yet these fellows are prized commodities, so what has been done with them?

I'd like to know what proper guidance, if any, Iestyn Harris was given at the Arms Park when he switched codes in September 2001. It struck me as though he was just seen as a genius who could be left to get on with it. One thing that used to get me tearing my hair out was when he played outside-half or centre and the opposition kicked the ball over his head downfield. You would see Iestyn just standing still, which is what they do in rugby league. The guy is one of the most evasive and silky-smooth runners you will ever see in either code at any level, but who was telling him that when a kick was put over his head at outside-half he had to work his socks off to get behind the ball and offer support to the full-back? It's really basic stuff, but it wasn't there with Iestyn.

My renewed involvement at the Blues had been down to Gareth Edwards, who is still a director there. When we chatted, he couldn't believe that I wasn't still playing a part on the coaching side at the Arms Park. Gareth went and had a word with Peter Thomas, who then came to me. Gareth has always had time for me, but he is also entangled in the politics of the Cardiff boardroom and his loyalty lies with Peter Thomas.

Gareth's legendary status in the world game is used to the full by the Blues these days. He tends to be a front for things they do across a range of playing and commercial matters and I know he often plays a part in trying to persuade overseas players to come on board with Cardiff. He's very professional in what he does and is full of good intentions.

Anyway, I soon realised that my return to Cardiff was never going to work because when I came back in it was as if I was seen as some sort of threat and I was given the most menial tasks to do. In one training session, I found myself playing number 8 just so I could offload a ball in a rather pointless drill involving the scrum-half Ryan Powell, now at Worcester, and the young back-row player James Malpas. It was a total and utter waste of half an hour when I could have been working on individual skills with backs, getting them to chip and catch off their weaker foot, improving their ability to pass off either hand or focusing on attacking running lines and angles. I know the players enjoyed working with me, but I felt I was continually marginalised.

Undoubtedly one of the biggest problems I had in all my time at Cardiff and latterly with the Blues was Bob Norster. Bob was a brilliant lineout forward in his day and I suppose you can't argue with what he achieved as a player, but it has to be remembered that when he played for the Blue and Blacks he was helped by some other outstanding forwards who played around him. You had names like John Scott and Alan Phillips, then there was Ian Eidman and Jeff Whitefoot, who were two of the finest scrummaging props around at the time; Kevin Edwards was a foil for him in the second row and then you had players like Gareth Roberts, Owen Golding, Bob Lakin and Howard Stone.

John Scott, who played at number 8 for England and who still writes a column in the *South Wales Echo*, will tell you that Bob was a superb exponent of lineout play but that he offered little else. Bob threw his fists around a fair few times in his playing days with Cardiff, but it was always in the knowledge that these guys were around him. I would never have classed him in the same bracket as someone like Ian Robinson, a great friend of mine, who also played second row and was a legendary, genuine hard man.

Bob was always immaculately dressed as a player, with his tie perfect and a handkerchief in his top pocket, and when he was having his photograph taken he would look to the side to hide the crookedness of his nose. I never knew Bob that well in the early days but as I played alongside him more and more for Cardiff he did little to raise his estimation in my eyes.

I recall a great friend of mine at Cardiff, the hooker Jose Souto who came up through Cardiff Youth with me. He had a brother called Peter who also played for Cardiff at the time in the second row, but Peter went north to St Helen's, which was no surprise because he was so athletic and powerful. Now, I had played alongside Jose, who was slightly older than me, way back in our time at St Alban's Primary School and I had a huge regard for him because he was a real honest and tough player who would have walked into any team other than Cardiff, but like me, Jose loved Cardiff and regarded it as 'his' club.

Yet whenever Jose would come into the Cardiff team to replace Alan Phillips, Bob would seem to spend the whole game whinging because he and Alan used to hit it off so well as thrower and catcher in the lineout. Too often, Bob appeared to moan at Jo during games if he felt his delivery at the lineout wasn't up to standard. It all seemed to knock Jo's confidence. For example, instead of a few carefully chosen words to try and give Jo a boost, like 'Don't worry about it, son, it will come,' the situation seemed to be just about what Bob Norster did or didn't think was acceptable. This type of situation was the clincher for me with Norster.

What's more, when it came down to it, Norster was a real worrier despite being regarded as one of the kingpins of the team. I remember when we went on the controversial World XV tour of South Africa in 1989, while the rest of us were just enjoying the experience of going to South Africa to celebrate the centenary of their union, Bob spent most of the trip worrying about whether he was going to make the Test side.

When he couldn't think of anything else to worry about I thought I would wind him up by telling him I was going to write a warts and all book about the affair. I then had him on the phone one evening begging me not to go ahead with it. He said I was a loose cannon who was going to drag everyone down into the mire with him. Of course there was no book, but I enjoyed squeezing every last drop out of making Bob believe that there would be.

Bob later became captain of Cardiff and his performance in that role was not to my liking. One time we were playing Neath down at The Gnoll, where they would always give us what for. It was a real tough place to play and teammates would always be crying off, but I used to love playing there because I found the atmosphere gave me a buzz rather than a scare.

Bob was captain that day and Neath were giving us a real going over. Every time Neath scored a try we would gather behind the posts and Bob would deliver his own inimitable team talk, where he would go down on one knee and bang his fist into the grass as he spoke. 'You've got to do this, and you've got to start doing that,' was the gist of his sentiments, but the key for me was that it seemed to always be 'you' and never 'we'.

Later that day when this was happening again, I brushed past him and said, 'What about you?'

Bob looked at me and I said, 'Why don't you do your fucking bit!'

From that day on, we never saw eye to eye and I would be surprised if he has ever fought my corner in anything I have done at Cardiff, which has obviously had its consequences because of the position of power he has enjoyed.

When I was released from the Capital Rugby scheme, he called me into the office and explained how my departure was partly down to finances and that they were keeping on Gary Knowles because half of his salary was paid by the WRU. It was my personal belief that finances were not necessarily dictating I go and I felt it would never have come to me leaving had my contribution been truly valued by the club.

Then there are some of the players Cardiff and then the Blues have brought in over these last few years. When you look at some of the disastrous recruitment that has gone on, it is clear to see that this has not been a strong point. Don't get me wrong, in more recent times the likes of current captain Xavier Rush, scrum-half Mike Phillips and the former All Black full-back Ben Blair have been quality acquisitions who have strengthened the squad. Blair in particular has impressed in the short time he has been with the region. If these fellows stick around and perform like they can for a good few seasons together with the other senior Welsh internationals at the Blues, then things may start to look far more promising.

But I can't forget some of the earlier signings before these guys, people like Kenneth Fourie, Dominic Van Vurren and Semo Sititi to pluck out just three. No disrespect to any of them, but in terms of ability I will never believe they belonged in Cardiff shirts or at the top level, but they came in at a time when the club or the region seemed to me to be content to settle for mediocrity.

Then there was someone like Lee Thomas the young fly-half who left at the end of last summer to go and try his luck at Sale. I don't want to savage a young player but he seemed too slow and without vision at Cardiff, yet he was given a contract after coming up through the youth system when what he could offer never justified it. They even brought Graham Henry's son, Andrew, into the first team at one stage, giving him game time on the wing. In my view, he wasn't up to it and the fact he was given the blue-and-black jersey worn by so many great players of the past I felt was not justified by his performance.

In rugby, like football, if you're not prepared to shell out for genuine proven quality, you will be quickly found out on the field of play. Everyone knows that the money in football has become mind-boggling but even in rugby these days, while earnings are still way below the round-ball game, the very top players aren't interested in salaries that do not net them six figures per year.

And there are certainly players at some of the Welsh regions who are raking in well in excess of £100,000 annually. I believe it took too long for this to sink in among those in charge at the Arms Park and they subsequently paid a heavy price in terms of results.

Yet while it is clear I am not a fan of Bob Norster, he cannot be saddled with all the blame for the struggles that have hit the Arms Park in recent years. There's Dai Young as well.

I've never really had a go at Dai in the past, and the truth of the matter is that I like him as a guy in the same way I do Geraint, and I will always have respect for people who have done what he has in the game. But the bottom line for me, and this is a personal view, is that I just do not see tight-head props as visionaries in terms of coaching rugby union. All their lives as players they have been head down, arse up, and then they think they can see the game when they hang their boots up, but, for me, they can't.

My view is that tight-head props should stick to their area of expertise if they want to coach. For heaven's sake you wouldn't catch someone like Jonathan Davies trying to hand out advice on scrummaging so why think an ex-tight-head can be a strategist on general play?

Dai should have at least started his coaching career as a forwards coach or a scrum doctor; there's plenty of work out there in those departments. But instead he was in a position where he could succeed Lynn Howells as head coach at Cardiff when in my opinion he had no business walking straight into a role of that magnitude.

What happened? Well, while he wasn't given much backing by the board financially for long spells, he was still badly exposed by results for three and a half years and even now, after he has been there for more than three seasons, there seems, to me, to be very few members of the general public totally convinced about him.

And you can't blame people for doubting him because they will always turn to statistics first and foremost. Any coach should live and die by his results record – I know I always have.

I remember during my brief comeback thanks to Gareth Edwards' chat with Peter Thomas, I was wired up to what Dai was saying during a match at the Arms Park. I could hear every single thing that was said and I disagreed with everything that was coming from Dai's mouth. Practically nothing he said was, in my view, constructive. This particular game I could see that the entire Cardiff back line was just shuffling sideways because I was standing behind the posts for most of the first half.

I could also see that the opposition openside flanker was standing up and across two yards to try and get outside the fly-half and push everything sideways. It called for a flatter ball to be spun to our fly-half so he could beat the flanker on the angle and apart from that we were also over-committing to rucks and mauls. I tried to get these messages across but, for whatever reason, he just didn't seem interested in my contribution; they never got through to the team.

On several occasions at half-time during matches in which we were struggling, the players appeared to be looking to Dai to say something and take the lead but to me he didn't seem capable of making clear what he wanted. But Dai wouldn't listen to me when I tried to help.

I would look at him pacing up and down and looking flustered but when I tried to get him to talk to me one-on-one he would just say: 'All right, mun, all right.'

He made me feel like I was badgering him which in turn made me feel uneasy. All I wanted to do was help, but if I'm honest I suspect that one of the reasons Dai didn't want to listen was because he feared what I had to say might be too technical to relay meaningfully to the players.

When Dai was captain under the coaching of Terry Holmes he was good in the way he spoke to the players, a good talker and a good motivator. He always came across well in that way and if he ever did a session it was well structured. But my experience of Dai as a coach was nowhere near so positive. Dai wouldn't see how to take the game forward. Defences were getting stronger and stronger in Dai's early days as head coach but in my opinion he didn't seem able to think his way out of a problem. Having said all this, I must re-emphasise that I like Dai as a bloke and have always got on reasonably well with him.

He is a dry, witty sort of character and we go back a long way. I remember him making his debut along with Richard Webster as a teenager at the 1987 World Cup and there's no doubt that he is one of the great Welsh props of all time. I do believe though that he has been at the Arms Park too long; in fact, I wonder whether the likes of him and Norster will ever leave the place.

I saw a quote from Dai in a newspaper article not so long ago where Dai described himself as a Cardiff man through and through. Well, he's entitled to view himself in any way he pleases, but in my view this is an overstatement. Dai came from Aberdare, he then played for Cardiff Youth then went straight to Swansea, so he never came through the Cardiff system like so many of us.

Yes, he's had a good few years of his career at the Arms Park, but Cardiff through and through? Not in my eyes. Dai's record as a coach is poor when all is said and done. I have always said there is a role for him at Cardiff because to a significant extent he has the respect of the players. But as far as I am concerned he is not the one to lead the Blues in taking them forward. The game is moving on very quickly, but I would never see Dai as the man who can stay one step ahead of the whole process.

For me, Dai is a forwards coach and no more and if you look at how the forwards have gone for Cardiff and the Blues while he has been in charge, they have always held their own and won enough ball to have won far more games than the team has actually managed. That says it all for me.

In my opinion the disappointments of recent years at the Arms Park have been down to the fact that the wrong people have been running the show. More recently I was staggered to see Rhys Williams given the captaincy last season; as far as I was concerned, this was a completely ill-suited appointment if ever there was.

Rhys has experience now and no doubt he put his heart and soul into the job, but if nothing else Rhys's weakness in the tackle should have stopped him ever coming into the frame. It was no surprise whatsoever to see former All Black number 8 Xavier Rush given the job at the start of the 2006–07 campaign.

You can't have a situation where the Blues defend for seven or eight phases in a Heineken Cup match before the opposition break through a weak Rhys tackle and score, with Rhys then expected to motivate the troops behind the posts when it was his mistake that let the other side in. The rumours were that nobody else wanted the job at the time he took it. What a sad situation if it is indeed true.

I believe Terry Holmes should have come back to Cardiff after Lynn Howells and that's not me touting for a job at all, it's simply because I am convinced he would have been the best man for the director of rugby role. The man commands respect. When he talks, players listen. And while he may not have the most technical of minds, he knows what he wants and he knows how to oversee a coaching team and a squad of players. Cardiff Blues should be one of the very best teams in Europe but in recent years they have shipped more than 70 points to Biarritz and then last season they failed to qualify from a Heineken Cup pool of Perpignan, Leeds and Calvisano which could not possibly have been any easier. And that after they had been forced to qualify for the top tier through a play-off against Viadana the summer before.

The purple patch the Blues enjoyed in the last couple of months of last season led a lot of people to say that Dai had turned it all around but I don't think that's an accurate statement. I watched one game when they played the Ospreys at home just after the end of the Six Nations Championship, a game the Blues won comfortably. Yet the Ospreys team that day was so ragged it left me in disbelief. There was no organisation there whatsoever.

Subsequently a Blues team desperately low on confidence was handed a major boost, practically without having to play particularly well. Dai then went on television to say how he thought everything had come off for the Blues that day. I disagreed strongly, I hadn't seen anything come off for them that looked planned, to my mind they had merely taken advantage of a staggeringly poor Ospreys performance.

But, whatever the reasons behind the win, it gave the Blues players confidence which enabled them to put a run of six or seven victories together. And that was the key.

I am strongly of the view that Dai's record dictates that he should have gone long ago, no question about it, and with Peter Thomas refusing to put him out of the door I believe he should have gone of his own accord. He should have stepped aside and allowed the Blues to bring in someone else above him while he concentrated on working with the forwards.

I bear Dai no malice whatsoever, nothing would please me more than to see him finally turn things around and put Cardiff Blues back to the top of the European tree. As I have made clear, Cardiff has always been 'my club' and I want success for the Arms Park like anyone would want for their hometown club. But I see precious little evidence that that it is around the corner, though I'd love to be proved wrong.

17

THE GREEN ARMY

Sometimes you go into something with pretty low expectations and it turns into an experience you wouldn't swap for the world. That's how I look back on the 2002–03 season I spent coaching Caerphilly Rugby Club, the Green Army, or the Cheesemen, as they are sometimes known.

I began as a part-time assistant at a club that seemed to be going nowhere but finished in overall charge of a team that reached a European final. Caerphilly are a little Welsh club who, if they exist for another 1,000 years, will never be fashionable, but what they achieved in rising through four or five tiers of the old structure of the Welsh club game was nothing short of phenomenal. By the time they rose into the old Welsh Premier Division at the turn of the millennium, they had developed their Virginia Park ground into a decent little place to watch the game and were a vibrant entity, an example to any club in the country aspiring to improve their status. Despite their achievements, however, they were still very much the poor relations in the top flight, their lack of financial muscle compared to Cardiff, Newport, Swansea and Llanelli dictated that they battled every year to avoid relegation.

However, when I took a telephone call from their team manager Gordon Pritchard one evening while I was still working in the Capital Rugby scheme, the chance to go up there and see what I could do appealed to me immediately. Once I had the nod from Cardiff, my mind was made up.

Chris Davey, who has guided the Wales Under-21 team to so

much success down the years, had left Caerphilly after several years of sterling service and the team was in the charge of two less experienced guys. Gareth Nicholas and Simon King, who is now the coach of the Pontypridd Welsh Premiership team, were both really nice guys and at first I was not asked to do anything other than just help them out, and I was perfectly happy with that. I knew Gareth and Simon from my junior playing days. Gareth, a Bridgend boy, had been in that East Wales Under-11 team that played West Wales on the Arms Park, which I mentioned earlier in the book, while Simon was a year older than me and I remembered him captaining the Wales Schools Under-15 side, which I didn't make.

According to Gordon Pritchard, the problem the club had was that Simon, who was an ex-number 8, was trying to coach the backs and not really getting anywhere. Gordon said he needed help, so I went up there assuming that Gareth and Simon had been fully briefed about my impending arrival. That was my first mistake. Immediately I walked into unrest. I don't think either of them had a particular problem with me personally but both claim they had been kept in the dark about my involvement and it caused resentment.

I knew Gordon from back when I was in the roofing business and we used to compete for work. I'd be out trying to get a job and would hear that Gordon was going around trying every trick in the book to get ahead, offering potential customers bottles of whisky and cup final tickets.

It was clear that there had been crossed wires when I arrived at Caerphilly, but I couldn't afford to dwell on it too much. I went there for £600 a month, which I was quite happy with, as that topped up my Capital Rugby wage quite nicely. I was quite impressed with the Caerphilly team initially. Gareth, who is no mug, had them fairly well organised. It was clear, mind you, that Gordon had been right about Simon – I don't think he could coach backs. I'm not surprised Simon has gone on to do well at Pontypridd and I would not suggest he doesn't have ability, but his position there is a more rounded one and he has staff at Sardis Road, such as the ex-Wales scrum-half Paul John, who can organise the backs.

One of the first things Simon did when I got to Caerphilly was slam a thick dossier of backs moves onto my desk, with dust flying everywhere. There were all sorts of technical drawings of set-plays and moves, and I appreciated his diligence, but there was no way I was ploughing through any of that. I wanted to take the players back to the basics; all I wanted to do was get them passing well, running some good angles and developing their movement off the ball. If they could improve on all those basic areas and prove they had a solid work ethic as well, I knew we would get somewhere.

All the time, I had in mind something I read in an autobiography by Sir Alex Ferguson. Fergie had said that one of the main reasons why the likes of David Beckham had gone on to become a superstar was because Fergie did not fret too much about mixing up his coaching sessions. The Manchester United boss argued that much of what he did was repetitive and basic but that it had had the desired effect of improving people like Beckham as a player. Ferguson admitted that when he first started out in coaching, one of the big mistakes he made was that he wanted to please all of his players by making sure they did plenty of enjoyable light-hearted drills in training. He said all of a sudden the structure started to collapse. He said it had been a big learning curve for him and he had realised he would have to be more single-minded. I tried to adopt a similar mantra and that was how I started going about my business at Caerphilly: I knew that if need be we could make things more complex and specialised at a much later date. To my delight, the boys responded to everything I did and totally bought into the direction I wanted to take them.

I took a hell of a gamble with my first decision, which I based upon the fact that communication at half-back is vital to any side. My best communicator was my full-back Justin Thomas, a player who looked like the next best thing when he was called into the Wales squad as a teenager in the mid-'90s. He went to Cardiff but lost his direction altogether – he's not the first to fall into that trap – and a spell at Newport also failed to reignite him, so by the time he wound up with Caerphilly he was playing part-time, having gone back to teaching, but I knew he had a lot to offer.

He had played fly-half in his younger days, so I switched him to number 10 straight away. Outside-half is a position of huge responsibility and not everyone can cope with the pressure of decision making that it demands; I know many a player who has subsequently gone to full-back to get out of that and I think this was the case with Justin. He had suffered a confidence loss and his skill level had dropped, but I had been through that sort of thing myself: the main thing was I knew Justin had a good reserve of ability that could be brought out of him; I felt he was good enough to be my fly-half and that all he needed was a run of games to get his timing back. I went with my instinct and Justin was magnificent for me, he really was.

We worked on his skill levels and his restarts. He also had this terrible habit of trying to clear the ball from deep by catching it and then taking two big strides forward before he put boot to ball. It cost him dearly earlier in his career when he played at full-back for Wales against England at Twickenham in 1996 and got a clearing kick charged down by Jeremy Guscott in the opening minute, which set England on the road to victory. But we worked on that as well, with me basically telling him to kick from behind himself.

The other elements of his game were fantastic: his passing, his distribution, his communication and eventually his confidence, which prompted him to try different things, vital at a time when defences very much ruled the roost. Justin was pivotal to our run later in the Parker Pen Shield, which I will come to soon.

I dropped Luke Richards in order to accommodate Justin at fly-half, which didn't go down great with Luke because when I arrived he was seen as the up-and-coming playmaker of the side.

Sure, he had great skills and to a certain extent he knew it; he always wanted to be the last one out on the pitch and would invariably come out dabbing his toes into the turf every few steps as if he was Glenn Hoddle. What he didn't quite understand was that he could sometimes be a liability in defence and I couldn't have that. Luke would make breaks, kick his goals, as well as kick beautifully from hand, but occasionally we would lose a game because some inside-centre had run through him three or four times in a match.

He brought his dad in to renegotiate his contract when it expired towards the end of my first season in the summer of 2002. Caerphilly couldn't afford to pay him what he wanted so he came up with this idea that he could be paid so many pounds a point, which was novel, to say the least.

'Give me £20 a point,' he suggested at one meeting.

'I tell you what,' I replied, 'I'll give you £20 a tackle!'

Luke and his dad were lost for words and a week or so later he left for Swansea.

Not long after I arrived at Caerphilly, Gareth and Simon resigned. They were unhappy that they had been kept in the dark about my appointment and that meant I was left to hold the baby, so to speak. Their departure wasn't solely as a result of me. My arrival, so I understood, was just the final nail in the coffin after a long line of upsets. I saw it as a great pity because while Simon has come back to good effect, Gareth, who I believed was a really promising coach, was lost for a long time.

I didn't feel ready to steer the ship by myself at this point, so the first thing I did was ring Terry Holmes whose talents had been going to waste since Cardiff had forced him out. I was happy on my £600 a month, I knew my limitations at the time and I told Terry that I would be happy to be his assistant if he could sort out a contract with Caerphilly. Yes, I had been a director of rugby before with West Hartlepool and Penzance and Newlyn, but at that stage all I wanted to do was concentrate on my own area of expertise.

Terry took some convincing, but what persuaded him to accept was something that you'd think would have put him off altogether. We had a European Shield tie away to Gloucester at their Kingsholm fortress and I asked Terry to come along with us and just see what he made of it all. I didn't hear back from him and unbeknown to me he made the trip that day on his own and just watched the game from the terrace. We were thrashed, leaking 90-odd points in the process. Their back-row man Jamie Forrester was absolutely outstanding and the whole Gloucester performance was a pleasure to watch from a pure rugby connoisseur's point of view.

My phone rang not long after the game. It was Terry. 'I was in the crowd,' he said, to my amazement.

'So, are you up for the challenge?' I replied.

'No chance,' he said.

But things would change.

The following week, the Cherry and Whites were back at our place and although they duly beat us again, we put on a vastly improved performance at Virginia Park. It was enough to convince Terry we were indeed worth a punt and after the game he came across and said he'd changed his mind and that he would like to take me up on my offer after all. Terry brought Tony Faulkner in with him as our scrum doctor and off we went.

To complete a good day, my mate Paul Turner, now coach of Newport Gwent Dragons but at Gloucester at the time, gave me a video of the match from which I was able to learn so much about the good things we had done.

Terry had negotiated a really good part-time contract, but as usual he knew what he wanted. After the three of us kept the club up in the Premier Division that season, our budget was cut and Terry decided to call it a day. So not for the first time, I was left on my own.

In the final season before the game went regional, we embarked on a fantastic journey in the Parker Pen Shield, which was effectively the third tier underneath the Heineken Cup and the

Parker Pen Challenge Cup. Some people belittled our achievement in reaching the final, where we lost to the French side Castres at Reading's Madejski Stadium, but I think that was a short-sighted way of looking at things. The bottom line was that it was the right level for us and as a part-time team on a shoestring budget, we worked miracles to get that far.

You could say we did get a bit lucky with the draw, coming out against three Italian teams in home and away ties along the way, in which we beat Rovigo in the first round and then Parma and Padova in the quarter-final and semi-final respectively. While some people snigger at Italian clubs, Parma's play-off win against Newport Gwent Dragons last season was proof that they have been upwardly mobile for some years now. Be under no illusion that for us to get the better of three fully professional Italian sides from their Super 10 domestic competition was no small achievement and we had a real battle in the semi against Padova, who actually beat us 33–26 at Virginia Park in the second leg, though it wasn't enough to stop us progressing on aggregate.

We found ourselves in the third-tier competition because we lost on a home-and-away basis to Harlequins in the Shield earlier that season but that episode definitely sparked us. Quins trounced us by 50-odd points at home, but when we went to The Stoop we were absolutely magnificent against the same side that we had faced a week earlier, except the great English prop Jason Leonard had been brought back into it. We ended up scoring six tries to their five and losing narrowly. If we had kicked our goals, I'm sure we would have beaten them.

The result was immaterial because of the thrashing we took in the first leg but I was far more encouraged by the kind of rugby we played. It was a phenomenal display in relation to our circumstances and I was proud to have played so well at such an illustrious venue. It was a defining moment of the season for me; I left The Stoop that day thinking that even though we were in the bottom-tier tournament, from now on it might just be that we could do something in it.

There was no pressure on the players – some of them were even playing on lower terms than in their original contracts because of the reduction in our budget.

A guy called Ryan Howells was playing for a pittance each week. He came to us for a trial and told me he just wanted a chance, so we put him in on that amount and he did a job for us. There were other decent performers dotted around the side. Paul Jones, the ex-Llanelli second row, was there and was a good stalwart. There was Mark Workman, an ex-Welsh Youth captain from Newport; Andrew Williams, the ex-Bridgend number 8; Justin Thomas; Roddy Boobyer, the centre who I have always thought magnificent ever since I saw him play for Maesteg against Llanelli in a cup match many years ago; and Neil Watkins, who was a fine second row.

I also managed to bring in a tight-head prop called Richard Skuse from Bristol because he was behind Andrew Sheridan, now of England and Lions fame, in the pecking order and Bristol just wanted him to have experience. Skuse went on to play tight-head for London Irish in the Guinness Premiership and he was one hell of a player for us.

There was also a scattering of others from the Bath academy who we managed to get in on the cheap, such as the centre Sam Cox, who went on to Bristol. Others, like Joe El Abd and Rob Higgett, who both went on to play for Bristol, were also key figures.

Players like these were helping us to build up a squad and they brought an added professionalism to our set-up. We were training three nights a week on a Monday, Tuesday and Thursday, and I also brought in Dean Parsons, who had played with me for Cardiff Youth. Dean was an exercise physiologist and had been a fitness adviser at Pontypridd and Neath previously. He really started to get the lads fit, which was the base on top of which we were able to build.

We also had some match winners in our Tongan players. There was a fellow called Holo Taufahema, who was a brilliant left-winger; Sione Tu'ipulotu, who played for the Dragons at centre last year and has now gone to play in Japan; and Feao Vunipola, the hooker. The only thing we had to do for them was keep them happy – if we did, they were brilliant players – which was not always easy, especially when they had not been given the money promised them!

We had a nice balance in the team of guys who had been at the club for a few seasons, academy players from England who had come over largely to get some experience and game time but who brought a welcome professionalism with them, a tactical controller in Justin Thomas at fly-half and the power of the Tongans. That's really where our journey began.

I did have one bad experience with a player I brought in who happened to be studying at Cardiff University and was a big athletic winger. He was a nice kid, but I felt his father mollycoddled him. In one of our games in Italy, we made numerous half-breaks and this kid was nowhere to be seen; it was as if he didn't want to know. All he had to do was keep up with the play and finish off some of those breaks we were making, and I watched from the side, getting more and more annoyed.

I don't normally pick on individuals, but at half-time that day I gave him an absolute roasting, effing and blinding and warning him to buck up his ideas. What I said clearly did the trick because he went out for the second half and played really well.

Sadly, that wasn't the end of it. He obviously went back to his father and told him about the rollicking I had given him at the interval. His father then wrote a letter to the club chairman explaining how his boy had been left bitterly upset by my outburst and that in all his experience of rugby he had never heard of such a foul-mouthed tirade – he didn't have that much experience then! He sent a copy to the Welsh Rugby Union basically calling for me to be sacked as coach of Caerphilly!

Unfortunately, details of the letter were leaked to the other players at Caerphilly and it didn't go down well. Before long, he stopped turning up and that was the end of the matter. I'm not particularly proud of the episode and I'll admit it was unusual for me to speak to somebody the way I did that day but as a coach I was quite entitled to do it.

Then again, I have never been afraid to speak my mind . . . I was once fined £1,000 by the Welsh Rugby Union for comments I made on television about referee Gareth Simmons after a Caerphilly match at Ebbw Vale. The background to the incident was that the WRU had called all the coaches in just a few days earlier to meet with the three full-time referees at the time. The idea was for us to talk about how we felt matches should be refereed with one aim being that we could put a domestic template in place which might benefit the national team. I said the one thing I hated was the number of times that the attacking team meets the last line of defence and is then penalised at the breakdown for apparently holding on to the ball. I argued that the 50–50 decisions were always going against the side on the front foot and that a big part of the problem was retreating defenders joining rucks from the side. The referees promised to bear my points in mind.

Come the Ebbw Vale game at their Eugene Cross Park home, a game that was an important dogfight between two teams at the wrong end of the table, Gareth Simmons, who had not been at the meeting but who was supposed to have had all our comments passed on to him, consistently blew against us after we had got beyond them. I went on television and said the meeting called by the WRU had been a total waste of time and that referees didn't understand the game.

I was called in by the governing body almost immediately and fined £500 with £500 suspended, though I ended up paying the second fine later in the season after I had another pop on the same issue in front of TV cameras. I just couldn't hold back because I felt so strongly!

* * *

It was May 2003 and what a memorable occasion the day of the Shield final turned out to be. Welsh rugby was going regional that summer and Caerphilly weren't part of it, so this was very much a last hurrah on this type of stage for all concerned. In a few months' time, Caerphilly would be a Welsh Premiership club with no way of playing in European competition. I'm not sure whether that fact dawned on too many people involved with the club.

The day got off to a worrying and somewhat chaotic start for me, which was typical of the way my life has gone. I had decided to start with Christian Ferris at hooker and have Vunipola as my impact player, who would definitely come on at some stage. It was a very difficult selection to make. I did not realise at the time that in Vunipola's mind this was his last big moment in rugby because he was close to retirement. For that reason, he didn't show up when we met. All I remember is spending the morning before we left for the game grappling with the problem. I rang him, but he wasn't having any of it despite my pleading, so I ended up speaking to his wife, who eventually persuaded him to come. It wasn't an ideal scenario because the team had gone up the day before and checked into our hotel five minutes from the ground, and Vunipola didn't join us until the Sunday morning, the day of the match. The whole episode was unsettling.

To make matters worse, our centre, Rob Higgett, had said during a training session a couple of days before the final that he felt something was wrong with his neck. The day before the game, closer examination by medics revealed he had actually broken a bone and so he was out of the game, meaning that Jarred Murphy, an Australian ex-rugby league player whom I had brought in from Melrose, came in at centre.

The final straw came on the morning of the match when, along with several other players who were all heading for our final team meeting, I got stuck in the hotel lift. You may laugh at the thought of it, but I certainly didn't see the funny side at the time as I am claustrophobic, a condition that appears to be getting worse for me with age.

I had been out the night before and had had a few beers as well, which hardly helped the way I was feeling. After a couple of minutes, while all the players were cool about the situation, I was down on my haunches in the corner of the lift with my head in my hands, sweat pouring off me and in serious distress. And all this just moments before I was due to take the lead at our final team meeting before a cup final. Eventually, an engineer got the lift moving again and we got out. Straight away the tension lifted, but since that day I have never set foot in a lift.

Gradually, the other two problems faded away as well. By this time Vunipola was with us lock, stock and barrel and by the time we were due to leave the dressing-room for the match he was saying his prayers and was obviously very switched on. And I knew Jarred Murphy wouldn't let me down as a replacement for Rob in the centre either.

In fact, as the boys went out they were all seriously motivated, even though some of them were playing for next to nothing, and others knew that with the game going regional the following season, their chances of earning a decent living out of rugby would soon be few and far between.

For the bulk of the first half, we lived with Castres, but the final score – 40-12 – didn't really flatter the French side. Ten minutes before half-time, we were clinging on for our lives, falling off tackles and desperately trying to stem their tide.

In the second half, we completely ran out of steam and they piled up their points tally, but there was never any disgrace for us. Here were Castres, a squad worth around £3.5 million and there we were, a tuppence ha'penny outfit who had lived with them for a time but eventually bowed to their obvious superiority. The fact that we had been fit enough to compete with them was a tribute to the work the boys put in with Dean Parsons.

Our fans were magnificent that day and I remember going over to applaud them with the players and having tears in my eyes, genuine tears. It meant so much to everyone connected with Caerphilly and there was a lovely touch when the Castres boys wandered over and applauded us as well. It was a great gesture that I didn't see as being the slightest bit patronising.

At the end of the day, all the French guys knew what we were about: they knew we weren't a Cardiff or a Newport, and that we scarcely had any right to share a field with them. The fact that we had given them a game was down to our outstanding fitness levels, but we were nowhere near as streetwise as them. Our tighthead prop, for example, a rough diamond named Darren Sweet, had managed to split their tight-head, the great Argentine Mauricio Reggiardo, away from their hooker when we slammed into one scrum. I asked him afterwards why he had not tried to do the same thing again and again and he just said he didn't know.

After the match, we went back to the clubhouse in Caerphilly, having been cheered off the bus and into the building, and we had a good old knees-up. As I contemplated it all later that evening, I knew we had really achieved something amid so many problems. I was gutted Caerphilly were going to be no more in their present form and that there seemed to be a lack of ambition among the club's hierarchy. They didn't want to be included in any merger for the new regions and were content just to go back to being a social rugby club, which I felt was a pity.

I was sacked by the club a season and a half later while we were in the Welsh Premiership. They didn't say publicly that I was sacked, but the reason they gave me for my dismissal was daft in the end. I was told it was because I had a habit of effing and blinding in front of the main stand when things weren't going my way and that there had been complaints. I had several good friends at the club who were very unhappy at my release and the team manager, Dai Phillips, resigned over it as well.

These days Caerphilly are under the umbrella of Newport Gwent Dragons and have been lost in the mix, but I'll always hold dear the memories of what we achieved there.

18

COACHES AND BUSES

At the height of the furore surrounding the sudden shock departure of Wales coach Mike Ruddock during the 2006 Six Nations, a cruel joke was doing the rounds.

'Why is Mike Ruddock nicknamed bus?'

'Because he's no coach . . . Boom-boom.'

Not the funniest, or perhaps fairest, gag, I'll grant you, but it does hint at a problem I believe exists in Wales: coaches tend to get ahead because of their ability to fit into the template that is drawn up by the Welsh Rugby Union. In my opinion, if you fit the criteria laid out by the WRU high-performance unit, pass the exams and learn all their ring-binder language, any experience you have in the game arguably counts as a bonus. And these criteria are generally created by people who themselves have little experience of coaching or playing at the highest level.

Let me emphasise that I'm in no way singling out Mike Ruddock here. I'm fond of him: he's an extremely amenable guy whose heart has always been in the right place and I mean that to sound complimentary rather than patronising. He always sat at the front of the class on the WRU's Level Four course, the one you need to pass if you want to coach at the highest level in Wales. But Mike is by no means the only person to have been put on his way towards a top position because he has scored well on a WRU course.

I can hear the cries of the hierarchy and others already: 'Ringo's just bitter he couldn't get through the Level Four course, so he's just hitting out at those who could . . .'

Fine, they are as entitled to their opinion as I am mine, but before

I go any further let me say I am big enough and ugly enough to admit that it was my own failing. I couldn't get through Level Four, I couldn't stick it out, I couldn't live up to WRU expectations. But that was down to the type of character I am: in other words, I had such disregard for the content of the course and felt the emphasis on writing essays and doing other assignments belonged on a university degree rather than anywhere else. I simply couldn't bring myself to complete it. I was on the Level Four course about four years ago though I have to say that although I totally lost patience with it, one of the reasons I left halfway through was because my daughter, Maddy, was due to be born and I had too many family priorities to attend to. That said, my experience of the course might have been different if I hadn't been tearing my hair out about what Level Four was expecting of me.

At the beginning of the course, Leighton Morgan, who was in charge as head of the WRU's elite coaching programme, introduced a fellow called Peter Treadwell to us. None of us had ever heard of him, though we were told he was there 'to play devil's advocate'. Not a good start because that suggested to me that he wasn't going to lead us in any way, or tell us anything we didn't know. He wasn't going to claim he knew any more about coaching than us; he was just going to be a sounding board for the thoughts we ourselves threw around. We were told he was going to bring in some lecturers, get us talking about the game from a coaching perspective and just generally set a few agendas. How insightful!

Ruddock was there, and Geraint John, along with Gareth Jenkins and Nigel Davies and a whole host of people I didn't know. Ruddock, as I said, would sit up at the front and had his hand up all the time. He came across as very ambitious and the way he was going about things made it appear as though he was on a real mission to get up the ladder.

I have a lot of time for Mike and always like talking to him, but so many times on the Level Four course he would put up his hand and what he would say made me wonder if it was the same person. He made me feel down because I was convinced he was just trying to be the person and the coach he thought the WRU wanted him to be rather than just himself, and that was the biggest problem for me. I always felt Level Four was primarily about coaching the way the WRU wanted you to coach, not coaching in a way in which you knew you could get the most out of individuals and a team. Coaching is such a subjective thing; look across all sports down the decades and see for yourself the different personalities and methods that have characterised successful coaches.

Brian Clough conformed to nobody and nothing, yet he was a genius ahead of his time. The current Wales football manager, John Toshack, has no formal coaching qualifications whatsoever, but he is good enough to lead his country and he was good enough for Real Madrid and a host of other top clubs around Europe. Unfortunately, these days Welsh rugby is more about the manual than the man.

What coaching badges did Carwyn James have, I wonder? Times have changed, people will cry. Of course they have, but the principles of being able to get the most you possibly can out of a team will be the same forever. The only certainty is that there are not, and will never be, set guidelines. I know that in football there are qualifications required before you are supposed to take over the top jobs but only this year we have seen that clubs have the power to make their own appointments, with Newcastle United and Middlesbrough giving their manager's role to Glenn Roeder and Gareth Southgate respectively. If only there was the same discretion in Welsh rugby.

Yet even as I am saying this, I must stress that I would have had far more regard for the need to complete Level Four if I felt it had been worth its salt. There was a book called *The Coaching Process* which has become the WRU's bible and seemingly contained all you needed to know about how to become a top coach. If I recall correctly, it was written by a Scottish hockey player and he came down one day to lecture to us, while the Union people told us how privileged we were to have him along. One of the central points of his talk was how David Beckham was supposedly an uninspiring leader. I couldn't believe the argument because qualities of leadership are a subjective field: what works in one environment may not work in another – it depends on the individual make-up of the group. Beckham might well admit himself that he may not be the sharpest tool in the box but quite often athletes forgo their education in order to dedicate themselves to their chosen sport. Their personalities and ability to speak in public will develop as they spend more and more time in the public eye. Beckham, to me, is an icon. I said to our lecturer that inspiration can come in different ways – for example, that Beckham could lead by example – but he replied by saying that he knew exactly what Beckam had said on the field because he had been analysed by professional lip-readers.

'Do you have lip-readers in the dressing-room?' I asked. He didn't like that.

At this stage, though, I got a dig in the ribs from Gareth Jenkins, the current Wales coach, and a few whispered words telling me to grin and bear it and just get through the course.

Gareth liked me and wanted me to get on. I was always one of the first into class because I lived locally and whenever Gareth came in he would make a beeline for the chair next to me. We used to sit together with his assistant, Nigel Davies, and in hindsight I wish my attitude had been more like Gareth's. I sensed Gareth had no regard for the content of the course or the people who had drawn it up whatsoever, but his attitude was that it was just something he had to get through if he wanted to progress up the ladder. He understood the political side of the game and that he had to grin and bear it even if the last thing he needed was a collection of lecturers telling him how to coach. And who can blame him for a stance like that? Here was the most successful Welsh coach of all time, the man who had led Llanelli to so much success down the years, the man whose coaching credentials should have been without question, having to sit through arguably the most mind-numbing and irrelevant nonsense. For years, Gareth headed up Llanelli, the best-coached team in Wales, often with limited resources.

I've seen Llanelli get the best out of players who never made it at other clubs, which is so different to Cardiff, which for too many years had a reputation for ruining good players. Also whenever I saw Llanelli warm up before matches, it was always highly structured and game-related. It's no coincidence they have been Wales's best side in Europe down the years because they have always had so much tactical nous rather than just being a side that played from set-piece to set-piece. Gareth was the only Welshman for the Wales job when it became vacant early in 2006 and I think it was the right appointment; he had to be given his chance.

The final straw for me came when when Peter Treadwell and Leighton Morgan started discussing regulation throughout the entire coaching scene in world rugby. I think it's a theory that has come from Loughborough University and to me it's complete and utter nonsense. I am deeply suspicious of such regulation because it smacks of academics infiltrating the sport of rugby union and engineering a situation whereby any top rugby coach must become an academic himself. Coaching rugby is not about passing exams. It's almost as if the world of academia resents the idea of a rugby player coming straight out of the sport and earning a salary without having sat years of exams in the same way as, say, a school teacher. It's as if you must serve your study time if you want a chance to get to the big money.

In my opinion, it is pity there is such scant regard for people who were born with the talent to represent their country at the highest level and had the dedication and diligence to actually achieve it. What about the years spent at the coalface of the sport where it really counts? What about the injuries, the operations, the commitment to travelling the world when it sometimes involves leaving your family for weeks on end? Are these not qualifications in themselves? And I'm not just talking about myself here, either. All this could apply to countless ex-players. There would be nobody more qualified in my view to coach forward play at the highest level than someone like my old mate Staff Jones, for example.

He played for Pontypool and Wales, but sit him in a classroom or a lecture theatre and he wouldn't last five minutes. I'm not suggesting Staff himself should coach, but there are a whole host of his ilk out there who would never stand a chance.

Like so many others who have had similar upbringings, Staff came from an Ynysybwl mining background and learnt his trade under the noses of the legendary Pontypool front row and the likes of world-renowned prop/second row Ray Prosser and ex-Wales and Lions number 8 Jeff Squire. I would doubt if any of those people have ever stuck their heads into books in their lives, but not qualified to coach? Don't make me laugh.

If it was up to me there would be a training course for coaches, but it would focus on teaching people to teach; in other words, lecturers giving advice on how to convey their ideas to players in simple language. Then, for goodness sake, let them get on in their areas of expertise.

Nowadays, you've more chance of getting the opportunity to coach a set of forwards if you've had your head stuck in a book rather than a scrum. Level Four had me charged with the task of producing 5,000-word essays. I had to get through huge amounts of reading and then put what I had read into writing from an educational perspective. I had to use the Harvard system to reference every single thing that I wrote. I found it incredibly difficult because I am not an academic. I left school when I was 16 with three O levels. I do not have a degree. I am not an ex-schoolteacher. I am a rugby player.

I played 32 times for my country all over the world in a position that allowed me to view games and strategies as they unfolded. Furthermore, I know how to motivate players and I know how to impart my knowledge on a level with which everyone is comfortable. I know rugby union. I will admit to being disappointed that I have not been able to contribute more. It frustrates me deeply because I can see things happening in games and often wonder just what the coach in charge is capable of doing about it. And so much of what we see, particularly at the highest level of Welsh regional rugby, is of a poor standard. And that in turn calls into question the standard of coaching.

On this topic, I'll say one thing straight away. Look at the improvement in the play of Welsh internationals Gareth Thomas and Stephen Jones since they went to France to play with Toulouse and Clermont-Auvergne respectively. Gareth, or Alfie, as everyone calls him, has come on in leaps and bounds: his career has entered an Indian summer, his skill level is higher than it has ever been and he now has the ability to chip kick with both feet. In four years at Cardiff, Alfie didn't seem to improve one jot as a player. In my opinion, when he was at Cardiff he couldn't kick a ball to save his life and yet now he's playing full-back for Wales and doing it brilliantly.

Stephen has experienced much the same. For starters, he has bought himself an extra yard of pace since going to France, but look at the things he is doing on the international scene nowadays. He's making breaks – remember that one he made against the French in Paris during the Grand Slam year?; he's dictating from number 10 with a whole new level of confidence; and he's kicking the ball out of hand further than he has ever done. Is all this a coincidence? Of course not. I would contend that it took French rugby to breathe a new dimension into his game, something the Welsh system had failed to do for years.

I worry about Gavin Henson's future in the Welsh regional game. As yet, it is arguable that Gavin has achieved surprisingly little in the game despite his celebrated status. And while much of what he does from now on will be down to him, just who is going to improve him as a player in Wales? If he wants to become a top-notch second five-eighth, he needs to develop more guts, confidence and ability, and find the time in a game situation to take the ball another yard forward when he receives it. What he tends to do now is either hand someone off and make an outside break, or kick the ball away too early.

I see in Gavin the potential to become a truly great player, but he needs to be nurtured by someone of revered standing in coaching circles.

Yet perhaps I am annoyed by all this because of the person I am; the player that I was. Nobody ever really coached me: I learnt as I went along from playing with and against the very best players. For example, when I partnered the New Zealander Craig Innes playing for the Barbarians against Argentina in 1990, we just seemed to have a telepathic understanding and I watched the things he did and used them to my benefit later. Craig was a direct running athletic centre who read my every move. He was a phenomenal player and I'm not surprised he moved into rugby league not long after that.

Another example of me making things up as I went along was when I started kneeing the ball over defences when my space was closed down quickly, something I saw in rugby league. I first tried it at Pontypool in a match against Swansea when I could see Scott Gibbs lining me up like a raging bull out of the corner of my eye. I dinked it over him, leaving him completely flat-footed, and from the confusion we scored. I also did it against Mike Catt in a game against Bath. He came up to me afterwards and admitted he just did not see it coming. It was such an effective little tactic.

I even used to find I could alter matches by taking up a certain position and bluffing the opposition into thinking I was up to something when I wasn't. They would then alter their plans, which in turn would make our lives easier. I remember Nigel Davies changing the position of the Llanelli back line when I was playing for Cardiff at Stradey Park one day just because I went and stood in an unusually deep position. All it did was buy us more time to clear from a dangerous defensive position, and all along I had no intention of trying anything outrageous, even though Nigel thought otherwise because of my reputation.

Someone like Gavin Henson can't play against the highest quality players because the Magners League still contains far too much mediocrity. I'll be accused of just trotting out the old cliché about how things are not like they were in my day, but I genuinely believe standards are declining in so many areas, although there are current Welsh players who I do love to watch.

You may not be surprised to know that Shane Williams is one of my favourites. I felt awful for him on the British Lions tour to New Zealand in 2005 because in my opinion the coaches made him look a mug by using him in a way that made him a sitting duck to have ten bells smacked out of him by athletic Kiwi second rows. Under Scott Johnson for Wales he would only be put up against those athletic second rows when the Welsh team had got themselves on the front foot first. Then he was in a position to cut those people to shreds. I refer you to what he did against New Zealand in that glorious World Cup game in Sydney back in 2003.

The Lions so rarely got themselves on the front foot as an attacking force, so the likes of Chris Jack and Ali Williams were able to hit Shane on a rolling start and close down his space before he had a chance to get into his stride. It was like going to fire a gun against an enemy bearing down on you only to find you have to assemble the weapon and load the bullets first. Shane was subsequently rag-dolled on numerous occasions and ignorant watchers claimed it was because he wasn't good enough for that level. Total nonsense!

I also love to watch the Cardiff Blues and Wales scrum-half Mike Phillips. All he needs to do now is take his game on a stage further so when he makes those breaks, which are fast becoming his trademark, he knows instantly what to do in terms of offloading, chipping and chasing, sidestepping or whatever. Too many times – and Wales's defeat at home to France in the 2006 Six Nations was a prime example – Phillips' magical breaks are wasted. Some blamed other players for not supporting him in that France match, but Michael has to know himself what to do to ensure those moments are capitalised on. In modern rugby, the type of breaks he makes are so rare, they have to be converted into points.

I always wanted first and foremost to entertain – I was once asked before a Cardiff game by two of my close friends what I was going to do for them during Saturday's game. 'We'll have a look at a left-footed drop goal,' I said. I attempted the feat from an impossible angle, kicking towards the Taff End of the Arms Park late in the game just to please my two mates, with the effort just dipping under the bar. When I saw them in the bar after they were in hysterics because I had the audacity to do something like that, but, as I say, I was there to entertain.

The famous back-heeled conversion I attempted in a match against London Welsh in December 1989 is still brought up by people today. It was borne out of a desire for showmanship, but there was also a bit of needle involved as well. At the time, London Welsh had a great rapport with Cardiff at committee level and there was always plenty of buzz around the fixture. We were winning comfortably and I had been handed the kicking duties, even though I had not played for a while because of injury and was rusty. I made a hash of my first three attempts – they were all from very wide out but nevertheless I mistimed them totally and I concede they must have looked awful efforts – then this renowned heckler in the crowd lost his patience with me and began to barrack me personally. He was on my case with comments like, 'You've got your slippers on again, Ring!' I had never really been targeted by this guy before and it got to me, so when we scored a try underneath the posts, I muttered under my breath, 'I'll show you, you bastard.' I decided to back heel it over at the Taff End and it hit the upright and bounced back over my head. Half the crowd laughed, the other half booed.

The funny thing for me was that I got good height on the ball, which was the hardest thing to do, but I hadn't lined it up properly. It didn't affect the result, but it did prompt my father to leave the ground early because he couldn't listen to the disapproving comments from the diehards. My mother thought it was great.

The committee, predictably, didn't see the funny side. They thought it was a simple provocation directed at a side that was starting to fall on hard times and which needed all the help available to get back to health. I was made to write a letter of apology to London Welsh, which I was happy to do because it gave me the chance to explain the circumstances involving the heckler and to assure them that it was not meant as a sign of disrespect to their club. I told them I wouldn't have done it with hindsight and that Welsh rugby needed a strong London Welsh.

Later, Terry Charles, chairman of the Cardiff committee at the time, passed the message on that I was banned from kicking for two years, which I thought was hysterical. What if we were in a semi-final and there was an injury and I was the only option to go for goal? To this day, I'm not sure whether it was a wind-up on Terry's part.

Like I say, I didn't make it to the end of the Level Four course. I became bored and angry with the whole set-up and when Jonathan Westwood left – he was backs coach at Newbridge at the time and we went back a long way – I thought, 'Good for you, mate. I'll be next.' I even scored low when they marked a training session I took at Caerphilly, but it was because I felt the whole situation was false. They put a microphone on me and spent the session walking around with notepads, making me feel really under pressure. The players didn't respond to me in their usual way either because they felt it wasn't about them doing things well but about making me look good in front of a panel of examiners. Basically, I was told my session was no good. One of their main gripes was that I hadn't empowered the players enough. When I was reassessed, I made a conscious effort to have a session with the players at the end, asking them questions about what we had done and seeking their views. And though, again, it was false, the WRU people loved it.

To me, I had always empowered the players, but in a more natural and informal manner; there I was being brainwashed into methods that were alien to me, methods I didn't believe in. From a career perspective I should have stuck out Level Four, but I cannot be false and go through a system for the sake of it, trampling over all my philosophies in the process. I've seen others do it and it's almost as if they have been institutionalised by the WRU. Their sessions are the same, they conform to the same programme, they even sound the same. They're welcome to it, but I will never be one of them.

I know I will never have a top coaching job in the future in Wales unless I have the Level Four to my name and I can't see me doing it unless they overhaul the course content and structure. But so be it. I think people have this idea of me that I am fiercely ambitious. Yes, I have ambitions, but I know my area of expertise is back play and I would simply like to be given a chance to coach in that sphere somewhere.

I have certainly never aspired to be the Wales coach – good job because it ain't ever going to happen. I hope Gareth can take Wales through to the 2007 World Cup with success, but I can't in a million years see Wales winning it. I would go for France; yes, even over the All Blacks. I believe they have the all-round game and they are the host nation, with a coach who has already said he is bowing out after the tournament. For me, everything points to them pulling off the big one. Good on Gareth for knuckling down on the Level Four course. I knew the same things as him, but I just couldn't hack it.

19

A QUICK HOP ACROSS THE BORDER

When I left Caerphilly, I was in limbo. It was halfway through the 2004–05 season so I started going over to Rhiwbina RFC, just across the road from where I now live, just to keep my hand in and help out on a voluntary basis. At first, the club officials looked at me as if to say, 'What's he after?' but I assured them I did not want to be paid, just to stay involved in the game and do whatever I could.

I had a phone call after a couple of sessions from Dave Hobbs, my contact at Rhiwbina, who I had known for some years, saying that the committee had met and felt I was stepping on the toes of the coaches who were already in place and they didn't really want me involved. He then asked me if I was prepared to travel, explaining that he had set up a team in the Gloucestershire village of Tetbury when he'd had a tyre business there many years before (I had actually gone there to open it for him). When I went to have a look, I liked what I saw. There was a tiny little clubhouse and it was a beautiful part of the world. Prince Charles's Highgrove estate was nearby and the whole area was extremely well-to-do.

Dave told me it was an hour from my house, which it was, and Tetbury's millionaire chairman, Steve Payne, looked after me financially. They gave me a car, which, for a small club like Tetbury, was a bonus.

I went on to enjoy a fantastic little spell with the club. We only played in South Gloucestershire Division Three and it was a really low standard compared to the rugby I was used to. Our first game was in November 2004 against a team from Bristol called St Brendan's Old Boys, with me having taken just one session since joining the club. Typically, we were short, which meant that I had to play, even though I had not kicked a ball for four years. I started the match at fly-half and finished it at scrum-half. I remember setting up a try for our left winger Phil Morris towards the end of the match. I could have gone round the last defender myself and gone under the posts, but I thought I'd give him an easy run in, so spun it out for him to canter home. When he ran back, he jumped on my shoulders and shouted, 'Yes! That's the first time I have ever scored!'

'But you're a winger!' I said.

I don't think he heard; he was too busy celebrating.

I told the lads beforehand that they would have to look after me to a large extent because I was so rusty and advanced in years and was quickly told that our flanker Ian Wood, otherwise known as Iggy, who had played more football than rugby in his time and was a Manchester United fanatic, would be just the man for that role. I didn't really get a good look at Iggy before we kicked off because I was so busy organising everyone else, but moments after the game started I did a double take – Iggy only had one arm. I say one arm but in fact his arm had been severed at the elbow. It was the first time I had ever played with a one-armed rugby player, but I was full of admiration for him. Iggy was an outstanding bloke. For someone with his disability, his skill level was phenomenal. He could do the lot, including jumping up to catch high balls.

I didn't know what to make of all these different characters to start with and half the time I couldn't wait to get back to my local pub in Rhiwbina to tell my mates stories, but Tetbury were no joke and the way we steadily improved was brilliant. We won that first game in Bristol 12–10 and it sparked an uproar of excitement among the lads, who had been bottom of the league up to then. Futhermore, our slow winger Phil Morris had got another try later in the game. We finished the season runners-up in the league, losing by a point or two in a play-off for promotion. It was incredible how far we had come.

The following year, we won everything and had the championship wrapped up two months before the end of the campaign, finishing the term with a tour of Malta. When I came back from Malta knowing my time at Tetbury was ending, I was very emotional about it. I miss the set-up terribly at times. I became quite close to a few of the boys and some of them even came to Cardiff to my local pub to give me a send-off a couple of weeks after we returned.

I hope now that I have gone that the team stays together and that they can bring in a coach who will continue to take them forward. I'll never forget the experience I had of walking into a situation like that and turning it around. In some ways, it felt like the classic film plot where a coach helps turn a bunch of no-hopers into a force to be reckoned with and I'm proud of what the lads achieved. The club was a real throwback to the times when rugby union really was rugby union. The boys used to run the clubhouse bar themselves, putting money in the till whenever they had a pint as if it were an honesty box.

I'd like to say thanks to Tetbury for the memories. I've never been afraid to try something different and more often than not I haven't regretted it. The Tetbury experience may have been low profile, but it was enriching in so many different ways. I know I'll always be welcome back.

I couldn't stick around for ever, though, and I didn't once I'd decided that an offer that had come in from across the Irish Sea was too good to turn down.

20

IRELAND'S CALL AND THE FUTURE

Ireland's call first came along back in 2005. A chap called Peter Manning, who was team manager when I was coaching at Cardiff, was good enough to send my CV to a club called Old Crescent, who play in the All-Ireland League in Division Two. When they eventually got in touch with me, they told me that they had tried a number of player–coaches who had not really worked out for them and that they now wanted somebody to fill the role full time.

I went over to Limerick, where the club is based, for an interview and snatched the job from a shortlist of three. Funnily enough, the first thing they asked was whether I had a gambling problem! I told them that I had had my moments along the line, but that, no, I didn't have a problem, I just put on a bet as a hobby and that it was far from outside my control. That was that one laid to rest!

Since taking up the job, I have been really impressed with the whole scene over in Ireland. The club provided me with a new four-bedroom house and a car was thrown into the bargain, which allows me, my wife Lisa and little Luca and Maddy to live comfortably.

The economy seems to be booming in this corner of Ireland at present and the fact that Munster are such a rugby power helps as well. I would find it hard to be convinced by anyone that Limerick is not first and foremost a rugby town. When I was there last summer, and I know that was a time when Munster had just won the Heineken Cup, six out of ten cars were driving around with Munster flags attached to them. The entire main shopping street was draped in the provincial colours. Rugby seemed to be oozing from everywhere, with the faces of the players all over the place. The town was buzzing and it felt good to be a part of it all.

When I first started in the July, I would go over for spells of four days just so I could start planning and getting my feet under the table by taking training sessions and meeting the players. Then in August we moved as a family on a more permanent basis, renting out our house in Cardiff.

It is not a glamorous setting by any means. Old Crescent is right next to the more famous club Garryowen, which plays in Division One, and we tend to get overshadowed by them and Shannon, who are also based in Limerick. We have a similar type of set-up to Cardiff club Glamorgan Wanderers: there is nothing flash.

Having said that, Old Crescent are very professional in the way they run themselves. For a start, I have sensed the players are far more committed to becoming the best they can be, even though they are not paid to play. They appear to be far less hasty to put their hands out and ask how much they are going to be paid than some in Wales I have known.

They are fortunate in that the Irish provinces have been set up for years and years and everyone knows the score. Rugby players in Limerick and the surrounding area have always known how it works – Munster is the pinnacle and if you make their squad, that is when you will get your privileges and not before. Consequently, you have players really aspiring to play for the province, not just for the kudos and sense of achievement but also because they know that is the only path to big money. There are no short cuts.

In Ireland, they have kept the sport amateur at club level, so far fewer players have ever tasted money of any significance – unlike in Wales where mediocre talent has been paid inflated money for donkey's years – and so everyone has just grown up with a different attitude.

For my first training session that July, about 30 players came along, which was so heartening considering that I'd been told the turn-out was in single figures a year earlier. I have a two-year contract and I would like to see that out and taste success, but I haven't looked too far down the line. What I will say is that I've been about a bit now and have plenty of experience under my belt. I know the pitfalls of coaching and it's been many years since Terry Charles told me to go away and make my mistakes. They've all been made now and I feel I'm ready to deliver from a coaching perspective.

But I will do it my way. My idea of coaching is improving people's ability, skills and character, and enhancing team spirit and organisation. It takes time to do that, and if you are given the time to get it right, you become a team with foundations that will keep developing rather than be a jumped-up squad that has bought its way to the top. The structure will also be behind you, which should keep you healthy for a long period. Time is something I have never been afforded as a coach, which is why I am hoping to work with Old Crescent for longer than two years.

Of course, moving to Ireland was a big step family-wise; I was always unsure how Lisa and the kids were going to get on. For instance, my daughter Maddy, all being well, will go to her first school out here. The kids are at the right age, though, where they will not be too disrupted and Lisa has been hugely supportive. She obviously had to leave her friends and I am acutely aware that she needs a life in Ireland as well, but she never showed any concern about going, which is a mark of the love she has for me and the support she is willing to give. I'm sure, being the person Lisa is, she will integrate comfortably. She is the sort of character who makes friends very easily. And so it's onwards and upwards towards the future.

I once told my great pal Alun Donovan, who I played with in the centre at Cardiff, that I was born to wear the number 10 jersey. Well, I achieved that for Wales, but it was cut short by injury and circumstances, and it didn't happen until the end of my career. Not becoming a long-term, established outside-half in the game from a young age and not becoming a British Lion are probably my only two regrets when I look back over my career.

At the time, missing out on the Lions was something I didn't dwell on; it only becomes an issue in my mind when I look back. Yet I would like to think for all my trials and tribulations, I did carve my own little mark in the history of the game as a player, and might do so yet again as a coach. Remember, I'm still only 43 as I write this book, a young pup in coaching parlance.

I also hope that all the people I have liked and respected down the years have liked and respected me back. It's strange but I often find myself wishing that my personality could be different to what it is. I really admire people who don't force opinions down people's throats but when they do speak always have something profound to say. I would like to be like that, but instead I know I can't keep my mouth shut. I have to give people my views all the time, they just pour out, and I don't like myself for that.

I also think I'm selfish to a certain extent, in that I would go totally mad if I couldn't still play sport. It's hard for Lisa at times when I just get up and go to play golf, leaving her with the kids and goodness knows how many other things to do, but I just always have to be doing something otherwise I would go nuts.

The qualities I do possess are that I am loyal, trustworthy and sensitive. And I like a laugh, a joke and a drink as much as anyone else. When all is said and done, whatever judgements people choose to make about me and my life, it is a life that has been lived to the full. Everything I've done, I've done my way.

And I've always tried to do it with style. Always with style.

MARK RING'S DREAM TEAMS

My Mates Team

15. Mike 'Mikey' Rayer (Cardiff, Wales)
Like me, Mike is Cardiff born and bred, so we share a special bond. We often wondered how much wearing the blue-and-black shirt meant to others.

14. Glenfield Webbe (Bridgend, Wales)
The driest, wittiest and shrewdest man I have ever met. He would have won 60 caps for Wales had he not been around at the same time as Ieuan Evans.

13. Kenny Poole (Glamorgan Wanderers)
Kenny Cool or Kenny Fool, he was everyone's mentor at Old Illtydians baseball and held the club together for years. The first person I would call for advice.

12. Martin 'Charlie' Daly (Cardiff)
My best mate at Cardiff and Lady Mary High School, and best man at my wedding. We were once inseparable around the Cardiff nightspots.

11. PJ Ward (St Albans)
Look him up in the Yellow Pages under Sevens specialist. A real 'have boots, will travel' character and surely a future Lord Mayor of Splott.

10. Paul 'Tommy' Turner (Newbridge, Wales)
A highly respected rugby genius. We have shared our views on the game over many a pint.

9. Jonathan Taylor (St Josephs)
Rugby mad and a political ambassador for Wales, Jonathan and I played together for Cardiff and at Lady Mary High School. I've never won an argument with him. A close friend of our family, along with his dad Bomber, his mum Margaret, his brother Jeff and sister Joanne.

8. Tony 'Clubber' McLean (Cardiff)
Named after Clubber Lang of *Rocky* fame, Tony was once my lodger (what a cook and cleaner!) and at 6 ft 4 in. tall and 18 stone, he always made me feel safe.

7. Paul Ring (Cardiff)
My brother, who I love dearly. I've never told him how proud I am of his achievements in rugby and as a husband to Angela and a father to Christy and Cara.

6. Stephen 'Potter' Franks (St Albans)
His first love is boxing, but he is well versed in the old rugby tradition of post-match banter with the opposition. A great solo artist with his harmonica.

5. Howard Woon (Llandaff)
My greatest friend and confidant. We are both regulars at my local, the Butchers Arms in Cardiff, and at any golf course we can blag our way onto.

4. Ian Robinson (Cardiff)
Another great friend and drinking partner, although I am starting to tire of the songs he sings about himself. One of the toughest,

roughest forwards ever to play the game, but he's never out these days without a comb in his back pocket.

3. Stephen 'Wally' Blackmore (Cardiff, Wales)
Very good friends with Jose Souto as well; the pair were inseparable. We had some memorable moments on tour.

2. Jose Benito Souto (Cardiff)
An ex-St Alban's Primary boy like me and a gentleman these days who would rather sip a glass of wine than a pint of lager. A hard man who inspired everyone.

1. Bob 'the Bolt' Newman (Cardiff)
If ever a young player joined Cardiff, Bob was always the first to welcome them. I am deeply indebted to him for pushing me to do weight training when I hated it.

Team manager: David Giles
David, an ex-Welsh international footballer who is now a successful TV, radio and newspaper pundit, is one of my closest pals and drinking partners. Dai Young thinks I feed him criticism about the Blues for his radio phone-in – Dai, it's all his own opinion!

My Best-Ever Team (all the players I have played with or against)

15. Jean-Baptiste Lafond (France)

I played alongside Jean-Baptiste on the Western Province centenary tour of 1983. A free spirit who represented everything I loved about playing rugby, he possessed awesome pace and was a good-looking bugger who had a way with the ladies!

14. Ieuan Evans (Wales)

I'm sure he'll be pleased to know he edges out All Black greats John Kirwan and Stu Wilson. Ieuan was the most evasive runner Welsh rugby had seen since Gerald Davies.

13. Jerry Guscott (England)

To me, Jerry was a natural 12 and I could never understand why he played outside Will Carling. I would have loved to have played alongside him at three-quarter.

12. Warwick Taylor (New Zealand)

I played against Warwick on the 1988 tour of New Zealand and was spellbound by his skill and vision. He taught me about the true intricacies of playing as a second five-eighth.

11. David Campese (Australia)

David is the most complete rugby player in the squad. He could have played any back position for Australia except scrum-half. Pure genius.

10. Jonathan Davies (Wales)

Jonathan beats the great Mark Ella by a whisker. He had it all: his confidence and ability to attack from any position on the pitch was sublime. He was one of those players who had an effect on all those around him.

9. David Bishop (Wales)

David just beats Terry Holmes. The two of them had a similar skill level, but I've gone for Bish because of his ability to kick with both feet. Bish was a total one-off.

8. John Scott (England)

Scotty was the best captain I ever played under. He knew when the time was right to switch on and off. He was a massive influence who always instilled confidence.

7. Michael Jones (New Zealand)

A total and utter flying machine at openside, Michael was in opponents' faces for 80 minutes and reputedly clocked 19 on the bleep test, so was supremely fit.

6. Mark Shaw (New Zealand)

Cowboy Shaw was another whom I was privileged to play alongside in South Africa. He was naturally hard and no-nonsense, and good on the back or the front foot.

5. Hennie Bekker (South Africa)

Hennie was just one of those athletic and giant Springbok second rows who I saw play on the World Tour in 1989. I would have hated to have been up against him.

4. Gary Whetton (New Zealand)

Probably the most athletic and committed lock forward I have ever seen. Gary took play in the department to a new level with New Zealand in the late '80s.

3. Gary Knight (New Zealand)

I'm not sure whether Gary ever got to beat John Ashworth in those sprints I talked about earlier, but given his supremely competitive nature it wouldn't surprise me.

2. Bobby Windsor (Wales)

I've used a bit of leeway here because I never really played with or against Bobby, but I saw him destroy so many opposition packs in his time and he was an unbelievable character.

1. John Ashworth (New Zealand)

John was a phenomenal competitor who never ever took a backward step. He was everything you could possibly want in a prop forward and more.

Replacements:

Andy Moore (Wales)

Andy was underrated in my view. He had great skills and a great attitude.

Mark Ella (Australia)

Only Jonathan could have kept him out of my starting line-up.

Didier Codorniou (France)

A centre who gave me the most torrid 20 minutes in Paris in 1985.

Sean Fitzpatrick (New Zealand)

Little needs to be said about such a legendary hooker . . .

Graham Price (Wales)

Pricey was a big influence on me in his latter years at Pooler and a colossus in his younger days. His staggering 12 Lions Test caps tell their own story.

Howard Stone (Cardiff)

One of the greatest back-row forwards never to be capped by Wales.

Mark Brown (Wales)
One of the toughest opensides I ever played against. He was lightning quick, always in your face.

Coach – Terry Holmes (Wales)
Honesty personified and the best man-manager I have ever worked under. He would command the respect of every player.

Assistant coach – Roger Beard (Cardiff)
I played for Roger for a long time at Cardiff and have nothing but respect and admiration for his methods.

Scrum doctor – Garin Jenkins (Wales)
Every team needs one because it remains one of the most important parts of the game. Nobody would be better qualified than Garin.

Team manager – Willie John McBride (Ireland)
He took on that role when I toured Bermuda on a special invitational tour in the late '80s. A great character and a legend.